THE
WITCHING YEAR

THE

WITCHING
YEAR

A MEMOIR *of* EARNEST
FUMBLING THROUGH
MODERN WITCHCRAFT

)))●(((

DIANA HELMUTH

SIMON ELEMENT

New York   London   Toronto   Sydney   New Delhi

**SIMON
ELEMENT**

An Imprint of Simon & Schuster, Inc.
1230 Avenue of the Americas
New York, NY 10020

Some names and identifying characteristics have been changed.

First Simon Element hardcover edition October 2023

SIMON ELEMENT is a trademark of Simon & Schuster, Inc.

For information about special discounts for bulk purchases, please contact Simon & Schuster Special Sales at 1-866-506-1949 or business@simonandschuster.com.

The Simon & Schuster Speakers Bureau can bring authors to your live event. For more information or to book an event, contact the Simon & Schuster Speakers Bureau at 1-866-248-3049 or visit our website at www.simonspeakers.com.

Interior design by Jaime Putorti

Manufactured in the United States of America

1   3   5   7   9   10   8   6   4   2

Library of Congress Cataloging-in-Publication Data has been applied for.

ISBN 978-1-6680-0298-8
ISBN 978-1-6680-0301-5 (ebook)

For Kim and Jacole.
My path would be so dark without you.

This is a work of nonfiction. Some names, locations, and descriptions have been changed to respect the privacy of those involved, and some timelines have been condensed for brevity. But if you find yourself asking, "Wait, did that actually happen?" Yes, yes, it did.

And a note on grammar: all spiritual practices have been intentionally capitalized.

Large parts of the neopagan movement started out as jokes, you know.

—ROBERT ANTON WILSON
AS QUOTED BY MARGOT ADLER

PREFACE

I don't know if we get to decide where our spirits sleep. There's a place where yours does, and that is simply that. This place is simply mine.

It is also probably someone else's, but I can pretend it's just mine for an hour or so. I think that's what you have to do to have a spiritual experience. Pretend something is uniquely yours—your relationship with God, the universe, your ancestors—when in fact you probably share it with a billion others. You need to feel like it belongs to you completely, that you have some unique relationship with it, in order to retain its sacredness.

The place I'm looking for is a bluff: acres of waist-high wild grasses arrayed like pews before an altar of ocean, thrust five hundred feet into the sky, with a row of ancient Monterey cypresses lined up on one side, like bishops. I first came here when I was fourteen. I have not driven back probably since I was twenty-one, about eleven years ago. The bluff is in a town that prefers not to be advertised, whose residents have a decades-long habit of tearing down any identification signs. (Of course, Google has found the town, and marked it by satellite, so anyone with a smartphone in their pocket can locate it within a few swipes. But the residents continue to tear down any on-the-ground directional sign-posts, perhaps more for the pride of tradition than for anything else.) I take one of the few turns I know because I happened to befriend people who taught it to me, and drive up the hill, saltwater to my left and honor till farm stands to my right. The cypress tree branches slice the sunlight over the road. My car darts from shadow to spotlight, like it's trying not to get caught. I'm not a local. I've never lived here. It's just where my soul got stuck.

At the top of the hill, I move by instinct. I don't do this for romance's sake; the town might be on the map now, but I still don't know the address for where I'm actually going. We are off the grid—some folks in this neighborhood don't have legal water meters, operating on a "don't ask, don't tell" housing policy. I used to navigate my way here by sight when I was a teenager (turn right at the eucalyptus grove, right again at the house with the buoys hanging on the door, left at the dirt pile no one is ever going to clean . . .), but these objects have either grown, died, or vanished entirely, changing the negative space around the road I used to recognize. I have no idea if I am correct now in my navigation. I take a left. Then, for a reason I can't explain, a right. Then another right. And just as I doubt myself completely and think I need to turn around, a tide of recognition rises from my toes to my ears. I know precisely where I am.

I drive straight ahead, and the meadow rises up to meet me.

The mighty waves of grass, which normally retain the color of pale amethyst through June, are almost completely blanched. A lack of rain, even with the fog rolling in to nourish the coastal bluffs each night, hasn't been enough to stave off the effects of California's now ever-present drought. It makes my heart ache. It makes me think about climate change and how powerless I feel trying to fight a catastrophic global emergency by voting every other year and putting yogurt cups in the recycling.

I pull over to the side of the road, and bring my car to a stop. The minute I open my door, the wind clambers into the cab, and begins yanking at my body, bringing with it the scent of the ocean below. It's not pleasant: unwashed clams and mussels, rotting kelp and salt. But it mixes with the scent of the cedar trees, and the sun-warmed dirt and the fresh grass. It picks up the hiking sweat from my own body, finalizing the blend. If this were a perfume, I'm not sure I'd wear it. But it feels like a path up to a front door, my front door. Home.

I walk through the portal of a rusted fence post, then approach the edge of the bluff, the wind making snakes of my hair. I peek down to the beach below, under the five-hundred-foot-high sand-colored cliffs, and see a dog walker and a picnicking couple. Their bodies are the size of seashells. The ocean is a glistening carpet of steel blue, stretching into the horizon, a few soft white lines of foam tumbling unhurriedly toward the shore. It eats up my entire vision, blending into the sky without a seam.

What the hell am I doing here?

I tried to go on a hike somewhere ten miles away but bailed at the last minute; it was crowded, I was PMSing. I don't know exactly. What I do know is I didn't feel right. So I got back into my car and drove here. If someone asked me why, I wouldn't have known what to say. *Why does someone go out of her way to visit somewhere?*

We have been in Covid "lockdown" for a little over a year. Every evening I pull on a pair of fuzzy socks, curl up with a bowl of vegan ice cream, and run a finger up and down a magic screen that tells me how many different ways the world is ending. I feel disconnected from reality. I feel spoiled. I feel tired. I feel annoyed at my own tiredness. I want someone to tell me what to do. I want to fix everything with a magic wand. I want to surrender. I want to not want absolution. I want a sign.

I wander along the cliff's edge as the wind pushes and pulls at me, through scrubby bushes and up into the thousand-acre meadow I walked a hundred times as a teen.

My traditional motto is "Nature doesn't give a shit about you," and when people say they feel at one with nature, I have a tendency to roll my eyes. Nature is a process, a constantly churning life-and-death cycle, an eternal, omnipotent web in which we, the living individuals, are pathetically small dust motes. To think otherwise is arrogance and idiocy. And yet I feel like the birds and the wind and the ocean and the grass are, well, at one with me right now, and if I'm very, very forgiving of myself, I can imagine the atoms we shared in a star a billion years ago. I feel unafraid, and I can't convince myself that I should be afraid. There are ticks. An earthquake could strike any moment, and the cliff could break off into the ocean, taking me down with it. I could trip in a gopher hole and break my leg and no one would hear me scream. A rabid coyote could be hiding in that patch of grass. But all of the worry feels muted, like it's shouting at me on the other side of a closed window.

I can practically see my sixteen-year-old body lying in an imprint in the grass, right there, in a cheap goth T-shirt and hiking sandals and jeans that don't fit because I could never get hip-huggers to work.

I have a sudden urge to talk to her. I try to imagine what she would ask me.

"Did you write a book?"

"Yes, and it was hard but wonderful," I'd reply.

"Did you get skinny?"

"No. But that's not how we judge beauty anymore. Don't worry, Lizzo is coming soon."

"Are you still stressed out all the time?"

I falter, staring at the grass. I would have to answer no, that I have not yet learned to live easily, I am not yet the embodiment of a Mary Oliver poem. But I don't want to admit this to her.

Which makes me turn back to the wind, the pale sky, and the tiny single cedar tree growing boldly on the tip of the bluff.

The wind curls around me. As it always does. Because we are on a cliff's edge. And that's where wind does poetic things like curl around the hair of privileged women who are desperate for answers to why they aren't happy, when by all accounts they should be.

I decide to stop pushing my luck. *Take the nice moment for what it is,* I think. *Don't make it more. Enjoy the pleasant walk down memory lane; these walks are not always pleasant.*

I turn around and walk back to my car.

A shiny piece of trash lying in the grass catches my eye, and I freeze.

Earlier this morning I had stopped at my usual grocery store to grab a few hiking snacks. I wanted a small can of yerba maté, the little twelve-ounce kind in a can. It comes in three flavors: grapefruit, cranberry, and . . . What was the name of the third flavor, and why wasn't it on the shelf? Oh well. I shrugged and grabbed another flavor, paid, and left the store, not thinking about it any further.

Seven hours later, I am on a deserted Northern California sea bluff, standing above flavor number three.

"Enlighten Mint." I read the label on the fallen can. Exactly the one I was looking for six hours ago, except someone else, right here, in this grass, has already drunk it.

I pick it up and glance around. The meadow stretches out in all directions, the brome and oat grass waving like the silky tendrils of sea anemones, oblivious and innocent. There are no other humans in sight. Just the slightly indented grass where I can imagine my younger body lying, here in the only place on earth where she never worried about anything at all.

I feel like a prayer has been answered. Except now I don't remember what the plea was.

I stare at the can.

I realize I am idolizing literal trash.

I shake my head and finish walking back to my car, my boots crunching in the gravel. I toss the can into a waste bag, duck into the driver's seat, and shut the door. The wind hushes immediately, like a candle being blown out.

COUNTDOWN to DAY ONE

Telling My Mom I Want to Be a Witch

Underneath my repression, maybe I have a closeted mystical side. Maybe I'm a rational Presbyterian on the outside, but an emotional Baptist on the inside. Given the right circumstances, maybe everyone is. Even Henry Kissinger.

—A.J. JACOBS

"So, when does the animal sacrifice start?" My mom asks me this cautiously, almost politely, as we stand in her kitchen. I'm mixing a batch of Cara Cara Orange and Chamomile Palomas, a recipe from a cookbook called *Floral Libations* given to me by my sister last Christmas. It is now, while we are churning up liquor and flower juice, that I decide to tell her I'm considering writing a book on Witchcraft. For a year. With myself as the subject.

"I think animal sacrifice is actually a misunderstood part of Voodoo," I reply. "I'll be doing Wicca, probably. The hippie Goddess religion from the sixties, reconstructed from pre-Christian Europe."

She seems mollified, but only slightly. My mother is a beautiful, sixty-five-year-old registered nurse who a few years ago abandoned a twenty-year career in the ER to attend herbalism school. She lives alone by choice in an ancient Victorian with a huge garden in rural Northern

California. Every time I open her fridge, I have to pick my way past at least fifty glass jars with labels like Helichrysum Tonic, Fire Cider, and Poke/Castor: USE SPARINGLY before I can find some milk for my tea. She adopts stray animals that turn up on her doorstep, which over the years have included a llama, a rooster, a pheasant hen, and one extremely vocal Bengal tomcat that refuses to be touched by anyone but her. One time I heard her say she'd left a jar of rose oil outside during a full moon, so the light could get in.

I don't bring any of this up. I care a great deal what my mother thinks of me, and I want her support. I have no intention of pointing out that if Witchcraft was a competition, she's already a clean fifty points ahead of me.

We are alone in the kitchen, but she still leans in to whisper, "Are you gonna start . . . worshipping Satan? Is that part of it?"

"No, that's Satanism," I say, squeezing half a lime into the pink-and-orange cocktail glasses, trying to avoid the rose salt on the rim. I remember an argument I'd had with an old editor; when I questioned her constant capitalizing of "god" in my first book's manuscript, she retorted, "Listen, I'm a Satanist. I'm not defending God, I'm defending grammar."

I turn back to Mom and add, "But you know Satanists aren't actually that scary."

Her eyes grow large. This was not the right thing to say.

"Anyway." I cough. "Wicca is basically a nature-based religion." I begin to paraphrase information from the other Witches I know, and everything I've absorbed so far from reading *Drawing Down the Moon*, Margot Adler's exhaustive anthropological study of twentieth-century neopaganism and Witchcraft that I've been reading in preparation for my spiritual journey. Adler was a Nieman Fellow at Harvard, an NPR career journalist, and host of the Clarion Award–winning radio show *Justice Talking*. She is analytical, objective, scrupulous. And in *Drawing Down the Moon*, you can watch her justify, to herself, over six hundred pages of dissertation-level research, why she wants to dance naked in the moonlight. As a person with control issues raised with science as my primary religion (but also raised in the granola-crunching, Tibetan flag–waving, hippie mecca of Northern California), I find Adler's takes very relatable. Some of us need something unimpeachably scholastic to bait us into the stygian depths of the "woo-woo."

I am a skeptic at heart, and by that I mean I'm a realist. Imagination has value, but at the end of the day, I take far greater comfort in things I can prove to exist with at least one of my five senses, or, things people with PhDs can prove, and then write about in very prestigious journals that I can quote whenever I need someone to believe I am smart. I'm sure I'd be a great atheist, if I didn't find atheism about as comforting as a blanket of upturned tacks.

You see, the trouble is, I'm a skeptic. But I am also tired of God being dead. The appeal of Witchcraft for me isn't about getting naked and dancing in the moonlight (in fact I fear I am becoming an increasingly rare breed of woman who actually likes her underwire bra). It's about the most sacred, serious, and unfunny obsession we all harbor: a desire to feel safe, to feel sure about our identity and purpose, to have power.

And that's probably why I'm doing this now. We are in a climate crisis, racism is pervasive, inequality is skyrocketing, the middle class is shrinking, and a virus is threatening to kill our most vulnerable and most of us still can't even agree on if any of this is a problem. Witchcraft represents comfort and agency in a world that otherwise buzzes with a thousand things I have no control over but promise to destroy my life. It tempts me to tame my inner turmoil and heal my uncomfortable relationship with spirituality by putting *me* in charge of it. It's a DIY ingress to divine comfort in a world of superstorms and daily economic uncertainty. I have been flirting with it my entire life, surrounded by Witches and occult shops and the leftover dregs of 1960s counterculture movements that clung to California's golden hills into the twenty-first century. And maybe it's just because I've spent a year inside reading story after story about some newfangled way that we're all gonna die, but I have a sudden and compelling urge to grab the helm of my spirituality and steer it straight into the arms of some divine being who will tell me everything is going to be okay. No—that maybe I can be one of the people *making* it okay.

The best part is that Margot Adler tells me that belief is not required in order for me to participate in this new world of Witchcraft and neo-paganism. I find this incredibly reassuring as I consider the task ahead of me. Granted, I have trouble reconciling Adler's assurance with a group of people who have told me that the location of the planet Venus during my mother's final push on the delivery table will have an effect on my fiduciary responsibility thirty years later. But that's a question for down the line.

Witchcraft is a kaleidoscopic spirituality, often pulling from traditions that claim to have survived in secret over millennia. Diving into Witchcraft provides the same sensation as discovering a forgotten path home, forging a connection with something bigger than myself, picking up a phone line to talk to my shapeless, long-forgotten ancestors. It feels like a way to find my unique identity in a world of increasing homogeneity—maybe even a way to discover pride in my European heritage. Without becoming a Nazi.

Thorn Mooney, author of *The Witch's Path*, says that the goals of Witchcraft are to transgress social and political boundaries, engage with magic for the benefit of the self and others, and interact with the spirit world. These goals are accomplished through the worship of pagan gods, veneration of ancestors, communion with land spirits, and/or the practice of personal development into "the sacred self." There are a host of traditions a Witch can pull from to fuel her Craft, from reconstructed Celtic to diasporic Mexican, modern African to ancient Egyptian.

However, the Bible is still the main book of sacred scriptures in America, and I'd be kidding if I said I wasn't terrified of the judgment of my evangelical uncles and Southern Baptist friends for undertaking this journey. It's this precise fear that I will be working through during the year. I sense myself starting to circle the drain on it here in the kitchen, but decide to keep it to myself. I'm not very confident just yet, and Mom does not look like she's ready to cheerlead.

"I think the point is"—I clear my throat—"it's about finding divinity within yourself and the world around you," I say, feigning a posture of authority. "It doesn't rely on belief in something like a virgin birth or a holy ghost, it's just about connecting to the . . . energy of the world."

(For the record, I have no idea what "energy of the world" means, it just sounds like something Witches say.)

Mom nods, watches me stir.

I need to stay positive. I remember yet another line Adler quotes, from a Witch named Bran Tree: *A witch is someone who can become excited over the feel of a pebble or the croak of a frog.*

"I'm just . . . turning hiking into church," I conclude, finally finding something we can connect on. "Turning my love of nature into spirituality. Easy." I hand Mom a glass of swirling sunset liquid, laced with flowers.

My mother inspired my love of hiking. I dedicated my first book, a backpacking how-to titled *How to Suffer Outside*, to her for this reason. This last statement seems to settle her nerves.

"Well, lemme know how it goes," she says, still looking at me cautiously but accepting the glass. We clink, and the pink tequila bounces in the tumblers.

"I will," I say, and stare down into my cup. "I just have to do it first."

COUNTDOWN *to* DAY ONE

Refusing to Call This Section "Which Witch"

*I didn't know it, but I was one of thousands of dormant little
witches all over the country, and years later, we would start to
show ourselves.*
—LORRAINE MONTEAGUT

I begin my journey by typing "best books for beginner witches" into
Google. Of course I am looking for divinity through the internet; it's
where I have found every other piece of information in my life: is this
poison oak, or MRSA; are all Targaryens immune to fire; do you really
need anchors for drywall; how to apply to UC Berkeley; what happens if
you don't do all your homework at UC Berkeley; does it mean anything
if you went to UC Berkeley. Why would I change course now? More
importantly, the Witchcraft community is alive and thriving online. This
is a decentralized folk spirituality after all, whose foundational belief is
that you should be empowered to connect with the divine yourself—no
intermediaries. It is an autodidact's dream religion, practically designed
for the autobahn of free information that is the internet.

And that's actually the problem.

As a template for my spiritual quest, I am using *The Year of Living Biblically*, A.J. Jacobs's best-selling account of his search for spiritual

enlightenment through living the rules of the Old and New Testaments as literally as possible. Jacobs is a forty-year-old Jewish man from New York, looking to connect with his roots, bring meaning to his life, and become a better father and husband. Although our paths are very different, I am ultimately seeking the same holy grail as Jacobs: spiritual fulfillment as a reward for following all the rules.

The trouble is, when Jacobs starts his quest, he has a two-thousand-year-old standardized tome of rules at his disposal. While it's true that the application of those rules are debated (often violently), they still come in a version so culturally ubiquitous you can find it in hotel room drawers, long after telephone books have become obsolete. Unfortunately for me, there is no King James Witchcraft Bible. There are no standardized Witchcraft texts of any kind—no hierarchy, no grand councils, no popes. If modern Witchcraft had a bible, it would probably be the internet. Just, the whole thing. As far as I can tell, the only thing that Witches agree on is that Witchcraft is the process by which empowered individuals shape reality with their will. Every other detail is basically up in the air. Witchcraft is, effectively, a "choose your own adventure" book.

There are, of course, prominent voices that have risen (and fallen) in popularity within the broader community, and hundreds, if not thousands, of Witchcraft books I can read. Most of their covers feature impressionist paintings of women standing on mountaintops in flowing robes, and have titles like *The Way of the Water Priestess*. I scroll through a few pages on Amazon and have serious trouble discerning which are fictional and which are instructional.

I consider that perhaps I shouldn't use the internet as a guide. I should be talking entirely to people, real-life Witches.

That wouldn't be too difficult to do. I live in Oakland, California. Prominent neopagan leaders like Oberon Zell-Ravenheart, Zsuzsanna Budapest, Starhawk, and Cerridwin Fallingstar are perpetually floating around in the coastal fog. Ninety-five percent of the girls I went to high school with knew their sun, moon, and rising signs by eighth grade, and 80 percent were reading tarot like Laurie Cabot by senior year. Starhawk's Reclaiming Witchcraft tradition was born in 1970s across the bridge in San Francisco, and its annual Spiral Dance festival still attracts thousands of circle-trotters every year.

I first heard about Witchcraft in high school from my friend Emma. Emma is a nerdy, doe-eyed marathon runner with a caffeine addiction and a crippling fear of authority. She currently lives in New England with two well-behaved children, a husband who drives a lifted Dodge Ram, and a kitchen that smells perpetually of Lysol and/or freshly baked cinnamon rolls. At first glance you wouldn't guess that she regularly goes upstairs and communes with pre-Christian deities.

At age fifteen, however, Emma and I were high school companions, and she was the first Witch I had ever met. Her mom had converted from Christianity to Judaism because she didn't like Christianity's vibe, and so didn't mind when Emma moved directly into Witchcraft for more or less the same reason. This made her a rare teen who was allowed to practice openly. At least, in the house.

When Emma first invited me over for a "ritual," I wasn't really sure what was going to happen. I was simply intrigued by any religion that involved ceremonial knives, and a quasi-religious reason to stay up past midnight. Plus, the whole thing had a very feminist air, exhilarating and exotic after I'd recently learned in social studies that all the world's major religions agreed on basically nothing except one thing: that women should be compliant, chaste, and concerned primarily with the happiness of their husband and children. Anything else was rebellion (and not the cute kind, with nose piercings and hair dye. The kind where they kill you).

Emma, like many American girls of her generation, was a Wiccan Witch—in fact, Wicca and Witchcraft were basically advertised as the same thing (leading to a great deal of consternation from non-Wiccan Witches, but more on that later). In Wicca, the deity in charge was suddenly, radically female. Okay, yes, there was also some sheep-centaur dude known as "the God" hanging around, but I barely noticed him. I couldn't get my eyes off the capital-G Goddess, a supreme deity in her own right, unshackled from incestuous brothers and unbothered by husbands whose favorite hobby was turning teenage girls into ducks and then mounting them. Emma offered her Fiona Horne books and her insight, explaining to her curious friends the main concepts behind this neopagan religion.* It was reconstructed from what historians had discovered about the "goddess cults" and traditional practices of pre-Christian European peasants (usually Celtic and Nordic). It was not anti-Christian, despite the supposed battle of the ages between Jesus Christ and those who dance with the devil in the pale moonlight.** Wiccans don't proselytize their faith and don't demand exclusivity (as in, you can be a part of another religion, and also be Wiccan). They also believe in reincarnation and a version of karma, expressed through something called the Threefold Law: whatever you put into the universe will come back to you at three times the strength of the original dose. That is to say, even if you believe you are justified, if you try to cause anyone harm, you will feel that energy returned to you. (If you are suddenly reminded of that final scene in *The Craft*: yes, exactly.)

Wiccans also believe that sex is sacred, and pleasure is a gift from the gods to be enjoyed and revered. You should feel encouraged at all times to seek what you want, and never forget that the earth is divine and everything from the top of a mountain to a grain of sand has a life force, echoing the principles of animism present in several indigenous African and Asian religions.

It was beautiful, like a basket of cherries picked from the best ideas from every world religion. And the person holding the basket was a polyamorous ecofeminist with psychic powers, an ironclad pelvic floor, and the ability to talk to dolphins.

Wicca's holidays were determined by the patterns of the earth and sky: equinoxes and solstices, full moons and new moons. But also, the mating cycles of livestock, and calculating when you should plant and harvest your fields. In short, the life-or-death concerns of a preindustrial farmer in Bronze Age Europe. For twenty-first-century American

* If there is a *Clarissa Explains It All* of Witchcraft, it's Fiona Horne. Or, depending on your generation, *iCarly*.
** There are many books about Wicca, and virtually all of them begin with a declaration that Witches don't hate Christians, don't worship Satan, don't have any kind of "black mass," any suggestion that they do has been a huge misunderstanding, and could we all please drop it now and have some tea?

girls, this Wheel of the Year was less about farm chores and more about when we should plan a party. But to our credit, the party always aimed to match the theme.

And then finally, there were spells. Oh my god. Spells were amazing. With a spell, you were granting *yourself* the power to attain something you wanted: protection, money, love, whatever. As long as it harmed no one, we could do what we willed.

Emma also introduced me to the main myth in Wicca, which consisted of an all-powerful "triple" goddess who would transition over the course of a year from Maiden, to Mother, to Crone, along with the horned God, who was either her son or consort (depending on the holiday).

"Isn't that kind of . . . incestuous?" I asked Emma, sitting on her bedroom floor as she laid this all out. Her room was painted twilight blue, her bookshelves overflowing with Lemony Snicket and Outlander books. It smelled constantly of lavender incense, and there was an Evanescence poster taped carefully to one wall.

"No, she doesn't have sex with her son," Emma explained patiently. "He transforms from her son to her lover as she transforms. The whole thing is a metaphor." I nodded, still confused but not wanting to say so. But compared to a virgin giving birth or a guy rising from the dead after three days cold, it wasn't such a wild belief demand. That's part of the challenge of religion, as far as I knew: your participation trophy hinged on having faith in the unbelievable. I wanted to try.

What I didn't know is that while my friends and I were standing in Emma's mom's Pottery Barn–catalog living room chanting, "Isis Astarte Diana Hecate Demeter Kali Inanna," thousands of other teens were standing in living rooms across the world, taking their first steps with Witchcraft, too. It was the early 2000s. So many people—but especially young women and queer people—were all dying of spiritual thirst, searching for a religion that respected our desires to be more than #tradwives and wasn't overtly associated with racism, pedophilia, and a modern crusade in Iraq. In Wicca, we were no longer ribs. Here is Goddess, created in *your* image.

However, although Emma was generous in lending her books, I

couldn't sink too far into the Fiona Horne style of Wicca. I felt like a child, matching colored candles with corresponding directions and memorizing goddess powers like they were spell slots. I couldn't even start to address the faith issue of if I believed the goddess was "real" or not. I wanted spiritual ecstasy. It felt like spiritual Pokémon. Meanwhile Emma was astral projecting. I moved on.

My second foray into Wicca was in my midtwenties, with a woman named Liza. Liza is a proud second-generation, eclectic Wiccan Witch, one of those rare people who actually practiced with family members growing up. Imagine Mrs. Weasly, if Mrs. Weasly was a gay punk who was really into comedy burlesque and purple velvet couches. I met Liza in 2010, when she was getting into fire hula hooping and finishing her master's in fine art. She invited me into the coven she ran with another person named Theodora. These two gave me tarot readings, had me binding yarn around candles on Ostara and invoking the Goddess. I knew most of the steps, and why we were doing them. But despite their generosity of time and spirit (and funds . . . Wicca tends to attract crafty folks, and ceremonies aren't cheap), I still felt like an outsider. This made no sense. I was going through the motions, but something kept preventing me from feeling like I belonged. I wanted to feel the divinity of the cosmos running through me. But I just felt like an imposter. I don't know if I was more afraid of doing something wrong, or of what would happen if I did something right.

Then Covid hit and they took the coven online. My world became a screen; the computer was where I worked, socialized, researched, watched TV, shopped, caught up on news. I drew the line at making it the place where I worshipped. I was grateful when the term "Zoom fatigue" was invented so I could finally put a name to that cotton-stuffed feeling behind my eyes at the end of every evening. Digital video communication, once touted as a science fiction miracle, revealed itself to be a nonnutritive substitute to in-person communication. When it came to Witchcraft on Zoom, it felt like trying to light candles underwater.

Ironically, it was during this time that I felt more called into spirituality than ever before. I decided to move in with Justin, my boyfriend of two years, in March 2020. We didn't know when we were browsing ads on Craigslist earlier that winter that whatever rental we managed to snag in Oakland's competitive market would effectively be our home prison for the next two years. But we got lucky. We landed the top floor of a duplex, a carved-up Victorian with a maze of oddly shaped, postage-stamp-sized rooms that initially felt useless, until their very closeable doors revealed themselves as a blessing by winter 2021. The property has a shared backyard and a few large fruit trees. One of my best friends, Joanna, a pop culture journalist and podcaster, managed to grab the vacant apartment downstairs, making us a full house. As the pandemic waxed on, Justin and I adopted two cats: Bird, a persnickety, owl-faced female, and Basil, an anxious, talkative orange tabby. We populated the backyard first with vegetable beds and then, after a few days of shoveling dirt and cursing at hardware cloth, four teenage hens. Taking care of the animals and plants became my quarantine hobby. And once caretaking lost its luster to distract me from solitary confinement, I suppose I thought I would try religion. Justin, a proud atheist who enjoys dressing up as a Viking shaman every Halloween with a suspicious degree of enthusiasm, was extremely supportive of the idea. In fact, the vast majority of my friends are atheists, and are simultaneously—almost confusingly—supportive of my journey. I am still trying to figure out how to unpack this without accusing them of wanting what I want: to be comforted by the divine. Nobody likes a name-caller.

So, this is me, covenless, painfully typical, midpandemic, actually attempting the journey into Witchcraft on my own.

Which means starting with Google and the anonymous data scientists who see my query and my results and file it away to better improve their marketing algorithms. But it's a safe relationship, me and the search engine. It has never let me down. Besides, this is how most people are getting into Witchcraft these days. We wish we were following the glow of lantern light toward a circle of cloaked figures in the misty woods. Instead, we are following the glow of computer screens toward teenagers with opinions. As Arthur Ashe says: start where you are.

)))●(((

If only one correct way of approaching deity were possible, there
would be one religious ideal. This will never happen.
—SCOTT CUNNINGHAM

Where I am is overwhelmed by the amount of content that exists about
Witchcraft. But I suppose that's par for the course when approaching
a decentralized religion whose goal is to allow every participating
individual to become, as Margot Adler wrote in *Drawing Down the
Moon*, "as the gods." I'm not sure where to start. Until this point, I
actually thought all Witchcraft was the same.

What an idiot.

As I research the timeline of Wicca's development, the first sect
I consider diving into is Gardnerian Wicca. This is, as far as I can tell,
the Catholicism of Witchcraft: the OG, the source, the purest shit you
can get on the street. Gerald Gardner, who founded the tradition in mid-
twentieth-century England, claims to have inherited it from a Stone Age
matriarchal cult that had kept its practices both uncontaminated and con-
fidential over two thousand–plus years of literal Witch hunts. And despite
the fact that, as far as I can tell, basically no one believes his story, most
still agree he has earned his title: the Father of Modern Witchcraft. The
practices he introduced in the mid-twentieth century have been passed
around from disciple to disciple, each person remixing and adding a bit
of this and that, to form much of the bedrock of modern Witchcraft in
America. I study the image of Gardner on his Wikipedia page. He looks
like a cross between Gary Oldman's Dracula and Doc from *Back to the
Future.* He looks unsettling. He looks happy to have unsettled you.

Gardner's books are not the oldest books on Witchcraft, though;[*]
that distinction would probably go to Charles Leland's *Aradia.* Pub-

---

[*] I'm not counting the medieval classics *The Discoverie of Witchcraft* by Reginald
Scot, or the *Malleus Maleficarum*, which are, respectively, medieval stage magic
tutorials and torture instructions for women who talk.

lished in 1899, *Aradia: Or the Gospel of the Witches* is a slip of a book, containing a dreamy Italian myth of how the goddess Diana, "Queen of All Witches," told her daughter Aradia to teach Witchcraft to the earthlings—like Prometheus, but with moonbeams. It contains a few spells for what I can only assume are the everyday concerns of Italians: prosperity, vengeance, and "How to Have Very Good Wine." Leland claims he received all this knowledge from a traditional Witch named Maddalena.* But it was Gardener who took Leland's writings (along with a few other characters) and expressed them as a living, breathing religion that he claimed had been operating in secret for centuries. I love this story. There is a legitimacy to it—if something survived thousands of years, it's impossible to question, right? There's just one problem: it's considered by most historians to be total bunk.

The Stone Age goddess cult theory, as I've come to refer to it, is the idea that Wicca descended, either completely or partially, from a prehistoric, shamanic, pan-European, matriarchal fertility cult, which survived attempted eradication during the "Burning Times" of medieval Europe. This theory goes by a few names, and variants of it are held by a few different twentieth-century historians, but the main face I keep running into is a Victorian Egyptologist and folklorist named Margaret Murray. A kind of founding mother of neopaganism, Murray did a great deal to legitimize Wicca as more than a weekend hobby for eager nudists, but a revival of a very real pre-Christian religion that used to dominate ancient Europe. What I find most remarkable about her is that she did most of her research during the World Wars, when university positions were quite rare, as all the people who should have been attending classes were busy murdering each other in the French countryside. Murray was primarily an Egyptologist; her research on Wicca was more of a side project, which to me makes it all the more impressive. Imagine if your weekend hobby became the foundation of the world's fastest growing

---

* The debate about the truth of this sentence cannot be overstated. Consider this footnote a symbolic space for the thousands and thousands of pages dedicated to questioning Leland's claim.

religion. I'm convinced someone needs to make a movie about her, like *Erin Brockovich* meets *The Mummy*. Which is why I'm extremely disappointed to learn that after decades of accolades, her work was discredited shortly before her death in 1963.

In the 1990s, Murray's work was further dragged into the mud by historian and commissioner of English heritage Ronald Hutton, in his book *The Triumph of the Moon*. Hutton (himself rumored to be a neopagan) argues that Wicca has more to do with freemasonry and man's hunger for theatrics, rather than with anything verifiably prehistoric. He concludes that Wicca is a valid religion. It's just that most professional academics don't understand how to study a faith that "occupies the ground at which nature religion, post-modern religion, and revived religion intersect," without, well, making fun of it. Hutton's book ripped the Witchcraft community in two, between those who wanted to continue to believe their rituals had descended intact from ancient, secret traditions and those who were okay with the idea that Gerald Gardner made them up. The effects of the conflict are still being felt to this day.

Finally, Gardner was heavily influenced by Aleister Crowley, the notorious early-twentieth-century occultist who founded Thelema, and whose goal in life was to "bring oriental wisdom to Europe and to restore paganism in a purer form." As far as I can tell, Crowley spent most of his life in a tower FaceTiming demons and pitching just about anything to the English upper crust on the condition that it made Christians nervous (kabbalah, yoga, tarot, sex magic, tantra, and so forth).

Which leads us to today. Most historians, and a healthy number of Witches, agree that Gardner was not actually pulling an ancient, mystical, earth-based religion out of the Dark Ages and into the light of 1950s England. Rather, Gardner was taking "material from any source that didn't run away too fast." Mary Nesnick (a disciple of Gardner's) explains that "50 percent of modern Wicca is an invention bought and paid for by Gerald B. Gardner from Aleister Crowley. Ten percent was 'borrowed' from books and manuscripts like Leland's *Aradia*. The remaining 40 percent was borrowed from Far Eastern religions and philosophies, if not in word, then in ideas and basic principles."

This seems to answer all my questions about how Indian nag champa incense, Italian tarot, the Chinese goddess Guanyin, and a tapestry of the Celtic Green Man all seem allowed to rub shoulders in the occult shops of America today. Perhaps this is the real meaning of Witchcraft: grab whatever resonates and doesn't run away too fast.

This should be a fun, uncomplicated year as a white person.

But fuzzy history isn't actually the reason I decide not to dig deeper into Wicca's original form. It's because Wicca didn't stop evolving after Gardener. Not even close. (And also, if I'm being honest with myself, it's that all ceremonies are to be done "skyclad," which is a fancy occult word for getting naked in front of total strangers. Call me a victim of the patriarchy, but I'm not ready to take off my pants in front of a crowd just yet.)

There are dozens of Wiccan sects, if not hundreds: Alexandrian Wicca, Algard Wicca, Seax Wicca, Dianic Wicca, Covenant of the Goddess Wicca, British Traditional Wicca, Welsh Wicca, Pictish Wicca, Celtic Wicca—the list keeps going. But that's not the worst of it.

I am also continuously reminded while surfing through blogs and book titles that while Wicca is a religion whose followers refer to themselves often as Witches, *Witchcraft* is not. You can be a Wiccan Witch, but you can also be a Hellenic Witch, a hedge Witch, a green Witch, a lunar Witch, an Egyptian Witch, a Luciferian Witch, a Norse Witch, a cosmic Witch, a shamanic Witch, a kitchen Witch, a Jewish Witch—virtually any ethnicity, religion, or adjective can precede the title. The African American practices of Hoodoo, Conjure, and Rootwork are also considered Witchcraft, as well as Brujeria, a modern version of Latin American Witchcraft that blends folk Catholicism with indigenous traditions. In Pennsylvania, there is a whole Christian Witchcraft tradition called Powwow that is at once practiced by white people and not considered problematic according to liberal Twitter.

Some of these branches share holidays and founding members. Some of them will call you racist if you conflate them with one another. Some of them were made up by thirteen-year-olds last year. I am trying to pay attention to the differences. I also feel like I'm reading a dissertation from an audiophile who's taken it upon himself to educate the masses on the subtle nuances between screamo and metalcore. It's complicated by the fact that for most of the twentieth century, all Wiccans referred to themselves simply as Witches, leading to very vocal uproar from the Witches who didn't relate to Wicca at all. I've come to see Wicca as a popular religious scaffolding around Witchcraft, but whether Witchcraft itself is a religion depends entirely on what tradition you're following.

So basically I feel completely lost on where I should start.

I come across a video from LadySpeech Sankofa on TikTok (the "home of modern witchcraft" according to *Wired* magazine), advising beginner Witches on their journeys to "start with your ancestors." She leans into the camera and croons, "Start with who you are; that's going to give you a very clear direction, and you'll more than likely avoid shit that don't belong to you." I take this as a very polite way of saying, "If you're white, stay out of POC traditions, please." Noted.

According to my birth certificate, I am French, Welsh, Portuguese, and German. I remember discovering this when I was about fifteen and feeling a rush of curiosity. Until then, I had been a standard-issue WASP, the same nebulous, milquetoast European mix that most white Americans claim as heritage. My ancestors (as far as I know) were mostly peasants, which is to say we had no money, which is to say no one has kept any great records about who we were and why we should be proud of ourselves. As I was growing up, the unspoken assumption I got from my family's lack of stories about where we came from is that we came from nowhere special, and we had nothing to be proud of. As time went on, and I learned about Native American genocide and slavery in the early United States, the beguiling void of where I came from turned into an ecru rainbow of white guilt. Then, around five years ago, my curiosity got the better of me and I did what every modern woman does when she feels the urge to discover herself: I mailed my spit to strangers. The results mostly matched with what was on my birth certificate. And I was confronted with the aseptic reality of genetics research. What your DNA doesn't tell you is specifically how most of your ancestors lived, what they did for a living, or what they believed was happening when they prayed. My ancestors' very desire seemed to be that the third, fourth, fifth generation of children they produced not know what came before them. I was supposed to be American, period: someone with no past, only a star-spangled future. This is the story of many white Americans. Even the most ethnocentric, burger-grilling, flag-waving patriots among us, when asked, "Where are you from?" will lift their heads toward the Atlantic, get a little misty-eyed, and declare something like: "I'm twenty-five percent Swedish." The truth is white Americans have no idea who they are. To go to our roots is to try and pull individual ingredients out of a melting pot. It's probably why we're both bad at it and sensitive about being told we're doing it wrong. I wonder how long it takes for blood to forget where it comes from, and what it becomes after that.

What I have gleaned about my ancestry, however, is enough to point me at Celtic and English-grown Witchcraft—which I take to be Wicca— with perhaps some nods to Germanic traditions. I try to find information about Portuguese Witchcraft and only get results about the Inquisition.

While this might appear to some as fairly sloppy sourcing, cobbling together a patchwork of unverified, pre-Christian traditions is indeed what most Witches are doing when they venture down the Crooked Path of the Craft.

In a 2020 Pulitzer Center article titled "Is Witchcraft Too Main-stream?" Claire Hogan quotes Deborah Blake, a Wiccan high priestess and author of *Everyday Witchcraft*: "Witches in general are sort of slowly veering away from the strictly wiccan [*sic*], and going more toward 'I would consider myself to be an eclectic witch now,' which values a little bit of everything." Hogan goes on to explain that when surveyed, most self-identified Witches identify as "eclectic," which is to say, they "adapt their beliefs from a variety of sources and traditions with a focus on the natural world." The more I research, the more I discover eclectic Wicca (sometimes called solitary Wicca) is not just some catchall, but its own respected branch of this religion. I'd like to lean into Wicca. I do want some religious backing for my spiritual experiment. I know I don't have to be a Wiccan to be a Witch, but considering how much modern Witchcraft was influenced by Gardner (whether today's Witches even know his name), in such an ocean of options, something with a little history and structure feels comforting.

But then the question becomes which books and study materials to start with; who will be my spiritual advisory panel? I feel I am doomed if I am to attach myself to standards like "the oldest," "the newest," or "the least likely to be crucified at an oral dissertation defense."

Finally, it occurs to me that this is a folk religion. So I lean into the folk aspect: I let it be a popularity contest. I will simply buy the top eight best-selling books that have "Wicca" in the title, along with Gardner's *Witchcraft Today* and Leland's *Aradia*.

I also call in as my advisers Meg Elison and Lauren Parker, two Witches in my weekly writing group who have been quietly observing my flirtation with solitary Witchcraft during Covid confinement. Meg is a Philip K. Dick Award–winning science fiction author, Wiccan, Thelemite, and Berkeley scholar. She drives a hatchback sedan covered in quotes from Neil Gaiman novels, and although I have not officially asked, I think her favorite hobbies (in order) are wearing cherry-red lipstick, sipping Dom Perignon, and telling me off. Lauren is a soft-faced anarchist crust punk who transplanted herself from Cleveland to Oakland ten years ago because it felt safer here. She is the owner of Star Anise Crafts, a feminist essayist, and a Wiccan turned chaos magician, which is a type of Witchcraft that purports you should use whatever ideas and practices are helpful to you at the moment, even if they contradict the ideas and practices you used previously. When I proudly showed her a selenite wand Justin gave me for my birthday—a magical branch that seems to glow with moonlight from within—her first reaction was to advise me not to put it in my vagina. Last I heard she was reading Agrippa and scouring the Bible for hidden spells.

Like fairies in a Brothers Grimm tale, Meg and Lauren will occasionally pop in to nudge me along with helpful advice when I need it the most. The books they have put into my lap so far are *Wicca: A Guide for the Solitary Practitioner* by Scott Cunningham and *The Spiral Dance* by Starhawk.

I throw all the other books into my cart, check out, and get up from the computer. Now I wait a few days for my spiritual journey to arrive, like a fevered late-night purchase of beauty vitamins on TikTok, promising to change my life.

JULY *and* AUGUST

DAY 1

Many novice witches discover they face challenges in developing
an individual and intuitive Wheel of the Year practice.
—TEMPERANCE ALDEN

For no reason at all, I decided to begin my journey on July 31. It's a day I had free to write, to take staged pictures of witchy books strewn across my office floor with captions like "New Project, What Could Go Wrong?" According to some, the best time to begin the traditional year and a day of Wiccan training is around October 31—aka Witch's New Year—because the earth is hibernating. Other traditions believe this is the worst time to begin because the earth is hibernating. Like most everything else in this religion, it's up to me to decide whose advice I want to take. I decide to stick to the day I had the courage to announce what I was doing on Instagram.

There is one problem with my choice, however, which I didn't realize until just a few minutes ago. Tomorrow is Lughnasadh.

I discover this while flipping through the sabbat calendar in

Cassandra Eason's *A Little Bit of Wicca*. The book is about as thin as an electric bill—clearly meant to be a primer on the Craft rather than an exhaustive authority. But it was one of the best sellers, and I'm trying to give them all equal time.

I learn that there are two types of holidays in Wiccan-style Witchcraft. The first are esbats. These are full moon gatherings where covens engage in ritual spellwork, reflection, and, I assume, lighthearted gossip and sampling of premium Trader Joe's snacks. The other type of Wiccan holidays are sabbats, the "high holidays" of the Wheel of the Year. Because of Wicca's focus on the cycles of the natural world, the seasons, the waning and waxing of daylight hours, I assumed all the sabbats fell on astronomical solstices and equinoxes. That's only half true. The so-called lesser sabbats are Ostara (vernal equinox), Litha (summer solstice), Mabon (fall equinox), and Yule (winter solstice). The four greater sabbats were pulled from Ireland's pre-Christian "cross-quarter" holidays, and to my novice eyes have the apparently arbitrary dates of Samhain (October 31), Imbolc (February 1), Beltane (May 1), and Lughnasadh (fucking tomorrow).*

I don't have anything ready. I'm barely even a Witch. I haven't cast one spell, I haven't read a single tarot spread, or communed with one pre-Christian deity. And one of the high holidays is tomorrow? I don't even know how to pronounce Lughnasadh. It looks like if mashed potatoes were a word. I have to work quickly.

I snatch every Witchcraft book off the shelf and start flipping through all of them with a pen, paper, and a stack of Post-it notes. There is some discrepancy about the underlying myth behind this holiday, but the most common one is that the Celtic god of light (Lugh) sacrifices himself in order to lend the rest of his light to the earth, ensuring the crops may continue to flourish throughout the remainder of summer. Some variations include: Lugh marrying the Goddess, or actually, Lugh

---

* Later I will find out the cross-quarter days do follow astronomical rules. Imbolc, for example, starts when the sun reaches fifteen degrees of Aquarius. The dates for this can fluctuate between January 31 and February 5. For ease of planning, it seems most Witches have agreed to pick a fixed day and go from there.

is not about to sacrifice himself, we're celebrating how great his mom is. But most authors seem to agree Lugh is doing something big and important for us all, and things are being harvested for the first time, and we should reflect on that.

I reflect on the fact that I have never harvested a single shaft of wheat in my entire life and wonder if I have ever even held a sickle unironically. The disconnection of my urban life with the preindustrial people who came up with these myths continues to feel more and more pronounced.

Fortunately, my Wiccan authors have thought of this.

Today, if you live in densely packed urban housing with plumbing, electricity, and a nearby grocery store that's part of an international trade network ensuring you have year-round access to bananas, the celebration is not so much about the literal harvest. The idea of a god figure lending the last of his light to protect the remaining crops is a metaphor to encourage you to think about sacrifices in your own life: to reflect on the results of what was sown months ago, and to consider what must be done to create great things and protect them from the fact that soon (I can't believe I get to say this) winter is coming.

I read through the rituals written by my cohort of Wiccan elders and feel like I'm having a nightmare about showing up to my SATs without studying. The scenes described are lengthy and lavish, with all the pomp and drama of an eighteenth-century oil painting. They include instructions on which way to walk around a circle, which direction to pass a chalice, who should kiss whom, and of course, songlike liturgy to recite. But I have no one to kiss. I am not a part of a coven yet. The preface of Raymond Buckland's *Complete Book of Witchcraft* (known fondly to many as "The Big Blue Book") says he welcomes solitary practitioners. But all his rituals assume you have found at least four willing people to join you on a Saturday night for a romping good time donning black robes, traipsing around a pentacle, clapping your hands, and singing, "Haste! Haste! No time to wait! We're off to the sabbat so don't be late!"

For Lughnasadh, all the books seem to agree that I need a yellow candle, some wheat shafts, and a loaf of bread (or some other symbolic block of gluten). Then there are optional items such as flowers, blackberries, star cookies, and dolls made of corn. That's just a trip to the grocery store. I can handle that.

The trouble is that I don't have the main altar tools. They include a cauldron, a pentacle, a chalice, a bell, a censer, a candle snuffer, an athame (a ceremonial dagger), a bolline (a different ceremonial dagger), and an unconscionable number of candles. This is in addition to the dolls, crystals, flowers, crowns, centerpieces, and other handmade Craft items specific to the season. I am once again reminded that Witchcraft is truly the religion of crafters. I don't know why I'm worried about finding a coven; I could probably walk into a Michaels and shout, "As I will it?" and just follow whoever shouts back, "So mote it be!" like a game of Marco Polo.

All of my authors iterate somewhere in their books that none of these ceremonial items are *required* to practice magic and be a proper Witch. But then they spend most of their time explaining how they all work together and how to use them, so I feel a touch double-crossed. I want to do this as correctly as possible. I figure I need to learn the rules before I break them.

Which means I have to go shopping. Quickly.

It's 4:30, but (and I chalk this up to the benefit of living in the liberal posthippie Goddess movement Bay Area) there are three occult shops within four miles of me, all open until 7:00 p.m. I get into the car with Justin, who has pointed out we also need a grocery run.

At Berkeley Bowl, the Bay Area's undisputed best grocery store, I buy blackberries and corn bread mix, thinking I can use the bread for both a corn doll and the traditional bread loaf. I am not very adept at arts and crafts, and I don't think I could make a corn doll out of an actual corn cob. Cutting a man-shaped blob out of a batch of "just add water" corn bread is more my speed.

I cannot find any star-shaped cookies, the store is out of flower bouquets, and the blackberry clamshell snaps open at checkout, the berries leaping all over the floor. I briefly wonder if it's a sign. I decide I don't have time to care. But the corn bread is safe. I can make corn bread work.

The occult shop I visit is called Ancient Ways, a humble storefront with a black sign on Oakland's Telegraph Avenue. I step inside and the perfume of ten thousand incense cones competes for dominance in my nostrils. The shop is small and dark, but the clerk gives me a bright hello, smizing above her mask. She is chubby and tall, with perfect, mile-long blond braids draped over her shoulders. She looks like the kind of person I would probably gravitate toward at a party, so we could play fuck, marry, kill with all the characters in *Lord of the Rings*. I feel safe.

The shop is 80 percent bookshelves, with a floor-to-ceiling wall of jarred herbs behind the counter and bowls of crystals and gemstones sparkling inside glass cabinets. I grab a forty-cent yellow candle, a twenty-dollar cauldron (a small brass pot that fits in the palm of my hand and is emblazoned with a pentacle), and an actual pentacle from a rack of necklaces. It's about the size of a quarter. I was hoping to find a weighty pentacle, iron and imposing, the kind of thing that could double as a trivet for a Thanksgiving turkey. Liza had one of these, and I always thought it was supremely badass. But they have none, so I settle for the necklace. I don't have time to be picky.

My eyes dart around for the athames, and finally I see two rows of them under the glass cabinet in front of the counter.

Athames are ceremonial daggers, often used to cast a circle around a group before rituals. Technically the sacred athame is supposed to be black handled, to differentiate it from the bolline, which is white handled and used for more mundane tasks like cutting cakes, or inscribing symbols onto candles. The daggers in the case before me are all over the place. One looks like flinted horn and obsidian. Another is wooden and blunt, like a children's pirate sword toy. I look up and see an elderly man has come behind the counter and spread his arms wide over the glass, watching me. He has wiry eyebrows and a bushy white beard poking from behind his surgical mask.

"I call that one 'my first athame,'" he chortles at the pirate sword, and pulls it out, pretending to slice his arm against the dull wooden blade. I smile in response.

This is it, I think. *This is my Ollivander, and I am Harry Potter, and he is going to connect me with my wand.*

"What are you interested in?" he asks kindly. I realize I am probably projecting all the confidence of someone buying their first dildo.

"What's up with the one that looks like it's made of plastic?" I ask, pointing to an opaque white athame that suggests a 3-D printer has gotten into the occult business.

"That's selenite," he says, passing it to me. I think it will be heavy, but it's light as a fistful of feathers. The material is glossy and foggy at the same time, moonlight made solid. It's only twenty dollars, and I think maybe this is the one.

"I should warn you, you can't get that wet. Selenite dissolves in water."

My eyes flick up to him, "Dissolves . . . ?"

"Yep, it'll just vanish if you get so much as a drop on it." He chortles. "Poof!"

I realize he is making a joke and attempt to chuckle in kind.

"No, but seriously, I left mine outside in the rain, and it can deeply damage the quality of the stone if you get it wet."

I hand it back. I don't want to risk tipping over a chalice of ale and ruining my sacred blade my first night out on the job.

"What about that one?" I point to a modest little double-edged dagger with a wooden handle that looks like it's been dipped in watercolors.

"You know, this one was calling to me to pull out for you, actually," he says, bending over to fish it out of the case. He rises and places it in my hand. It's small and light. It's obviously cheap. I try not to read into the implied insult that he thought it would be perfect for me. Especially since he'd be right. I'm mentally adding up my collection of objects and already feeling nervous about swiping my credit card. I grasp the hilt of the blade. I don't feel a breeze in my hair or a warm, tingling feeling. But I don't get a bad feeling, either.

I turn it over and read a little label that says Made in Pakistan. I think about the hands that have touched it. I wonder about fair labor practices, and their effect on my ritual. I wonder what I was expecting:

that everything in here would be made from well-fed Irish grannies and Instagram sylphs? *And* be affordable?

I put the athame on the counter with the rest of my items.

"You look like you're getting the whole starter kit," he remarks, eyeing the candle, the cauldron, and the pentacle I've collected from the rest of the shop.

"Yeah, tomorrow is . . . um . . . you know, I actually don't know how to pronounce it."

"Lammas!" the woman chirps brightly from the end of the counter. The two of them chuckle conspiratorially.

Lammas is the other (Catholic) name for Lughnasadh (I later read it is pronounced LOO-nah-sah), but I think many Witches prefer to say "Lammas" because of its forgiving lack of Celtic consonants. I appreciate that these two are giving me permission to do so, as well.

"I don't have anything ready, so I'm trying to get it all together today," I say, gesturing to my splayed starter kit on the glass counter. "You don't have any larger pentacles, do you?" He shakes his head in response.

"Okay. I'm sure it will be fine. I mean, I'll be the only one there, right?" I laugh.

"The Goddess will be there," says the man, making eye contact with me. He is no longer smiling.

A beat of silence passes where I feel like I am supposed to say something back, but I don't know the line.

"But she's pretty understanding," says the woman, breaking the silence.

I blink over at her, grateful. "A for effort, right?" I ask. She nods and smiles at me.

Ollivander rings me up for seventy-six dollars and I try not to squirm. I understand this is still cheap in the relative scheme of things, but this is a lot of money to me. And it isn't even everything on my list. I am grateful they happened to be all out of chalices. I quietly plan to use a large, opaque black goblet embossed with chubby roses that I have at home. It's technically one in a series sold at Central California's famously garish midcentury hotel, the Madonna Inn. It was given to me by Liza before she moved away (or, rather, she was getting rid of it, and I asked if I could keep it). It's currently holding sticky change and dust on my living room windowsill. Tonight I'll wash it three times, and tomorrow I will use it to toast pre-Christian gods.

"Welcome to the Craft," he says, kindly, as I make my way to the door.

"Thank you," I call over my shoulder, and I mean it.

I duck back into the car. Justin had decided to wait here, despite my saying it was perfectly fine if he wanted to come inside.

"You smell like a Witch," he says as the incense fumes fall off me like loose powder.

I pull out my little bag of trinkets and begin to show them off.

"That's a kirpan!" he says brightly when I produce the athame.

"No, it's an athame," I say, defensive. "What's a kirpan?"

"A ceremonial dagger worn by Sikhs as a reminder to always be ready to fight against injustice." Justin had a nerd affair with Sikhism during his religious studies class in college, and still carries around the lore at all times.

I suddenly notice a belt clip on the back of the dagger's sheath and remember the Made in Pakistan label.

"Oh my god," I say. I put my head on the steering wheel. It is day one, and I am appropriating already. "I didn't know what else to do! My other options were a children's toy, a ninety-dollar goat horn, or a stone that literally dissolves in water."

He raises his hands in immediate defeat. "I'm not an expert! It just reminded me of a kirpan."

Later I go home and Google "kirpan," and notice that all the daggers are curved. I also text Meg and ask her what she thinks. She fires back: *If it's not curved, it's not a kirpan.*

I retort, "And the belt clip? What about the Made in Pakistan label?"

She texts: *Being made in Pakistan does not make something a kirpan.*

I consider how panicked the mere idea that I am appropriating has made me. She suggests it's not helpful. This makes me bristle. I know only a handful of things at this point, but one of them is that Witchcraft is full to bursting with cultural appropriation. Everyone seems to be talking about how it is ever-present and constant.

So it feels responsible (or at least, easier) to feel bad about everything I'm doing, until proven otherwise.

That's not what's being asked of you, she replies when I try to explain this. *There's nothing wrong with doing research. Being paranoid is not "the work."*

DAY 2

*The altar is sometimes round, to represent the Goddess and
spirituality, though it may also be square, symbolic of the
elements. It may be nothing more than an area of ground [or] a
cardboard box covered with a cloth . . .*
—SCOTT CUNNINGHAM

I start prepping my altar for the Lammas ritual around 9 p.m., after the sun has nearly set.

I don't have a yellow altar cloth, but I do have a yellow silk veil from an old dance costume. I hesitate to use this, because I really like it. It was hand dyed by a teacher, and if any candle wax or juice drips were to stain it, I would be upset.

It becomes suddenly obvious that for precisely this reason I should use it. I feel so disconnected from the necessary sacred objects I purchased at Ancient Ways yesterday that sprinkling in something that actually means something to me feels important, if not critical.

Next I try to find a clean surface. Every single table in my house is covered in cat toys, long-suffering orchids, and fat stacks of old magazines that I refuse to clean up on principle of their belonging to Justin. The cleanest table in the house is probably the dining room table, but using that feels insane, because it's in the middle of the house, and I'd have to ask Justin to lock himself somewhere else because I don't want him to see me practicing Witchcraft.

Eventually, I settle on my office, since it's the only place in the house that's both truly mine and has a door that shuts. Although to call it an office is generous: really it's a nook, all of four by six feet. The walls were painted Pepto-Bismol pink by the landlord, and along with three bookshelves and a computer desk, a very large cardboard box sits against the far wall, full of T-shirts from an old podcast project. The box is one of those objects you put down in your house on the express promise of taking it somewhere else someday, and then, since there actually is nowhere else to take it, and it's not hurting anybody, it slowly becomes part of the landscape until you forget it was never supposed to be there at all. I weigh the idea of building an altar on something I consider technically speaking to be trash, but my desk is covered in monitors and keyboards, and there's simply no other free space. I carefully pull the yellow silk veil over the box, tuck in the corners, and it looks quite legitimate. I feel a swell of optimism.

Then I open several of my Wiccan best sellers to their respective chapters on building an altar and promptly lose my mind.

Everyone seems to agree that the four elements must be represented: salt for earth and the north; incense for air and the east; a candle for fire and the south; and a bowl or chalice for water and the west. But after that, the consensus among the authors about what is critically necessary, and what is merely a suggestion, crumbles like a stale cookie. In addition to the four representations of the elements, there's the chalice, the bell, the athame, the (other?) chalice, a variety of taper candles, pillar candles, a smudge stick, and the cauldron. That's all before the optional/not-optional Lammas-mandated apple cider, which may or may not go in the chalice and thus may or may not represent water and may or may not go on top of the pentacle in the center of the altar, which thus may or may not still be able to properly represent the west.

I need to pick one road map and stick with it. I decide to put all the items together on the altar in the order recommended by Scott Cunningham in *Wicca: A Guide for the Solitary Practitioner.*

This book is widely considered to be the pioneer text for solitary

Witches—which is to say, people who wanted to become a Wiccan but didn't know anyone who could usher them into a closed coven (which is to say, me). Plenty of Witches, especially Gerald Gardner's most famous disciple and author of most of his liturgy, Doreen Valiente, spoke about a desire to open Wicca to the public in the mid-1900s. But it was Cunningham who actually wrote the book on it in 1989. He argued that Wicca is too important, too beautiful to limit itself to those who are fortunate enough to have covens to initiate them. For his efforts, he has become a legend. I've met numerous Witches who barely recognize Gardner's name, but all of them know Cunningham. He is the Bernie Sanders of Witchcraft, smashing the occultism 1 percent and handing out free ~~health care~~ spells to the weary masses. His Wikipedia photo shows a calm, nerdy white man in his prime, with oversized eighties glasses, a soft smile, thin hair, and a porn mustache. He smiles peacefully back at the viewer, hand resting thoughtfully on his chin, as if he's about to tell you how lovely you look today. He died in 1993 of an infection complicated by AIDS. He was thirty-six.

With Cunningham's urtext in my hand, I lay out my altar according to his instructions, taking special care to mimic his diagram.

I step back. It looks like a Whole Foods threw up on a Renaissance fair painting. I sigh.

The Goddess will be there, I remember the man from the occult shop telling me. *But she is forgiving*, the woman added.

This is just not working. I want to play by the rules; I really, *really* want to do this "correctly," but I realize I'm at a point where following the letter of the law is going to defeat the spirit. So I decide to listen to the other half of the altar-building advice given by the Wiccan experts who take so many chapters to describe how to do it perfectly: I don't actually have to do what they say at all.

I swipe everything off the top of the yellow silk–covered cardboard box and start over. I still represent the four elements with their suggested items. But rather than obsess about where to put all the candles, the bell, the athame, and my Madonna Inn–embossed chalice of apple juice, I just pretend like I'm decorating.

Finished, I step back and observe my creation. It still looks awkward. The box is sinking a little in the middle under the weight of the cauldron and my incense burner. But it doesn't look crowded. There's some kind of flow to it. It looks like a proper altar.

Pleased, I sit down cross-legged in front of it. Before starting the ritual, I decide to read as much as possible so I don't have to be referencing a book every two minutes while I'm in divine ecstasy. However, the rituals for Lammas in the books I'm reading all invariably reference earlier chapters in said books about how exactly Wiccans cast the sacred circle in which ceremonial magic is performed. These chapters are long, detailed, and extremely serious. It is 9:30 p.m. I am hungry. I am tired. I kick myself for not doing this earlier, but mostly I just want to get it done.

I suddenly remember Cassandra Eason's book and grab it hungrily, taking back all the teasing I did yesterday about it being as thin as an electric bill. Her instructions to cast the circle are blessedly succinct, and nevertheless completely sincere.

The circle represents a space between worlds, outside of time, a sphere of energy that protects its inhabitants and allows magic to be raised in a cone of power, and then sent out to actualize the intentions of its creators. It should ideally be nine feet in diameter. But since I don't have that kind of real estate in my closet-office, I'm just going to aim to make it round, and big enough that I can take a step or two and stay inside it. I quickly realize this means it will have to encompass my entire office, and everything in it, including all my books, my computer, four years' worth of tax returns, the cats' veterinary records, a filing cabinet of external hard drives and Scotch tape, shipping supplies, and a trash can. At first this feels profane, but I decide to go for it because a) this room could use some energy cleansing since all I ever do in here is grit my teeth and swear at emails and b) casting a rhomboid does not appear to be an option.

I have my map in hand, but, before I cast, I am supposed to stand and turn to each direction of the office and call the corners. This means holding my arms in the air and whispering, "I call on the guardians of the watchtowers of the east, to aid me in this working," for all four respective directions. To be clear, Cunningham isn't suggesting I whisper. I'm whispering because I don't want anyone else in our building to hear me. But I also want to say it out loud.

As I do this, I also realize that when I imagine the watchtowers, I am actually imagining the little element towers that pop up above the stones in the final Egyptian tomb scene in *The Fifth Element*. I try to shake this off, instead forcing myself to imagine a series of great, mysterious stone pillars, under an alien aurora sky. Catching the cue, my brain, like a helpful idiot, produces the starry cut scene in *Avengers: Endgame*, where Black Widow flings herself off the eternity cliff. *Please stop doing that*, I think. *This is religion, not the movies. Get serious.* I press on.

Following Eason's instructions, I sit back down cross-legged in front of my cardboard box, waving my hands and saying over and over, "May only goodness and light remain here and may this area be dedicated for the greatest good and highest purpose." It does feel quite grounding. I have never heard myself chant before. There is something powerful about declaring something aloud, instead of simply repeating it in your head. *Okay*, I think. *This is cool. I can do this. This is getting real.*

Eason's book quickly fails me, though, as she doesn't mention how I should *use* the athame to cast the circle. I know from having watched other Witches that there is definitely a way I'm supposed to do this. D. J. Conway spends several pages talking about what a big deal it is, and I was hoping to push that book off to another day, but instead, it appears I must drop Eason and pick Conway back up for more detailed instruction.

Immediately I realize I have called the corners wrong. At least according to her. I probably should have cast the circle first, before calling the watchtowers. I decide to pretend I didn't read that.

I stand up, dagger in my "power hand" (my dominant hand), and begin to cast the circle. I really do feel something here. I visualize a blue-and-white flame at the end of the dagger tracing along my floor, cutting through the air to the great beyond. My mind once again jumps up like an overeager assistant and attempts to offer me an image of Will Parry cutting into Lyra's world in Philip Pullman's *The Subtle Knife*.

I said stop it, I tell my subconscious.

As I walk, my right forearm feels alive with the unusual amount of attention. But then I realize I'm not drawing the circle evenly. My line is a bit wobbly. I imagine a wriggling, unfinished cut between worlds. The idea that I don't believe in alternate dimensions is suddenly belied by the fact that I'm genuinely spooked. Yes, I'm sure this is all just the power of visualization, but what if I have done something really wrong here; what if it is all real, it's not just my imagination, and I am fucking with powers wildly beyond my grasp? What if I'm the metaphysical equivalent of a toddler who accidentally lowers the parking brake in a car and rolls down a hill? Probably not. But if I am, the consequences suddenly feel too risky.

I stop, swivel around to the top of my invisible circle, and redraw it again—carefully. I then sit down in my imagined sphere, trying to force a sense of calm over myself. Then I read that I am supposed to have four taper candles to represent the four watchtowers within the circle. And also, I have to pee.

Almost all the ritual instructions say that once the circle is cast, you pretty much can't leave unless you cut a special door with the athame. I don't know if I'm supposed to cut the door where I started, or anywhere at all. I waste five minutes looking for this answer in the stack of books now piling up next to my altar before giving up and deciding just to hold it.

The truth is I end up switching back and forth between books so many times, any sensations of transcendental energy or *the gaze of higher powers* is quickly and completely lost. It is impossible to maintain a sense of ceremony while flipping pages, trying to determine who is right about which order to light the pillar candle, the taper candle, and the incense.

It's not all stress, though. Some of the lines in the rituals suggested by my authors strike me as so beautiful I find myself momentarily choked up.

I hover my athame over the incense bowl and say, "May the blessings of the God be upon this incense, symbol of air. May I always listen to the spiritual inspiration that whispers to my soul." I know that doesn't sound like much to read, but try saying it out loud to yourself sometime. To *hear* yourself promise to take your own dreams of spiritual fulfillment seriously carries an unexpected weight.

I also read, and then reread, and then finally as instructed say aloud: "By the bright circle of the golden sun, by the bright courses of the glorious moon, by the dread potency of every star in the mysterious zodiac's burning girth, by each and all of these supernal signs, I do call and command you with this sacred blade." This is directed toward the old ones, which is to say the God and Goddess, Wicca's ultimate polar energies of the universe. I fade at the end, my voice washed out by a sensation of egomania. I can hear the peanut gallery commentary on my little scene here, "Yes, there she is, everyone. Here in this two-bedroom duplex, the pudgy admin assistant will control starlight."

I make a mental note that immodesty might be the only crime among the Wiccans.

After what feels like about forty minutes of preamble (I'm not sure, I left my phone in the other room to underscore the idea that I am supposed to be outside of time), I get to the part where I am actually supposed to do things related to Lammas.

At Conway's advice, I decide to take a few moments of quiet meditation, breathing in cleansing energy and breathing out negative energy. I'm pretty sure this practice is cribbed from Buddhism. I'm also pretty sure I need a break, so I do it with genuine relief.

After a few minutes, I open my eyes and look at the yellow candle, in the dark silence of my now-sacred office. I think about sacrifice. Mine, and those I might make to achieve a dream. I think about other people who have sacrificed things for me, my success, my happiness. My mom. My friends. My partner. Past lovers.

I feel a ball of warmth hum into life in my chest. I have always tried to remain grateful and aware of all the ways in which I'm lucky, and to acknowledge the people who have helped me get along in life. Nobody does anything alone, and anyone who pretends they do is probably a narcissist. But this is more than gratitude. Yes, I have been wronged, and cheated at various times in my life, but I realize what I'm feeling while reflecting on everyone who has ever made a sacrifice for me is: loved. *Profoundly* loved. I am more loved than I ever considered I was. It's not something we are often asked to stop and consider.

I read another incantation: "This candle represents the harvest within my life. Those goals I have worked on this year are now nearing completion. I accept the harvest of all those that work to my good and reject any harvest of those that would work against me. I prepare myself—body, mind, and soul—for the time of winter and rest." Saying this aloud is truly so lovely, so comforting, it feels like an hour of therapy packed into sixty seconds. For a brief moment, I am consumed with the warm, rare dual sensation of respecting myself and being certain I am loved by others.

I take a scrap of paper and write down a few wishes for the upcoming year, considering what I might have to sacrifice to achieve them.[*]

I decide those sacrifices are worthy. I then put the paper into the cauldron and gingerly put a match to it, raising my Jiffy corn bread over the smoke and chanting a few things about the horned god (at Cunningham's suggestion). I think I would normally do this over the pillar candle that represents him, but he's one of the candles I left out in order to preserve the aesthetic (and structural integrity) of the box, so instead I just think about him really hard.

What Roderick says to do next is eat the bread, imagining the virtues on the paper going into your body, your future. This feels like the most symbolically meaningful thing in the entire ritual, and it's the only time my brain turns off. I am literally devouring something infused with my dreams so I might make them come true.

The rest of the ritual—the Simple Feast (or Cakes and Ale)—involves bread eating and the sipping of apple cider. So basically I just keep eating the bread, and permit myself to sip the apple juice in the chalice. I'm hungry, so this is nice, and it means I don't have to read any books for another minute. I am supposed to leave a little bread on the plate and cider in the cup for . . . I'm not sure whom, I think the fairies. Most of the authors agree I should do this, although no one can tell me why or

---

[*] Later I will find out that according to Buckland, you're not supposed to do magic on Sabbats, you're only supposed to celebrate. But I don't know that yet, so I do magic anyway.

exactly for whom. I decide to take it outside later and leave it at the foot of a tree overnight, because this is something I've seen other Witches do.

Eventually I stand up and release the corners by ringing the bell in their directions. I'm ringing a bell because I forgot to buy candles that are supposed to represent the directions, so I can't blow them out to signify their release. Instead I say behind the tinny chime of the bell, "Hail to the guardians of the north. Thank you for your protection. Until we meet again, farewell." I realize I am unclear if I'm supposed to do this for the elements, or just for the guardians. And also, it occurs to me that I don't know what a watchtower actually is, or who the guardians are. Nevertheless, I turn to four spots in a circle and raise my arms and try to mean what I'm saying.

At the end of the ritual, all my book advisers agree that I should do something called "grounding," by placing my hands on the floor, or concentrating on a stone, so I can "discharge the energy raised during working." I sit down, lean forward, place my hands on the floor, and repress the urge to chuckle. I feel bad about this, but it's true. I do not feel remotely glowly or ecstatic. I spent so much time trying to tee up a traditional ceremony I completely lost touch with any mystical experience. I thought I could follow only one book, but nothing matched what I had available, even with a day's preparation. My altar looks very clean and sacred (if crowded), but the floor surrounding it looks like a Barnes & Noble on Christmas Eve.

I stand up and uncast the circle by sweeping the dagger left to right, ending facing east. I feel palpable relief once it is all done. And also some guilt. That felt like a shitshow. I didn't feel the fluid brain dance of oxytocin and wonderment I expected a Witchcraft ritual to feel like. I felt like I was scrambling for purchase on a bunch of jagged, metaphysical rocks.

I need to read more about each of these steps, and why they are important . . . and what all the inconsistencies between these authors really means. I need to figure out how to stay in touch with an authentic sense of reverence while adhering to the instructions, which were designed, I assume, to lead me there.

I think I need to talk to another Witch.

DAY 3

Exactly what the present-day Witch believes
I find it hard to say.
—GERALD GARDNER, 1954

There are no agreed-upon standards,
even among Witches of the same tradition.
—THORN MOONEY, 2021

The next morning, I am trying to get a more detailed understanding of what a watchtower is, and why Witches invoke them during ritual. The "calling of the corners" was a part of every Wiccan ritual I remember practicing with Emma and Liza, but I never really asked what they were. D. J. Conway simply calls them "a term sometimes used to describe the four directions in a magical circle." Nineteenth-century French occultist Éliphas Lévi Zahed, on the other hand, says they are elemental energies that a magician invokes and directs in a magic circle. He refers to them more specifically as "demons."

I have two hours to contemplate the idea of myself as an unwitting demon summoner as I drive down to Santa Cruz later that day to visit my friend Bridget, a European expatriate and yet another former teen Witch visiting home for a few weeks. In high school, I remember her bedroom had a dog-eared copy of Joseph Campbell's *The Universal Myths*, and other anthropological texts that sought to find ancient, universal (and thereby defensible) constants of magic and mystery throughout the world's religions.

We haven't talked about Witchcraft in about a decade. Many of my friends who were open Witches as teens slowly went dark on their practices as they grew older. They didn't necessarily stop believing. But Witchcraft became more complicated than the fun, sage-scented smashing of the patriarchy it was when we were sixteen. Issues of cultural appropriation, fake histories, and the realization that paychecks often hinged on our appearing nonthreatening eclipsed desires to be a spiritual rebel. So today, as I climb onto the sunbaked redwood deck of Bridget's uncle's house, I'm ambushing her with a topic we haven't talked about in years.

"Oh, it's way too much ceremony. Why do you think I left that shit?" she says when I explain how much trouble I had trying to *get into it* on Lammas, how I felt I like I could never memorize all the rules, and how I'm mildly worried I'm summoning demons.

"Did you ever find ecstasy through ritual?" I ask, wiggling in my patio chair. The wind chimes flutter a few notes into the breeze, and the scent of wildfire smoke settles lightly around us, the incense of climate change. We checked the government apps and Twitter this morning to make sure the fire is still far away. We don't talk about it.

"Not through Wicca," she says, popping the cigarette she'd been rolling on the glass patio table into her mouth. "I liked the principles behind it, but the rituals were just too much. I think all the Witches in the fifties and sixties were raised Catholic, so they had this urge to bring in all this ceremony into it, because that's what they knew. That's why those books are like that."

I consider pointing out that Raymond Buckland, aka Mr. Blue Book, was technically raised Anglican before he brought English Witchcraft to the United States in the 1960s, but decide to let it go.

"It's too much work to put together, every other month and every full moon," she continues, blowing out a cloud of American Spirit smoke. "Plus, I didn't have enough money for all the tools. You need, like, twenty thousand candles every week. It just got exhausting."

"But that's the thing," I say, leaning in. "I really want the ceremony of it all. I like ritual. I want to build a liminal space where, like, magic actually happens. But I'm unclear where the divine ecstasy actually comes in while you're putting on a play with this many steps."

"That was the question for me." She shrugs. "But it sounds like you had something happen."

"I did?" I shake my head.

"Based on what you described, I think it was pretty normal," she says.

"That was normal!?"

"What are you looking for, exactly?" She narrows her blond eyebrows at me, takes another puff of her cigarette.

"To feel like I had the power to make all my dreams come true. To feel like all the atoms in my body remember what it was like to be inside the core of a star right before it went supernova."

"That's cocaine," she replies. "Not religion."

"Helpful," I say dryly.

"Why don't you try again?"

"I probably will. I just really want to do it right, you know? I want to do what the experts say. But then when they do, I'm annoyed by them, and feel like everything they suggest is too hard and too silly. And then they say, 'You don't have to do what I suggest, just trust your intuition.' But what the fuck does that mean? What's the difference between intuition and letting your mind backtrack into problematic stereotypes and total fantastical bullshit?"

"It sounds like you don't trust your own intuition," she says, staring at me.

"Do you?" I stare back.

There's a pause between us. I break first, turning my head to look at the treetops in the smoky light.

Finally, I ask her what I really want to know: "Are you still a Witch?"

She shrugs, takes another puff from her cigarette. The wind purrs a bit between the redwood branches. "I guess it depends on who you ask."

))) ● (((

DAY 13

Witches feel that they are following the path of the Goddess by
helping other people, animals, and even the earth itself to heal.
—D. J. CONWAY

Despite Timothy Roderick's express request not to skip ahead in his book *Wicca: A Year and a Day*, I skip ahead to day 138, where he covers the themes of Lammas. I didn't have time to do any of the rituals the day of, so I'm backtracking a little. I justify this by saying it is still the season and I'm committed to living more in tune with the earth.

Roderick says "the central symbol of Lammas is sacrifice . . . sacrifice involves one form of energy giving itself up so that it can transform into something else." He encourages me to review this concept in every area of my life, especially around mundane, nonspiritual tasks, like eating food.

One teaching is something he calls "pagan grace," where I am encouraged before every meal to consider the substances that are about to sacrifice themselves so they can nourish me and become part of my life force.

After preparing my breakfast, per Roderick's instruction I sit down at the table to eat, and deny the urge to pull out my phone and surf Tik-Tok, like I normally would.

I look at my bowl of oatmeal and think about it. I ponder the swollen bodies of each individual oat, the plump blueberries, even the microscopic bugs alive in the yogurt (although I find it counterproductive to my appetite to think about them too long). After a minute or so, I take a bite and chew. I feel the texture of the food in my mouth. I find myself thinking about how plants can turn light and water into calories, and what a magic trick that truly is.

Very quickly, though, my mind moves from the poetry of photosynthesis to thinking about the people involved in producing this meal, and their sacrifices. As a dutiful listener of NPR, I assume the agricultural industry is one big theme park of human rights violations, from the undocumented immigrants who picked the blueberries, to the pesticide-exposed farmers who milled the oats.

I put my spoon down. These thoughts make me completely lose my appetite. And there isn't even any meat in this meal. It's not that I'm thinking about labor and food politics for the first time in my life. I read *Fast Food Nation*. I saw *Forks over Knives*. I am awake. But, ironically, it's not something I tend to think about before every meal. Most of us don't. If we did, we'd probably never eat.

Shit. I know what's coming. I know this next part. This is the part where, for the sake of the earth and all its creatures, I become a wild-foraging vegan. Many Wiccans are vegan, or at least vegetarian, because that is the most obvious interpretation of Wicca's commandments to harm none and save the earth. I might even be willing to become a vegan, except for one problem: I don't want to lose all my friends. The entire rest of my year could be about this single topic: You never realize how central food is to your interpersonal relationships until you pick up a new diet. This is because, despite what nutrition bloggers like to insist, food isn't about nourishment. Food is about emotions. Rejecting someone's homemade meal is the equivalent of rejecting a homemade valentine. Insisting someone make a special dish for you at a dinner party is wildly self-centered. I know this because I was vegan for about a year in my early twenties. Well, I say vegan. I did away with cheese, butter, milk, and ice cream easily enough. The exception came about once a month, when I would eat bowl after bowl of tofu and noodles before screaming at the nearest bystander: *"Dear god please take me to a field, I am going to eat half a cow and ride the rest home!"* Whereupon they would usher me gently to the nearest burger joint, I'd scarf down greasy red flesh, feel horribly guilty, vow to be good, and then the cycle would repeat next month.* I finally stopped the near-veganism when I

---

* Yes, I know about B supplements and nutritional yeast. But I have also gotten in trouble with supplements before, over-potassium-ing my way into heart palpitations and falling victim to a three-week menstrual cycle because of too much spirulina. Don't at me.

did a year of study abroad in Egypt, because veganism is impossible in a country where the waiters ask you questions like, "Do you want the meat or the chicken?"

I should be a vegan now, in my thirties. I shouldn't care about offending other people with my dietary choices. I could never, in a hundred years, ever kill and eat another living being, so I am sure I don't deserve to eat meat. The only way I've been able to consume chicken since we got the four backyard hens that I refer to every morning as "my little sugar baby doves" is by placing my brain in a very deliberate and carefully calibrated state of cognitive dissonance. I also don't want to go back to a diet that had me obsessing over supplement regimens, skipping meals, and having every misstep cause a wild pang of guilt. I wanted to pat myself on the back and say I was saving the earth, but mostly I felt like I had an eating disorder.

Besides, nowadays a lot of people are very quick to tell you veganism is hardly harm-free. It doesn't solve the abuse of undocumented migrant workers who harvest and pack vegetables, or the carbon footprints of overseas food shipping chains, or the water demands of crops like almonds, which are a huge cause of the California megadrought. My friends would probably be supportive, but ultimately I don't want to give up cheese ever again, unless the whole world can agree I'm a hero for doing it.

I blink into the oatmeal. It is turning into a cold lump. I feel like I'm making excuses.

Guilt is not the point of the lesson I'm supposed to be learning. I'm supposed to be understanding that life feeds on itself, and this cycle is normal, natural. You can pick apart the "and ye harm none, do what ye will" Wiccan rede to death, but this is only to your own detriment. "If you want to go this far, everything, by its mere existence, hurts something else," Thea Sabin, author of *Wicca for Beginners*, says to those who might examine the harmfulness of their every activity to the point of freezing in place.

But I can't run from the fact that most Wiccan authors agree that Wicca's goal is to protect the earth and all its creatures. And going about the world in a state of constant anxiety and shame about food does not actually make the world a better place. There is no scale where someone is measuring my internal turmoil to judge whether I am a good or bad person. The only thing that matters is action, or the lack thereof. Which is to say: guilt is pointless—unless it is fuel.

The solution here is the middle path: I just need to be more thoughtful about what I buy, ensuring it's from good companies that give their employees fair wages and treat their animals well. How hard could that be?

Wicca has very few rules, but two of the big ones are: no evangelizing and no harming others. However, there is nothing said about proselytizing *about* not harming others. In fact, the spirit of that sentiment is arguably encouraged.

I run this line of thought over dinner with Justin later that night, after a ten-minute conversation (from his perspective, perhaps a soliloquy) about whether the chicken we're eating was raised in a pasture or a cage, how we need to do more research on the supply chains of our spices, and why I only want to buy organic from now on.

"Congratulations," he says, stabbing his shake-and-bake with a fork. "You officially sound religious."

DAY 17

Sometimes—especially for those of us who've been around for a while and are pretty set in our ways—things make us uncomfortable just because we think they're, well, kind of stupid.
—THORN MOONEY

There is something else sticking in my head about my Lammas ritual that has nothing to do with sacrifice or harvest, and I am having trouble letting go of it. It's when scenes from fantasy movies kept entering my mind as I attempted to perform more serious religious tasks, like casting a circle, or calling the watchtowers. Cunningham openly encourages visualization in all parts of your practice. But sci-fi movie scenes do not jibe with my concept of serious religious ceremony.

I'm not quite sure how to bring this up to anyone. I don't know what I'm more worried about: looking foolish, or having my problem be dismissed entirely, because almost every single neopagan I know is also a hard-core fantasy nerd.

"And a kinky fuck, too," Eleanor says when I chat with her about this on Slack after she tells me she's trying to determine which of her coworkers were high school goths based on their current haircuts. "That Venn diagram is practically a circle." Eleanor is one of my oldest friends, and a fellow teen almost-Witch. Like me, she seemed content to show up at our more dedicated friends' parties, dutifully chanting, "Isis, Astarte, Hecate, Inanna," over candlelight, munching on mac 'n' cheese until 2 a.m., and debating the ethics of hexing boys we didn't like with DIY Voodoo dolls.* As an adult, she worked in the costume department at the Dickens Fair, San Francisco's village-sized, Victorian Christmas festival. Despite the volunteer women essentially cosplaying as good Christian tradwives of yesteryear, she discovered that behind the scenes, more or less all of them were pagans (and boning each other).

In *Drawing Down the Moon*, Adler has several interviews with various Witches and pagans who openly acknowledge their gateway into paganism was some franchise of fantasy, whether it was *Sabrina the Teenage Witch*, or *D'Aulaires' Book of Greek Myths*. Oberon Zell-Ravenheart, one of the fathers of neopaganism, lifted his Church of All Worlds directly from the sci-fi novel *Stranger in a Strange Land*. Many years ago, Emma, the friend who first introduced me to Witchcraft, quietly confessed to me that *Harry Potter* is what sparked her journey. "Of course, the magic in *Harry Potter* has nothing to do with real life, literally nothing at all," she added, wide-eyed. "But if I'm being honest, my desire to get into Hogwarts is how I eventually found Wicca."

---

* Yes, I know. We lived in the suburbs, and no one had taught us the term "cultural appropriation" yet.

"Well sure. Nobody gets really into *Beowulf* in middle school because their social life is going well," Eleanor replies to me today. "It starts as a form of escapism. But then maybe you find something there in the fantasy world that actually resonates with your spiritual side, and so you take it back with you into reality."

"I agree," I say. And then after a pause, I carefully venture, "But, like . . . don't you think that's a little silly?"

"Depends on whether you consider the creative a pathway to the divine," she replies. "IMO Catholicism is just live-action role-playing tyranny based on fantasy, until they create a city-state with its own military and a basement full of secrets. I'm curious why you're so invested in historical legitimacy."

I don't feel like I'm explaining myself correctly. Something suddenly just feels very wrong about this little spiritual journey of mine, and I can't quite articulate what it is.

I don't think there's some grand coincidence that I had a tendency to lose myself in other worlds as a young person, and as an adult I'm finding myself experimenting with neopaganism. I know some might split hairs here at the categories of what I call fantasy: Greek myths are certified historical, and franchises like *Practical Magic* and *The Magicians* are pure fiction. But to the kid sitting in the back of the bus, diving inside a book because their real life is basically a nightmare, those two things become the same drug. In fact, one might seem more legitimate precisely because it is historical. And that's where the trouble can start.

Eventually I sign off, staring at my reflection in the black screen.

Because the historical lineage of Witchcraft is perpetually fuzzy, the admittance that fiction got you in—or you are imagining something fictional while doing it—feels cringey. No, not cringey. Dangerous. I need the lines between fantasy and history to be firm, not blurry, because history is real, fantasy is fake, and to blur the line between fantasy and reality is to be literally insane.

The commonplace love of fantasy among neopagans and Witches does not feel like a permission slip to use fantasy imagery in ritual. It feels like the opposite. The implication is that this entire religion is just a fanfic, a LARPing event that went a little too far, and started cosplaying as a real religion. As far as I know, real religions are old. That is about the only thing that differentiates them from fake religions. But through age, they gain hegemony, which is to say a critical mass of souls insisting they aren't playing make-believe. Witchcraft doesn't have hegemony. More often than not, Witches pride themselves on being outsiders. And I have never taken comfort in being an outsider.

I need Witchcraft to be more than a bunch of nerds running so hard into another world to escape real life they decided to bring the fiction back with them, even if I was one of those nerds growing up.

Especially because I was one of those nerds growing up.

I text Meg later that evening, asking if she ever feels like her religion is delusional.

Her reply says, *You feel like you are in danger because you sense you are engaging in escapism. But you're not escaping into something fake. This is real. There are real people on the other side of this door.*

DAY 19

The primary bond between pagans is imagination.
—MARGOT ADLER

I might not be able to forgive myself for engaging in a religion that most consider little more than fantasy. However, I can talk to someone who seems allergic to the idea of feeling shame for anything. Today I've arranged for a phone interview with the man who adapted the Church of All Worlds religion from the pages of Robert A. Heinlein's midcentury sci-fi novel *Stranger in a Strange Land*: Oberon Zell-Ravenheart.

To say Oberon is an important figure in the modern neopagan movement is an understatement. He's more like a founding father, viewed with the same respect (and caution) with which poli-sci majors regard characters like Thomas Jefferson and George Washington. Born in 1942, he was a gifted child who took to tales of magic and science fiction, coining the term "neopagan" in college to describe the myriad of new religions that were bubbling up from the 1960s counterculture movement. Although not a Witch in name (Oberon identifies as a wizard), he has been initiated into several Witchcraft traditions and spent the bulk of his life working for the legitimacy and freedom of all neopagan faiths. In the 1960s, he worked alongside reconstructionist leaders in the Norse, ancient Egyptian, Druidic, and Wiccan movements (among others) to form the Council of Themis, the world's first neopagan ecumenical council, whose goal was to bring neopaganism out of the shadows of college dorm rooms and safely into the public eye. Along with his wife, Morning Glory (herself a Witch who passed away in 2014), the pagan power couple spent the latter half of the twentieth century on their fairy-tale-style compound in Northern California. They made unicorns of their pet goats using a long-lost horn-shaping technique, and popularized the term "polyamory" to more easily describe their group marriages. In 2004, they founded the Grey School of Wizardry—a virtual school deliberately fashioned after Hogwarts where both teens and young adults can take classes in real-life magic.

It also bears noting that among the founders of neopaganism, Oberon is one of the few who is still alive. He currently resides in the Longhouse, a pagan sanctuary in rural Washington, writing his memoirs and ensuring the Grey School runs smoothly.

We get on the phone, and he tells me he is painting while we talk. I can have all the time in the world for this interview. His voice is confident and clear—it's hard to remember that he is nearly eighty years old.

I open with a question that's been on my mind for some time: "Why do you think Witchcraft has risen in such wild popularity, while other forms of neopaganism have remained relatively quiet? Not that they're not growing. They just don't seem to be growing as fast. Like, why do you think it's Witchcraft and not paganism that's getting all the fame?"

"Well, because Witchcraft is more sexy," he replies without hesitation. I think he has been asked this before. "It sounds really cool. It gets a lot of media attention in movies and TV shows. Not necessarily accurately, but people have heard of it. You'll never see any media about pagans, and I think that's because Witchcraft is not a religion. Traditionally, it was a practice, a Craft. Paganism is a religion. My own little prejudice is that it's not just a religion, it *is* religion. The word itself means 'relinking'; it's supposed to be that which connects everything and puts all the pieces together. That's what religion is supposed to do, and that's what paganism is all about. But unfortunately, due to the enormous influence of 'Churchianity,' religion has gotten a bad name for people. A lot of people don't even like to be identified as religious. They say, 'I'm spiritual but I'm not religious.'"

This resonates. I know people who have memorized their astrology charts, have altars of crystals at home, and will casually talk about manifestation at a party—but would look at you like you just laid an egg if you characterized that as religion. Millennials and Gen Xers are the generations that lost comfort in organized faith, regarding it like an ex-lover, or a bomb in rapid need of disarming. Perhaps this is why I'm so uncomfortable getting into Wicca specifically. I don't know how to think of religion as anything but bad.

He pauses, seeming to answer my unspoken reflection. "In actuality, however, the surveys indicate that people who identify as being pagan are the same actual numbers as the people who identify as being Witches. It's just not as popular of an identification."

I almost want to laugh at this. We are so afraid of being called religious. But at this point it's more semantics than anything.

"I'm the opposite," he says. "I'm not particularly spiritual, but I'm highly religious, so that's a little bit different than what many people understand."

"Can you explain what you mean by that?"

"Spiritual is juxtaposed to material," he says. "Spirituality, spiritualism . . . it's all about the world outside of this one. The New Age movement is a good example of that. They're very spiritual and they reject the material world. There's almost an antipathy toward actual life and living in this world. Paganism is exactly the opposite of that. We're very earth oriented and life oriented. The best way to understand paganism, I think, is as a 'green religion.' But we are a disorganized religion. We like it that way, but a lot of people don't really know what to make of it."

When I ask him if he ever felt embarrassment at the idea that so much of his religion's roots came from fiction, his response is straightforward. "We are creatures of story. Storytelling was one of our earliest magics. These stories became myths and legends . . . and science fiction is also mythology. It's the mythology of the future, in which we're telling stories of what might be: both positive and cautionary tales."

"Right," I reply. "So then, what's the difference between *Stranger in a Strange Land* and, say, the Greek myths? Both are equally legitimate stories in your eyes?"

"Exactly," he replies. "You've got visions in stories, lessons, and teachings based on the past—a fictionalized version of the past, that lends itself to storytelling. I don't see any difference between the stories of Arthur or Jason and the Argonauts, or Heracles, or any of these things."

"So one of the things I have felt in my own life," I say, "is that because something is drawn from fiction, I feel it is illegitimate. And I know that with Wicca especially, there was this push to legitimize the religion by proving its presence in ancient cultures. Then when Margaret Murray's work got trashed and Ronald Hutton wrote *Triumph of the Moon*, everyone just went, 'Oh well, whatever. We're still gonna do it anyway.' So in that context, what do you think makes a spirituality legitimate?"

"Well, whether it works for the people, obviously," he says, as if this is the simplest thing in the world. "I mean, that's kind of the only criteria. If people find meaning and significance. If they can draw life lessons and shape their lives and are inspired by the stories that make it legitimate. I mean, what else? How else would we judge legitimacy if not by actual ability?"

I finally get up the courage to ask the question I really want the answer to. "Were you ever nervous about going public with this stuff, your religious movements?"

"No."

"No?" This is not the answer I wanted.

"No, I don't really have any sense about things like that. I really don't." He laughs. "I've never had enough sense to not be open. It probably got me in a lot of trouble over the years. Morning Glory and I lived right out there. I guess that I figured out that I could afford to do that because I'm that crazy, and many people can't. They really can't afford to be public. They might lose their jobs or get in trouble with somebody or something, and I just never worried about that. I was very public at my work, and I had a very public, corporate kind of a job for many years. I eventually became supervisor of services and all kinds of stuff. Everybody knew that I was pagan and people were basically just coming at me for advice. They would ask me to do readings or consult with me."

"So you set yourself up as a little bit of a beacon."

"Precisely. I just felt that was important . . . the beacon needed to be out there. I was willing to do it because I just didn't have any natural sense of caution or fear, or good sense, or anything like that."

I skate past the part where I want to ask him, "Hypothetically, how do you stop caring what other people think when you feel like so much of your success in life has depended on other people's opinions of you?" and instead say, "Do you have any advice for a budding Witch?"

"That would really depend on the Witch," he says. Which is a fair comeback.

"How about . . . when you were first getting started with all of this . . . Is there anything you wish you could go back in time and tell yourself?"

He pauses for the first time.

"I would look at the things that I would now find embarrassing from my older person's perspective. Top of that list would be my arrogance. It's just amazing when you know a little more than other people, it's so easy to fall into the trap of thinking that you are just hot shit, and anybody who doesn't know what you know is just an ignoramus. I fell into that category. I find it embarrassing now, so I would advise you not to do that."

Don't be so arrogant you embarrass yourself, I note in my internal ledger. *Got it.*

"When you know you don't know everything," he says, "you keep learning. And there's always more to learn. That would be my higher level of advice. Learn everything, study everything. Regard everybody as a potential teacher. When you are the smartest one in the room, you can get really contemptuous of other people. But at some point, you realize there are lots of other criteria by which people may excel. Somebody may be incredibly talented at music or art, or absolutely astonishing at human relationships or something else. We have to give credit to all these things as values. You shouldn't think, 'Well, I'm better than everybody else because I'm good at this one thing.' Humility can allow you to put what you've got into service and understand that that's our function."

We say our goodbyes, and I sit with my notes. I take from this interview that practicing Witchcraft—or any "alternative religion"—more or less requires you to become the benevolent genius CEO of your own spirituality. This necessitates a "fuck you" attitude toward mainstream society and a deep surety of your own internal compass. I think for some people this idea is liberating. To me it sounds like being given just enough rope to hang myself. I don't want to trust my own internal compass. It feels like a road map to trouble. I don't really know yet how it will get me into trouble; I'm just sure it's going to happen.

Later that night, lying in bed, I scroll through Instagram and discover two friends have the Covid Delta variant. "We are in a race," says a news article from *Oaklandside*, with images of health care volunteers setting up pop-up vaccine clinics.

Everything is shutting down again.

DAY 21

*The final price of freedom is the willingness to face that most
frightening of all beings, one's own self.*
—STARHAWK

Lauren Parker, my chaos Witch mentor, is texting me, asking how
it's going.

Instead of texting back *I'm fine*, I decide to be honest. Which is to
say, I admit I can barely get started because of how frustrated I am at the
lack of Wicca's historical legitimacy. This is compounded by a sudden
monsoon of advice. I'm discovering the hard way that I know a lot more
Witches than I thought, because they are all coming out of the wood-
work, telling me to disregard this author, read this one instead, watch
this YouTube channel, follow this or that Instagram celebrity (who take
turns calling me either a divine goddess or a spiritual colonizer, depending on the day). The minute I share an opinion, they launch into twenty
others. It's not that I think they are all wrong. That would actually solve
the problem. The trouble is I think they are all probably right, and since
I'm new, I am wrong. But the messages are inconsistent, coming all at
once, and sometimes contradict each other. I feel like I'm drowning. I
am also starting to wonder, in a religion where everyone is encouraged
to do everything differently, where and how does community happen?

Atheism has never looked so sexy, I text Lauren.

It's called the Crooked Path for a reason, she replies. *Remember, your
goal isn't to be the best Witch, it's the most accurate Witch to your spiritual needs and your journey. Honestly, this is gonna be your challenge:
you have to stop working from a place that is about making some invisible
teacher happy.*

I think about this for a while. She's right. I do want to make an invisible teacher happy.

But there's no avoiding it anymore. My Wiccan authors keep telling me I have to do what works best for me and my spirituality. And the truth is, I don't know what that is.

It's time to—shudder—go inward.

DAY 23

The mind, then, is the greatest instrument of magic.
—DOREEN VALIENTE

According to Conan the Barbarian, what is best in life is "to slay your enemies, to see them driven before you, and to hear the lamentations of their women." According to Scott Cunningham, it is meditation. It leads to knowledge of oneself, a calm emotional state, a clear heart, successful spellwork, and "usually precedes every magical act and rite of worship." In *Drawing Down the Moon*, Adler observes that just about every definition of magic includes the word "will"; the ability to concentrate it, shape it, and use it to manifest your desires into reality. Personal will is a Witch's Play-Doh. And to control your will, you must first know, and then control, your mind.

So a few days ago I decided to begin a daily meditation practice. Just five minutes where I try not to let my mind wander to the last wrong thing someone said on the internet, what I still need to finish at work, or how much I probably need to vacuum the carpet I am trying to meditate on.

There are several suggestions in my books on how to meditate, but they all boil down to the same thing: clear your mind and focus on the breath.

You would think that for someone who works from home and has no children, five minutes of quiet meditation would be a relatively simple task. And yet three obstacles are continuously in my way: my pets, my partner, and myself.

A year and a half of Covid has been a learning experience for Justin and me, as we slowly turned our house into a twenty-four-hour, two-person coworking pod. We are careful and conscientious, dropping off a plate of lunch when the other is slammed with a deadline, and listening for the muffled sounds of a video call before starting the washing machine. However, the minute I sit down on the floor of my little cubby-office and set a five-minute timer on my phone, he seems to receive an invisible notification. For the past three days, at almost precisely two minutes into my meditation, the following sequence of events take place: I hear his footsteps down the hall, he approaches my office door, my eyes fly open, I squawk like a chicken caught laying an egg, exclaim something like, "Jesus Christ, out of all the minutes in the day how do you always pick these five to come say hi?" he jumps, scuttles off into the other room, I sigh, pause the timer, get up, go find him, apologize for being short-tempered, watch him insist it's fine even though he's looking at me like I'm the lava monster in *Moana*, and then feel tense for the next hour.

After three days in a row of this, we agree on a closed–office door policy, where if either of our office doors are closed, it signals we are in a "do not disturb" mode.

The day this was enacted, the notification that once alerted Justin that I was attempting to engage in the path to inner peace now alerts the cats. The minute they hear the door handle click shut, they immediately drop whatever pressing business they are attending to elsewhere in the apartment and rush to my door, mewling passionately to ensure I know that, thank god, they are just outside should I need them.

This has led me to go meditate in our "attic": the top floor of our carved-up Victorian duplex that came furnished with pink-and-purple shag carpet, a black light, and an alcove of glow-in-the-dark sticky stars. A perfect place to get high. On life. For the past few days, I have been climbing the ladder, setting my timer, and closing my eyes.

This has allowed all distractions to be removed, except for one: me.

In high school, I had an acquaintance who once made the mistake of telling everyone that if she was asked "how do people swallow," she would suddenly be unable to activate her own gulping reflex. Naturally we asked her all the time and watched like curious scientists as her throat quivered, having forgotten how to be itself. She would stare at us, wide-eyed, betrayed, gasping like a fish out of water.

This is how I feel after five minutes of thinking about my own breath.

Breath is what meditators tell you to focus on when you're meditating. It's just about the only thing you're allowed to think about. But I've noticed as soon as I do it, I start to feel like I can't do it anymore. I try counting the seconds between inhales and exhales. I try various combinations of moving air through my mouth and nose. I try visualizing celestial light entering my body as I inhale, and muddy smoke exiting my body as I exhale. None of it really works.

I'm in some kind of awful feedback loop. I sit down, think about my breath, feel like I can't take a full breath, then get up after five minutes and spend the rest of the day gulping the invisible air in front of me, more anxious than before.

DAY 26

Persevere.
—SCOTT CUNNINGHAM

An hour into a movie last night, Justin finally turned to me on the couch and asked, "Are you all right?" in response to me huffing air like a kid with asthma who was just asked to run a 5K. I tell him it happens for the rest of the day after every time I meditate. To which he replies, as gently as possible, "I don't think that's supposed to happen."

Annoyed at my progress, or lack thereof, I decide to change things up today.

I set my phone to stopwatch, climb the ladder into the attic, and instead of sitting, I lie down.

Immediately, my back pinches. My eyes open. That's interesting.

I sit up into my normal position. It's still pinching, just a little less. Like there's a splinter in the left part of my low back.

I lie back down again. It hurts more when I inhale.

I ponder how I have not noticed this until now.

Something happened to my back about a year ago, making it difficult for me to walk for a few weeks. I assumed it was a hiking injury I got after a trip to Utah. I spent hundreds of dollars on massage, acupuncture, and chiropractic. It all helped a little bit. But it never went away. The pain faded from a debilitating injury to a small but ever-present voice whispering in the background of my life. For lack of any other solution, I trained myself to ignore it.

But now I can't ignore it. I am lying down and not allowing myself to do anything else but be in my body. And I'm realizing: of course, I've been ignoring my body. My body hurts. It hurts a lot.

I attempt some stretches to work out the splinter, and find a few that help. This is not the boneless surrender of the masters. But if bending over and reaching toward the right so hard my armpit feels like it's about to break off is the only way my lungs feel full, I'll take it.

After doing what probably looks like the gymnastic routine of the possessed, but breathing fully and deeply for the first time in months, I descend from the attic.

Justin passes me in the hall. "How did it go?" he asks cheerfully (for at this point, we know that if I've just descended from the attic, I've been doing something witchy).

I pause. "I think I need an MRI."

DAY 29

Be patient with yourself during the unfolding of your process.
—TIMOTHY RODERICK

After a few days searching, I find a doctor on my insurance plan who agrees to help me look inside my back and see what's been pinching for a year and a day. She cautions that the insurance approval process might take three weeks, even with her recommendation.

With the wait in mind, I give myself permission to change my focus to spiritual growth tasks that are not so dependent on the muscles in my torso.

Today I will try getting in touch with *energy.*

"Energy" is potentially the greatest word in the English language. It has the depth of "mystical," the friendliness of "vibe," and the versatility of "fuck." It can mean almost anything, or nothing, depending on who is using it and how. According to my Wiccan authors, it is either the force that emanates from the Deity, or in fact the Deity itself. The only thing that is really agreed on is that everything has energy. Thea Sabin can't help but compare it to "the Force," quoting Obi-Wan Kenobi's line in *A New Hope*: "It's an energy field created by all living things. It surrounds us and penetrates us. It binds the galaxy together."

Scott Cunningham describes three types of energies, which he refers to as powers: personal power, which is the energy within your own body; divine power, the energy that comes from the gods; and earth power, the energy that comes from (you guessed it) the earth. Some Wiccans consider these energies the same thing, just residing in different compartments, as it were. Today I will try to get in touch with all three.

Energy work is the first part of Wicca that feels intuitive to me. Not because I believe in "the Force" as introduced by George Lucas, but because I have always felt that people, places, and things radiate an energy. I can walk into a house, pick up a book, or meet someone's ex, and have an immediate opinion about their energy. I always assumed this meant I was a judgmental snoot. But if being a judgmental snoot has prepared me for Witchcraft—what news.

To begin, I step outside into the backyard. Thea Sabin, like most Wiccans, suggests energy exercises be performed outside to better tune oneself with the natural world. The day is bright and cheery, already warm at 9:30 a.m. The chickens see me and begin squawking, pacing the end of their run, wondering aloud why I am just standing there and not giving them treats. I toss a handful of dried mealworms over their fence to settle them, enjoying the sight of their happy pecking. Next I situate myself under the plum tree and close my eyes, recalling Sabin's instructions.

The first step she recommends to get in touch with your personal energy is to rub your palms together, and then slowly spread them apart. Simple enough.

I bring my palms together in front of me in a prayer pose, focusing on the warmth that grows where they touch. I then start rubbing them back and forth until the friction of the heat increases to a pleasant, toasty warm. After about ten seconds, I stop, and slowly spread my hands apart.

This is the part that I'm not sure "actually" happened, or is psychosomatic, because Thea Sabin told me it would happen. Maybe it doesn't matter. As I move my palms away from each other, I feel something ever so slightly resistant. I assume this is the effort from my arms, moving painfully slow in a position they virtually never assume. But the real interesting part is when I try to push my palms back together again, I feel some tension. Like two negative magnets pushing toward each other. There is distinctly more tension when I try to push my palms back to meeting, versus when I pull them apart.

Fascinated, I stand in my backyard, giggling like an idiot, rubbing my hands together and then pushing and pulling them apart as though working a batch of invisible taffy.

I don't yet know what this has to do with spellcraft. But it is fascinating.

Once I can feel my own energy, I graduate myself to discovering earth energy. Sabin suggests the best vector for this is plants. I recall what Oberon Zell-Ravenheart said about paganism being "green religion," a religion deeply grounded in the physical world. What could be more literally grounding than trying to feel the energy of a plant?

I have heard the term "green witch" tossed around, and despite not having looked it up yet, I like it. I am a backpacker with a garden and four shelves of kitchen space reserved for tea. Green Witchcraft is where I'm comfortably certain my Crooked Path is heading. Experiencing the energy of plants feels like the first step to making it official.

I scan the tufts of green across the garden, looking for my first connection. Ah, yes. The oregano.

My oregano plant is large, proud, and potted, because I want to ensure I can take it with me between rentals. I grew it from a clipping seven years ago, given to me by an older friend, who got it from her husband's grandmother, who brought it over from Greece nearly a hundred years ago. "It might not take," she told me when she first handed the pot over. "I've given clippings to other people from the mother bush, and they all died." A few weeks later, when my clipping began shooting off tall stems and snuggling the butts of honeybees in its little white flowers, it was impossible not to feel like Demeter herself had come down from Olympus and chosen me.

So today, when I walk up to the oregano, close my eyes, stick my hands out in front of it, and feel no energy at all, I'm devastated.

I frown and pull my hands back, making sure I'm oriented in front of the little shrub correctly. Sabin said this was as simple as putting my hands a few inches away from the plant's leaves, calming myself with a few breaths, and opening myself up to its energetic force. I try taking a few steps backward and forward. I clear my mind and review the information I'm receiving from all five of my senses, becoming super aware of everything around me. I close my eyes. Nothing happens.

This is embarrassing. According to Sabin I'm supposed to be feeling something zippy. But I don't feel anything at all.

I open my eyes and glare at the oregano, feeling betrayed.

SEPTEMBER

>)) ● (((

DAY 33

When a Wicca is outdoors, she or he is actually surrounded
by sanctity, much as is a Christian when entering a church or
cathedral.
—SCOTT CUNNINGHAM

*Y*ou *could take mushrooms,* Eleanor texts when I tell her about my
failed engagement with the oregano. *It might turn your backyard*
into a Salvador Dalí chicken park, but it'd work.

Drugs feel like a little bit of a cheat, I text back. *I feel like it's impor-*
tant to do this sober.

Suit yourself, she says.

Today I aim to begin planning for the next holiday I will encounter
in my Wheel of the Year: Mabon. This is the second harvest festival,
known to most Americans as the fall equinox.

I feel a bit bad for Mabon. It has all the aesthetics of Halloween
(squashes, corn dolls, changing leaves, candles), without any of the fun
bits (candy, Jell-O shots, an excuse to dress up like a sexy lobster and egg

your principal's car). Interestingly, I read that Mabon was not considered by Gerald Gardner to be a high Wiccan holiday—Gardner pulled his holidays straight from the Celtic cross-quarter days, none of which were solstices or equinoxes. Instead, it was a Witch from the 1970s named Aidan Kelly, working in the Wiccan tradition known as the New Reformed Orthodox Order of the Golden Dawn, who created the Wheel of the Year as most neopagans know it today.

Kelly explains his process in a 2017 article on Patheos.com: "Back in 1974, I was putting together a 'Pagan-Craft' calendar—the first of its kind, as far as I know—listing the holidays, astrological aspects, and other stuff of interest to pagans. We have Gaelic names for the four Celtic holidays. It offended my aesthetic sensibilities that there seemed to be no pagan names for the summer solstice or the fall equinox equivalent to Yule or Beltane—so I decided to supply them." Once finished, he sent them to Oberon Zell-Ravenheart, editor of *The Green Egg* (the largest neopagan journal at the time), and they became Witchcraft canon.

It is widely hypothesized that Aidan Kelly named Mabon for Mabon ap Modron, a character in Welsh mythology who was stolen from his mother, taken to the underworld, and eventually saved by King Arthur's gang. I read Mabon ap Modron's entire Wikipedia page (twice) and discover precisely zero references to squash. Why Kelly chose Mabon to represent the autumnal equinox and second harvest festival of the Witch's calendar eludes me. In fact, it eludes many. There is an argument between Witches debating if the word should be used at all. One side argues it's appropriative of Welsh culture. The other side argues it can't possibly be cultural appropriation, because so much of modern Witchcraft is from the Celtic lore across the British Isles.

Mhara Starling, probably the most famous Welsh Witch online today, posts a helpful response to this after several requests to weigh in. She says, politely and after a long preamble: "I've got bigger problems when it comes to Wales than to worry about whether or not neopagans refer to the autumn equinox as Mabon."

She also concedes not every Welsh person would agree, and we should be respectful of each Welsh person's wishes.

I recall that according to my mother, I am a quarter Welsh. I ask myself if I care. I discover I do not. Onward we press.

The real point here is that I will not be caught short again, like I was with Lammas. In the spirit of better planning, I am trying to come up with a list of what I'm now referring to as "significant pagan locations" where I can spend this sabbat. I don't want to be locked in my office with a cardboard box again, and unfortunately, pagan sanctuaries continue to elude me. I've already emailed five in California and received no response. (I'm assuming they are ignoring me because of Covid, but that might also be me trying to protect my ego.)

I text both Emma and Lauren about this problem, asking their advice.

Lauren replies, *Have you thought about going to Salem?* And this gets me excited, because I have been waiting for an opportunity to spring into my speech.

Salem? I reply. *But those women weren't even Witches. In fact, they were insisting they were Christian the whole time they were being indicted. Isn't it pretty ironic to build a witchy homeland on their legacy? By doing so, aren't we committing the same offense as their captors, and denying the wishes of the falsely accused victims? How did Salem become a place where actual Witches connect?*

You have given this some thought.

I have.

Salem is the home of Witchcraft because Witchcraft in the modern zeitgeist is a community of weirdos bonding about abandoning Christianity, she taps back. *There is no homeland. So we made one. It was easy to put it there.*

But isn't a place where Christian women insisted they weren't Witches and got burned anyway for being Witches a pretty dumb place for a witchy homeland? I retort.

Nobody actually got burned at Salem, she replies. *They were hung. As for Europe . . . women were burned for Witchcraft whether or not they were Witches. And most weren't, they just owned land or were Romani or just happened to be someone's least favorite washerwoman. But those women become symbols for the persecution of women. And*

Witchcraft is about reclaiming female power. So you kind of end up back at square one.

I grumble. I can't plan a trip to Salem on this short notice, but I wonder about Samhain, the Witch's new year, also known as Halloween. I switch over to Emma, who lives in New England, and ask her what Salem is like in October.

Hell, she replies. *You do not want to come here on Halloween. It is goth Outside Lands. There's trash everywhere, you can barely get through the crowds. I thought I was going to have a panic attack just walking around.*

I see, I reply, a bit disappointed.

But as for a Wiccan sacred place, you know, you've already been going there, her text bubble reads. *It's nature. I don't know if you're aware of this, but your favorite hobby has been, for some time, pretty damn witchy.*

She's right. I know she's right. Sort of. A deep connection with the earth is one of the few things that Witches seem to universally agree is important. At the same time, I know a lot of Witches I would lovingly describe as "indoor cats"—tarot-throwing, tea-sipping, pentacle-wearing cat moms without so much as a potted mint on their windowsill. They have their kinks, but putting everything in a bag and getting spanked by nature for three days isn't one of them.

Hiking and backpacking isn't sacred for every Witch, I tap back.

No, she replies. *But that's the great part about Witchcraft. Everyone connects with nature in their own way. You get to make it your own. It's pretty obvious you've felt pulled by nature for a long time. So just keep going.*

I briefly consider telling her about my failed experiment with the oregano and then change my mind.

Backpacking, while being a favorite hobby, might also help with meditation. Roderick encourages people who have trouble meditating in stillness to try slow, mindful walking. What's more, walking doesn't hurt my back. It's stillness that is causing me issues. When I'm moving, nothing hurts.

I begin prepping for my first pilgrimage.

))) ● (((

DAY 39

No one comes between you and the gods. Wiccans have the
responsibility and honor of forging bonds with the gods for
themselves.
—THEA SABIN

Before I head out into the backcountry next week, I figure I should do a bit more prep work for getting in touch with deities and elements. A Witch is basically a Wi-Fi router that picks up on these energies and channels them to her will. I haven't even thought about them since Lammas. I feel like I'm falling behind in class. This is unacceptable.

At the center of Wicca is the Goddess, and I need to get to know her. Wiccans believe the Goddess can wear a different mask, as it were, depending on what culture she is in or what is needed of her. Scott Cunningham informs me that "every goddess is resident within the concept of the Goddess; every god in the God." Hence some Witches have a particularly strong relationship with a specific deity. However, some Witches avoid the naming of her entirely, and find it better to think of her as simply Spirit or Source, from which all life springs. Once again, there is no correct way to do this. It's up to me how I'd like to approach the relationship with the divine source of all energy in the universe. Hooray.

I have never had a close relationship with any deity. After some reflection, I decide I prefer to keep her a bit shapeless. I flirt with the idea of exploring a relationship with the goddess Diana, but I don't think my heart is in the right place on that one. (Imagine meeting a woman named Aphrodite who was, like, *really into* Aphrodite.)

Beyond the Goddess, there's the pagan God. This is not the Santa-bearded, cloud-dwelling highfather that I was introduced to in Sunday school. Instead, I am invited to visualize him as a flirtatious woodsman, a noble king, or a rippling-muscled warrior. I can choose my favorite scenario, but it all seems to be some variant of a man who is golden, passionate, fiery, and burdened with a constant erection. Timothy Roderick spends two pages referring to him as "the Inseminator."

However, as the minutes tick by, it dawns on me that what I'm actually reading is a detailed road map for divine, nontoxic, positive masculinity. The God is bellicose, but he is not belligerent. He directs his strength for building and fructifying, leading and sacrificing, supporting and nurturing. He loves the Goddess and accepts her love, and works with her to bring their potential to life. "The God is the fully ripened harvest, intoxicating wine pressed from grapes, golden grain waving in a lone field, shimmering apples hanging from verdant boughs on October afternoons," says Cunningham. I flip back to the cover to ensure I have not accidentally picked up a Danielle Steel novel by accident. I still don't quite know how I'm going to approach him. But I definitely respect him.

The elements seem easier to approach. I don't have to imagine them, I have seen them with my eyes: earth, wind, fire, water. Being able to summon their spiritual essences during ritual without laughing or thinking of a Luc Besson movie is a goal I'd still like to achieve, and there's some work I can do on this.

I pull *The Spiral Dance* off my office bookshelf and start reading through the exercises designed to help me get in touch with the elements. Like Cunningham's *Wicca*, this book is a famous, foundational text for many a modern Witch. It was first published in 1979 by Starhawk, who I associate closely with the 1960s hippie movement, and its claiming of the Witch as a symbol of women's rebellion against male control. Starhawk is antiwar, anticapitalist, antipatriarchy . . . basically what Pat Robertson thinks every woman in the Democratic party is, Starhawk actually is. Mostly, she advocates combining social justice issues with a Goddess-based spirituality. She has wonderful advice on how to connect yourself with the divinity of nature, and as an avid hiker, I find myself bedazzled and nodding along with much of what she says. I also have trouble taking her seriously, because her name is Starhawk. Which makes me feel like an asshole.

Nevertheless, I settle in to perform some of the exercises she lays out. I have found if I sit cross-legged on the floor, spine upright, completely still, I have about three to four minutes before my back wants to give out. This is partially, I'm realizing, due not to what I'm now just calling "my pinch," but to upper back muscles that have more or less atrophied during my yearlong Covid marathon of sitting in an office chair. Every time I sit up and straighten my spine, my shoulder blades whine like babies awoken from a nap. Scott Cunningham says teaching your body to meditate is part of the path; despite neopaganism's frequent portrayal as a bacchanal of flower-crusted socialism, there is a rather large expectation of discipline here. I persevere.

As the sun pours sleepily into my office windows in the late afternoon, I take turns facing east, south, west, and north, dutifully visualizing what Starhawk suggests. Her first note in *The Spiral Dance* is to find the elements within yourself. For example, while considering the element of fire, she suggests I imagine the sparks of electricity within me, the tiny combustion of my cells burning food for energy. She also suggests I say, aloud, "Hail Tana, Goddess of Fire!" I do not know who Tana is, and I'm tired of interrupting my spiritual meditations to look things up, so I just say it and vow to look it up later, hoping I'm not accidentally invoking yet another demon.

I do similar exercises for air and earth. But have a moment of pause before water.

Water is the element I've always had the most trouble with. It's the easy answer I can give if anyone ever asks me what element I dislike the most. (Which no one ever has, because what kind of question is that, but the point is I have an answer ready.)

Water is spooky. It hides between things, it seeps in between cracks, it drips coldness in the places you aren't looking. It can go from comforting you to killing at just the right speed that you won't see it coming. One of my earliest memories is the sensation of being pulled out into the sea by a riptide, my mother's arms tearing me from the ocean's mouth and flinging me back onto the beach. When I was eight, I dove into a pool too fast and perforated an eardrum. To this day, I can't descend more than a few feet underwater without my ears thumping in warning. I have a perpetual fear of dark water, which feels like a prudent evolutionary instinct, but it's compounded by a semiregular nightmare of falling off a boat and drowning. In my adult life, plumbing issues are almost constant. The last two years, the last two houses I've lived in have burst pipes, usually over the holidays. It's not anything I'm doing, I swear. I put traps in my drains and have never flushed a baby wipe in my life. Even as I write this now, our downstairs neighbor is dealing with a burst pipe in her ceiling from our bathroom sink. In every vacation house I've rented for the past five years, a tub has overflown, a sink has stopped, or a pipe has exploded. This has prompted a series of jokes from friends that I'm no longer allowed to go on vacation until I learn to control my water bending (although Eleanor, daughter of a handyman, helpfully pointed out that perhaps it was not my latent supernatural powers causing the problem, but the result of a succession of tourists treating their vacation bathrooms like garbage disposals, leading to rather predictable results in ancient and fragile septic systems). It got so bad Justin started calling me "Squirtle." Finally, I'm a Leo. I don't really know how that's related, but when I told an astrologer friend about this, she asked my sign, leaned back, and said, "Ah, that makes sense."

But today I face west, close my eyes, and try to imagine water. I imagine the water inside of me already, keeping me alive, the water in my blood, in my brain. I try to find "the calm pools of tranquility within," as Starhawk suggests. But even when I imagine a serene ocean vista from the top of a cliff, all I can think about is what lies beneath. Because that's the thing about the ocean. It lies. We treat it like the ultimate symbol of serenity. But just a few inches beneath that lapping, spangled surface is a frigid, black-hole hellscape that smells quite literally of corpses and shark poop.

I open my eyes and see little dust motes floating in front of the window, like confetti from an opened packaged.

Yes, I'm aware there's probably a metaphor here. But sometimes just living your life one day at a time is enough.

DAY 52

I am a very bad witch. A witch is by definition one with nature.
—AUGUSTEN BURROUGHS

It is the midnight before my Mabon pilgrimage into the backcountry. My friend Shannon and I are sitting in my hatchback, still as stones, the engine idling. The thermostat informs us it is thirty-nine degrees outside, and the wind is shaking our car like a giant toddler rattling a toy. We are in the eastern Sierra Nevada mountains, staring at a sign illuminated by my car headlights: Campground Closed.

Shannon is a friend from dance class. I used my wild powers of deduction to uncover her identity as a Witch one night while we were chatting outside the studio, and she kept referring to the rising moon as "her." Shannon teaches sword dancing and West Coast fusion belly dance. Her specialty are acts that require full-face horror makeup, thigh-high skirts, and sticking your tongue out at the audience. She's also my hairdresser.

It has been hard to find a friend who will join me in backpacking. I'm still too scared to go alone, and a jolly weekend of shitting in a hole in the woods that you dig yourself is not an easy sell for most folks. Shannon, however, has agreed to go with me. Or it might be more like I'm going with her. She was practically jumping up and down at the idea. She started backpacking a few years ago, inspired by the trips her late mother took as a young woman. Best of all, she's not going to make fun of me if I start talking to trees. Or, possibly, the wind.

Which is definitely talking to us right now.

This storm, and the Campground Closed sign, is about number seventy-three in a series of mishaps over the past few days. A week before we left, Shannon's car broke down, I discovered I had purchased the wrong permit, and as we approached our start date in Kings Canyon National Park, we kept getting warned about snow. Then it exploded in wildfire.

I started shifting plans, trying to find a trail in California in September that wasn't smoked out. With our time off work already locked in, I didn't want to waste the opportunity. Eventually I found an opening: the Ansel Adams Wilderness had some available permits. I called Shannon, and she agreed.

However, in my haste, I forgot to check if the campground at the trailhead was actually open. It's not. And now that we are here, there's a big sign saying we'll be fined if we try to sleep in the parking lot.

A gust comes out of the dark and hits the car like an open-handed slap. I look down at the thermostat. It's descended to thirty-three.

"Do you, uh . . . want to see if we can find a hotel back at that little town we passed?"

I can barely finish the question before she blurts, "*Yes.*"

I turn the car around and start to drive us over the potholed forest road, leaves roiling in the headlights.

I'm going to sleep outside tomorrow, I think. *Why is this my hobby?*

"I'm sorry I didn't look up if the trailhead campground was open," I say.

"Oh, it's not your fault," she says, almost cheerful. "I did not want to sleep outside tonight anyway. We just have an excuse now."

I wonder how often our lives are the results of someone else's prayers.

DAY 54

Witches have formulae for producing this form of auto-intoxication, of escape into the world of faery. It cannot be induced, however, if people are unsympathetic, as many Saxons were, to these powers, which they thought devilish.
—GERALD GARDNER

It's day three of our trip, and officially Mabon.

You have a lot of time to be alone with your thoughts in the backcountry, which is part of the challenge in my opinion. But you're also surrounded by beauty. I have thirty pounds on my back and yet I have never felt lighter, walking parallel to a granite cliffside while pine needles whistle in the trees and sagebrush cheerleads at my ankles. The weather has been clear and relatively forgiving since the first night's windstorm. My back doesn't hurt. Nothing hurts. Everything feels sacred, washed clean by sunlight and wind. I'm not stuck at home with my imagination, trying to visualize things that aren't there, or forcing myself to sit still, pretending to ignore my body for the sake of spiritual enlightenment. I have never felt more in my body. My lungs feel like beating wings. My heart is a drum. I am out of my head, in the world.

But I also have mild altitude sickness. We're at around ten thousand feet. "Thin air" is a wonderful excuse to give to anyone asking why you're crawling up a hill your hiking partner seems to be prancing up like a fucking doe, and it's one I've given before. But I'm not making excuses this time. I have intermittent nausea and persistent insomnia; I haven't slept for the past two nights despite the day's hard work; I can't finish a meal, but my stomach roils with hunger every hour. I am having a good time, I swear. But I don't feel entirely like me.

Today Shannon and I are planning to make camp at Waugh Lake. But when the trees finally part at the first vista in the late afternoon, we see with some horror that it is gone. I don't know how else to say that. It is an ex-lake. Where a lake clearly should be, instead there is an empty bowl the size of two football fields and the color of charred bones. We teeter in our boots, staring at it like it's a dead body, and agree we cannot stay here. It takes us a half an hour to walk its longest side, a sense of cursed foreboding hovering over us. We plod on until it is behind us and we reach a superdeveloped backcountry campsite behind a dam, with several flat, barren patches of rust-colored earth. Designed for hikers with livestock, it's far from scenic, but it's flat, and there's a creek. As far as backcountry campsites go, that's basically a Hilton.

I begin to set up my tent and think about land spirits. I can't tell if my depression at the folly of man is what made me feel like Waugh Lake was cursed, or if it's something else. D. J. Conway and Timothy Roderick write pages about the spirits and deities associated with various elements, aligning water specifically with nymphs and undines (a kind of elemental mermaid). It's hard not to feel like something was silently screaming as we walked past the bone-dry bottom of the lakebed, even if we couldn't hear it. Conway says elemental spirits are real, not seen by the eyeballs but by the "inner-eye," or perceived by intuitive feelings.

But try as I might, I don't think I can accept the reality of nymphs and undines any more than I can believe in the tooth fairy. Partially because, what if they were real—what would I say to them? What would I offer them? "I'm terribly sorry about the desiccation of your home, here's a Clif bar?" Even if they're real, there's no way to approach any of them without feeling like I owe them something I don't know how to repay. I don't think they'd be satisfied with, "Don't worry, I vote Democrat."

I set my tent up and throw my sleeping bag inside, then pull the bandanna off my head and wander over to the creek to wash the layer of dust off my face. I try to tell the water I'm sorry about the lake. It tinkles past, oblivious. Insentient. I rub some of the icy moisture over my eyelids, the back of my neck. It feels incredible, like a baptism. I say thank you to the creek, and it's an uncomplicated act of spirituality, because I genuinely feel grateful it exists. As you walk up to any trickling body of water in the backcountry, the energy does change. But I don't know if this is just my mood brightening at the thought of cold, clear water on my roasted limbs. What is the difference between a sense of relief and witnessing the realm of spirit?

On my way back to the tent, Shannon passes me and says she's going for a dip in the creek. "Scream if you feel hypothermic!" I encourage her.

Back at our tents, I am alone. A bird flits about on the ground nearby, pecking. The wind tussles the needle-tufts of the pine trees. It's probably around six o'clock, about a half hour from sunset. There's a particularly flat granite rock nearby, and I pull my little sleeping pad on top of it, to stretch out my legs. After a few minutes pulling sinews and bending joints, I notice the light in the sky swelling to a lovely gold. Shannon is still gone. I am alone.

The landscape feels like it's staring back at me, waiting for something. I feel like I'm in the middle of an arena.

I don't like this feeling. So I decide to meditate. I do this with some trepidation. A curious thing about the backcountry is that it looks serene, but being there is anything but. You are no longer at the top of the food chain; you are at the mercy of the weather and the rhythm of the forest. It is prudent to keep one's guard up. Shutting my eyes feels counter to this. But still, if there was ever a moment to become one with nature, it's probably now, alone, at sunset, overlooking a meadow scores of miles from the nearest freeway.

I close my eyes and start to breathe. I try to rinse every thought from my mind and bring myself aggressively here, now. I review my senses, one by one. Breathing in and out. In and out. In and out. I focus on the smell of the sun-soaked, pine-dust air. I focus on the wind tickling and cooling my skin, the dull thumping pulses running through my legs. My mouth tastes like iron and sour water, dust and meat. I hear the gentle tinkling of the creek, the thin pine needles above me whirring, and birds chirping. But I see darkness. I want to see something else. I want to be here, in the world, with all five senses. So I do something not normally recommended in meditation: I open my eyes.

This next part gets a little difficult to describe.

I open my eyes and I see what I can only describe as God. God is beaming, pushing, glowing between the individual needles of the pine tree across the creek. God is the symmetrical ray of light, illuminating the granite wall that towers over the right side of our camp. God is the visible aura surrounding every single rock and plant and tree in my field of vision. God is the air. God is everything, glowing, pouring, floating, waiting. I see him because I want to see him. I see him because he is there.

My eyelids suddenly feel very hot. My throat feels full, like it's closing.

I gulp a breath of air, blink rapidly, and look around. I'm nervous for Shannon to see me. This is silly, because she of all people wouldn't care. But I still feel self-conscious. The sensation of feeling spiritual, without feeling silly, is a hard one to break. I wipe two tears from my eyes and stand up, patting the dust off my khakis. I roll up my sleeping mat.

I turn back one more time before walking away from the rock. The view is the same: the golden hour of sunset illuminating a picture-perfect Sierra Nevada landscape. Gorgeous. Holy, even. But supremely terrestrial. It is not what I saw a moment ago.

What if I have been making this too hard the entire time? What if God is simply the light? What if it's that direct—what if that is enough? That feels like such a cop-out, though; an atheist defending themselves against a mystical experience by asserting it is "the miracle of the mundane." I am tired of this idea. We strip the supernatural of its undefinable power—and allure—by implying it's the same thing as folding the laundry. I don't want to pretend the mundane is divine. I want the divine to be divine.

But I'm full of endorphins, running on no sleep, and starving. *I'm just hyperemotional*, I think. Did I see God? My imagination is running away with my mind. I decide this is enough mystery pondering for tonight.

An hour later, Shannon and I are back together at camp, huddling over our mac 'n' cheese in the growing chill of night.

"Should we do . . . like . . . a Mabon thing?" I ask. We didn't bring a whole altar. There was no way I was carrying all 746 of Raymond Buckland's recommended altar pieces in my backpack while ascending a 15 percent incline at 9,000 feet. I was prepared to fight about this, but then discovered Shannon is yet another Witch who cares very little for formal rules in the face of practicality.

"Mabon is about balance," she says. "It's the fall equinox, when the day and night are equal length, and the earth prepares to go into darkness. We should think about the parts of our lives we want to bring balance into, and what we need to prepare for before the season of rest."

We spend thirty minutes chatting about things like balancing work and play. Removing stress. Improving focus on people who are important to us. Our career goals. It's really not so different from any conversation two women might have catching up over drinks at happy hour. We're just doing it in a darkening forest with headlamps on. Shannon pulls out a surprise baggie of Halloween-sized Hershey's bars and opens them to share. We feast.

A few hours later in my tent, after some flirtations with sleep, I wake up needing to pee. I wiggle out of my sleeping bag, unzip my tent, and peer out into a wonderland of silver and shadow. The moon is an industrial spotlight, turning the forest into a labyrinth patchwork of bright splotches and dark voids. I don't even need my headlamp. I squeeze myself out of the tent door and rise into the numbing air.

My skin screams at me, assaulted by the temperature difference even under layers of clothing. My nose is attempting to bolt back into my face. I hastily find a tree and do my business, all the while in wonder at how surreal everything looks.

I want to stay awake and commune with nature. This feels like it should be that moment. I am in a mystical underworld, equal parts dark and light, a world I earned entry into through suffering. I am completely awake, every sense searing with information. But I'm freezing. And I'm terrified of every snap and crunch that comes from the shadows. I do not feel relaxed. I do not feel like dancing in the moonlight.

I look up into the sky. The moon's round, ice-white body stares back at me through the black-lace veil of the treetops. "Pretty" is not the word. It looks cold and austere, like it could kill me. Or at least, wouldn't care if I died.

I don't understand how Witches feel they can talk to the moon. How could this conversation ever be two way? There is no dialogue here. I feel like I'm being commanded, and the commandment is very clear: "You are not supposed to be out here. Get the fuck back in your tent."

Which is precisely what I do.

DAY 55

Today, Witches, healers, and many others understand that crystals are "alive" in their own way, capable of communicating their ancient wisdom with us if we are open and receptive to their messages.
—LISA CHAMBERLAIN

Ducking into my hatchback before we head home from backpacking, Shannon pauses, reaches down to the floor of the passenger seat, and pulls out a creamy green stone the shape of a miniature lemon slice.

"Did you drop this jade?" she asks, holding it out to me.

"No," I respond, staring at the little stone in her hand with genuine shock. This is not the kind of rock you drag in on your hiking boots. "I've never seen that before."

There is a pause. We look at each other.

I pray to any god that will listen *don't, don't, don't . . .*

"Well, here you go!" She hands it to me like a gift.

I force a smile.

What I haven't told Shannon, or most of my Witch friends, is that I hate crystals. I have about five that have wound their way into my home over the years. In Northern California, crystals are like spliffs. You don't really have to be into them, someone will kind of just keep offering them to you. I have always accepted a crystal gift with thanks because the point of a gift is to accept it, and to be happy someone thought of you. But crystals and I are not friends.

I think the entire power-stone-vibration trend is New Age snake oil at its peak, second only to pet telepathy in its nincompoopery and deceitfulness. My working theory is that our society has fallen victim to some kind of Dwarven Illuminati. They convene once a month somewhere in the American Southwest and, on the understanding that people want but can't afford things like diamonds and gold, pick a new mineral to dress up into a spiritual artifact and proceed to trot it out to every occult shop and hipster boutique in the world. There it proceeds to prey upon people's (who are we kidding, it's women's and queer people's) desires and insecurities, promising them shiny hair, a cranked-open third eye, or even just a basic sense of calm if they wear it as a necklace or drop it into their bathwater. Amethyst fights anxiety. Amber helps you heal from disease. Moonstone turns you into that calm, glowing princess version of Sailor Moon in the opening credits where she's looking over her shoulder and the wisdom of the universe dances in her eyes.

I don't tell my Witch friends this. I know what I sound like. Besides, crystals aren't really hurting anybody, so why pooh-pooh someone's good time? But it's getting hard to bite my tongue, because, actually, crystals do hurt people. Jade was recently referred to by *The Guardian* as "the new blood diamond." Crystals aren't owned by any one culture; they encompass all types of Witchcraft and New Age spirituality and are familiar enough to get lumped in with any layperson's love of jewelry. This broad application means everyone is grabbing for them, leading to overmining. If I were to tap into the energy of most crystals, I think I would find nothing but suffering—I don't understand how anyone can find anything different. Working with crystals feels simultaneously like a required part of Witchcraft, but also counter to the broader commandment to serve and save the earth. I don't know how to balance this.

I stare at the pale green stone. It's very cold.

"Are you sure this wasn't meant for you?" I ask Shannon hopefully.

"Nope!" She smiles firmly and closes the car door. She seems happy for me, as though a tiny leprechaun were snoozing in my hand.

Fuck.

⟩ ⟩ ⟩ ● ⟨ ⟨ ⟨

DAY 58

Crystals hold valuable information, and they are connected to the world of the infinite, the past, present, and future, as well as to other realms of energy that we don't have access to.
—VALERIA RUELAS

My Wiccan books have surprisingly little to say about how to work with crystals, despite what a huge part they seem to play in modern Witchcraft. So after grappling with my profound dislike for the jade I now possess,[*] I reach out to Valeria Ruelas, author of *The Mexican Witch Lifestyle* who also runs an Instagram shop selling crystals, candles, and other necessities of Brujeria. When I introduce myself and tell her I'm a skeptic of Witchcraft, she seems instantly taken aback; like she does not have time for this kind of bullshit. "If crystals are not working for someone, it's usually because they have a mental blockage." She's driving while talking to me, but her voice comes through over Bluetooth strong as an iron bell. "Spellwork doesn't work with people who think it won't work." Then she softens and tells me, "It takes time. I had trouble with candle magic at first, you know, I'll admit that. But you gotta keep working at it. If a crystal isn't working, like you're not getting anything coming off of it,

---

[*] I'm only guessing it's a jade. I spent half a day learning that color counts for almost nothing in the world of gemstone identification. You can have pink sapphires, yellow moonstones, blue topaz, etc. My stone is probably either jade or something called aventurine. Both stones are supposed to attract good luck. I learn that fact and give myself permission to stop researching.

sometimes you just need a bigger one. If you have some tiny little crystal and you aren't feeling anything, try more."

I also call Liza, the leader of the coven I spent some time in while in my early twenties, and she more or less says the same thing. "You feel a kind of warmth," she tells me when I ask her what it actually means to work with a crystal. "You can feel some energy coming off of it when you hold it in your hands or near your body. That's how I know it's charged, and that I have a connection with it. But hey, if you don't feel it, don't force it," she says casually.

I talk to Liza about my issues with the crystal-industrial complex, and while she's aware of the issues around jade, she points out that there are dozens of low-cost, high-energy crystals (like quartz) that come from the United States and aren't known for being particularly exploitive.

I still feel like the landscape of ethical assurances is murky. A 2020 *Cosmopolitan* article titled "Buying Ethical Crystals Shouldn't Be This Hard" validates my feeling, laying out how difficult it can be to trace the sources of all these sacred minerals; there is no certification of welfare on most of them, as there is with diamonds. When crystal shop owners ask their sources about their mining and labor practices, they are more or less relying on them to pinky swear they aren't doing anything unethical.

I was raised on *Captain Planet* and *FernGully.* You can't tell nineties kids to trust the pinky swear of a mine owner.

At the end of the day, I come across an article by a woman named Hibiscus Moon, a former science teacher and mineral shop owner who likes "to play with crystals to create ripples in the space-time continuum that alter future realities in the third dimension . . . and beyond." Hibiscus Moon cares very much about where she sources her shop's crystals. However, she also points out that while more and more people are asking her about the ethics of the crystal industry, those same people never seem to inquire about the crystals used in the microchips inside of their cars, computers, and cell phones—items far more widespread and whose industries are notoriously unethical.

Touché, Hibiscus Moon, I think. I do not remember the last time I thought about the ethical implications of my car battery on the space-time continuum.

However, my final defense is that crystals feel optional. Cars and computers don't. I don't need cassiterite on my altar to be a functioning member of society, but I do need a smartphone. How else am I supposed to lie in bed all night and look up everything I'm supposed to feel bad about?

OCTOBER

))) ● (((

DAY 63

In old Europe, Samhain was a time in which the herds were
thinned through ritualized slaughter.
—TIMOTHY RODERICK

I have a confession. I hate October.

I am aware this is an opinion bordering on excommunicative for my identity as both a woman and a budding Witch, so I usually keep it to myself. It's not that I don't like pumpkin spice lattes and leaf piles and scarves. I'm not a monster. What I don't like is fear. I don't understand why that's such a radical concept for some people, but there you have it.

And that's what October is in America. It's fear season. Where I grew up, October wasn't about celebrating the thinning of the veil between worlds or taking the time to cherish our beloved dead. October was (and is) the season of pranks and jump-scares, a blowout sale on one-upmanship for getting a rise out of people. I'm an exceedingly jumpy person at base level, so this time of year tends to be hell.

Also, despite years of protestations, I have not figured out a way to convince my friends and family I really, really hate horror movies. (Yes, really. Yes, all of them. Yes, that one, too.)

Maybe this is because I was the youngest in my family. I was four when my older sisters and cousins (ages eight to fourteen) wanted to watch *Jurassic Park*—a righteous request, and not even technically a horror film. "It's not that scary," I was assured. When I fell into wallows and shrieks as a glistening T. rex terrorized two screaming, hapless children in a Jeep, forcing my aunt to turn off the TV and send everyone to bed early, I was the brat who had ruined everyone's good time. And I knew it. I have a million stories like this. People put on a movie they swear is not that scary and then stare at me for an hour and a half while it plays across the room, waiting to see if they were right. They're never right.

Nobody likes being the wet blanket, so I learned to keep my fear a secret as I grew older. A lot of my friends were goths in high school.* And goths love horror. So October was a time of great and terrible joy. For one month of the year, I learned the best strategy was to keep my head down and make believable excuses about why I couldn't go into the haunted house, or how to suppress a panic attack after being pressured to go inside of a haunted house.

In my late twenties, I was armed with a new vocabulary. I started saying I had minor anxiety, and horror was triggering. That got most strangers off my back. But without a real diagnosis or medication, no one who knew me took me seriously.

October is also—by pure coincidence—the time when every job or serious romantic relationship I've ever had has come to an end. This month is one long slog of painful memories. When I learn that Samhain is called the Witch's New Year, the doorway to shadow work and rebirth, it's the first part of neopaganism I have no questions about. I

---

* I probably would have been a goth in high school too; I loved fishnets and black eyeliner, I listened to Nine Inch Nails on repeat, and absolutely no one understood what I was going through for at least eighteen consecutive months. However, I didn't have the budget for Tripp pants, I was allergic to hair dye, and there was the notable issue of my finding skeletons discomfiting, so it never really took.

feel like I've already been living that rhythm. And this is not a part of the beat I enjoy.

Finally, here's the real tragedy of it all: I hate horror, but I *love* Halloween. I love costumes and frivolity and celebration; I love that our society suddenly insists children take candy from strangers. I love going to themed clubs and breaking my eardrums to bad EDM and cheering for the best costume and drunkenly ordering a hot dog at 2 a.m. while trying to fix my friend's Morticia Addams eyeliner. Not that I'm going to be doing any of that this year. The Delta variant is in retreat, and a few people are going to clubs. However, a large portion of my family works in health care, and one conversation with them about overflowing wards and resigning nurses is enough to keep me inside.

But I can't stay in the house, not completely. This is the season of the Witch. Witches go apeshit for Halloween. And regular people pretend to be Witches. Samhain is the final harvest festival on the Wheel of the Year, treated by most Witches with the same significance as Indians treat Diwali or Jews treat Rosh Hashanah. I am practicing referring to it not as Halloween, but as Samhain.* It's no longer just about jump-scares, but also ghosts, séances, and glowing, twirling, morally questionable magic. The veil between the worlds is whisper-thin and beckoning.

I have spent my entire life trying not to engage with any of this.

Again, I refuse to feel that this makes me weird. This is not complicated.

I don't want to scream, I don't want to surround myself with morbidity, and I don't want to talk to dead people.

And I definitely, definitely, definitely don't want to see if they can talk back.

---

* If you're curious, it's pronounced SOW-in, because anyone who thought the French had a sadistic pronunciation pattern never met the Gaelic.

DAY 66

The word "witch" doesn't always mean the same thing.
—FIRE LYTE

"Why are you only reading books that are thirty years old?" Meg asks me after I responded to her question about what authors I had picked out to serve as my spiritual advisory panel. I asked her to review some of my pages in our weekly writing group. But instead she's commenting on my sources.

Her eyebrows furrow at me as I reexplain my premise.

"It's not my fault all of the most popular books about Wicca happen to be written before 1999," I say defensively.

"You are keeping yourself in the dark with this reading list," she says, looking me in the eye. "You need to branch out. Immediately."

Meg is not the first person who has suggested this to me. She's just been the most direct.

I've been on this Witchcraft journey for about two months, and the differences and similarities between the religion of Wicca and the broader Witchcraft actually being practiced by most people today is impossible to ignore.

I recently discovered an online "blacklist" of Wiccan authors and their various transgressions (such as cultural appropriation, perpetuation of the burning times myth, pseudoscience) and was disheartened to discover nearly all of my current authors were listed. Although, if I'm being honest with myself, it's not hard to see why. There has been a large amount of cringeworthy content in some of these books. I've been ignoring my instinct to brush past it, because I am here to push past feelings of doubt and allegations of stupidity. If I stopped reading everything I thought was a little off, I might stop reading entirely. But it's getting harder to ignore. You can attribute much of it to age, but when

D. J. Conway says that Witches who don't want to work with baneful magic are cowards, and even my beloved Scott Cunningham takes deities from Hawaii and inserts them into Wicca, it's hard not to grit my teeth. I think the Jungian idea of universal truths and myths is an escape hatch from the idea that you have appropriated a piece of someone else's culture and taken it out of context.

I'm also getting annoyed by Wicca's binary focus on the hard, fierce masculine and soft, fertile feminine. It's out of place in a world where everyone under twenty thinks you're a freak if you haven't at least once questioned your gender. At first I really liked the Crone aspect of the tripart Wiccan Goddess. There are precious few role models for older women in our youth-worshipping society. I walked into my thirtieth birthday party feeling like Melisandre in *Game of Thrones* walking into the dawn after the zombie battle, ripping off her ruby, and keeling over in the snow to die. Wicca's reverential attitude toward the aging female form felt like a warm hug from a friend whom you've done wrong, a road map that allowed me to see aging not as a loss of beauty and intelligence, but an actual gaining of wisdom and dignity. The real issue I have in connecting to the Wiccan Goddess lies in her Mother aspect. I don't want to feel anything but joy toward the first deity who has ever looked like me. But I find myself continuously unmotivated to reach out to her and form a connection, partially because her divinity derives almost exclusively from her ability to create life. Meanwhile, I have no desire to become pregnant. I'm in my early thirties, and the reality that I might not ever have kids is imminent. This leads me to wonder if I am a woman and I never have children—according to Wicca, do I have any divinity at all? All of this makes me want to explore other forms of the Witchcraft Goddess.

It's also interesting to note that anyone who has ever equated Wicca with Witchcraft is on this blacklist. That basically means every white Witch who was writing before the year 2000. When Wicca was getting started in the forests of England in the 1940s, the Craft *was* the religion, and conflating Witchcraft and Wicca was the norm. As the neopagan religion hit American soil, several people—especially practitioners of Rootwork and

Hoodoo—became exhausted with their Craft being constantly confused with European Wicca and asked everyone to please stop.

According to Raymond Buckland in 2011, "The word *Wicca* is generally directed to those who still follow the Old Religion concepts, worshipping the gods through the Wheel of the Year, in esbats and sabbats. The word *witchcraft* has come to be relegated to those who wish to work magic and only magic."

This is why the line between Witchcraft and Wicca is so blurry and has been so hard for me to find.

What's true is that if I am to truly grasp the heart of the modern Witchcraft movement, I need to step outside of the confinement of Wicca. Besides, most of my Wiccan books have shockingly low coverage of topics like astrology, tarot, and crystals. And that's 99 percent of WitchTok.

There are a galactic number of books about Witchcraft in existence, far more than Wicca alone. For necessity's sake, I once again employ the popularity filter to narrow them down. I seek out the all-time best-selling books with the word "Witch" or "Witchcraft" in the title—not Wicca.

Later that day, I step into Walden Pond Books, my local mom-and-pop bookstore. The scent of wooden floorboards and old paper embraces me, so rich it creeps behind my surgical mask. I begin the joyful task of perusing, and discover the store has approximately twenty-seven thousand books in stock with the word "Witch" in the title.

None of them are the books on my list.

The occult section has about five books in it, looking tired and forlorn. Above it, I notice bitterly that the "women in Christianity" section has a whole shelf to itself. Astrology has two.

Disappointed, I walk back toward the front entrance, past *Hour of the Witch*, *A Discovery of Witches*, *The Witch's Heart*, *The Once and Future Witches*, *Everyone Knows Your Mother Is a Witch*, and a sign declaring Patricia Lockwood "a modern word witch," and out to get my books about Witches.

After visiting three different occult shops, I at last have my new spiritual advisory panel, a fresh canon of sages. I am excited. I feel nervous, like I'm graduating to a new, modern level of the Craft. Some interesting trends: the median publication date has drifted closer to 2010, sales numbers are much higher overall, and there are far fewer male authors. As time goes forward, you can watch American Witchcraft distance itself from the word "Wicca," at the same time it becomes more female dominated. We are also exiting the realm of ivory-towered theosophy and entering the world of folk magic and DIY. One of the "books" is actually just a tarot deck. Another is more or less a laundry list of spells. Identity-based specialties—such as green, house, or kitchen Witchcraft—suddenly appear, and have been selling radically well over the past several months. (It's almost as if everyone has been locked in their homes for two years and is keen to learn how to make vacuuming spiritually fulfilling.)

I am also finally encountering a name I recognize from the shelves of my teenage Witch friends growing up: Silver RavenWolf. RavenWolf was something of a Wiccan shepherdess to a generation of people who happened be in the throes of puberty at the same time *Practical Magic* and *The Craft* had made it to basic cable, and decided they wanted to see the truth behind the Hollywood versions of Witchcraft. Today, according to anthropologist and Witch Kathryn Gottlieb, merely referencing Silver RavenWolf in some circles is a sure way to get yourself laughed out of them. Her critics hold that she is a proponent of the (debunked) Stone Age goddess cult myth, bashes Christianity, is guilty of several acts of cultural appropriation, and conflates Wicca with Witchcraft (this last one confuses me, because for better or worse, it's very obvious to me that Wicca is the primary bedrock of modern American Witchcraft, but I guess we're not supposed to acknowledge that fact too loudly). Regardless of your opinion of her, RavenWolf was one of the first writers who departed from the self-important, academic tone that characterized most twentieth-century books about the occult, and instead wrote in the language of her audience (that is to say, teenagers). She applied magic to boyfriends, eating disorders, anxiety, homework, money, sexual consent, self-harm, even acne. She often included sections for parents, helping to affirm that their daughters were not, in fact, worshipping Satan and there was no need to panic. This is probably why, despite whatever is said about her now, her encyclopedia-weight tome *Solitary Witch: The Ultimate Book of Shadows for the New Generation* remains one of the top-selling Witchcraft books in existence.

I research the backgrounds of the other best-selling authors and make a few interesting discoveries: they are all white, and, most interesting of all, although they don't say "Wicca" anywhere in their book titles, they are all still Wiccan.

There is one exception: Juliet Diaz, a Taino American Bruja—the only person on my list who isn't white and doesn't directly associate with Wicca, although she still writes about the neopagan, Celtic-derived Wheel of the Year.

This is not what I was expecting. I feel the emotional equivalent of having prepared myself for a year abroad only to discover my scholarship has been canceled. I'm not really sure I'm going anywhere new.

DAY 68

While some grew up initiated into family religions, many have been disconnected from their ancestral practices for a generation or more, so White spirituality sometimes serves as a sort of scaffolding for mystical exploration.
—LORRAINE MONTEAGUT

Modern Witchcraft places a strong emphasis on bringing us back to our roots. There's heavy usage of words like "reclaiming" and "ancient" and "tradition." I find myself thinking about legitimacy and lineages—who is allowed to do what, and how they found out about it. What does going back to your roots mean for people whose parents were born far away, who raise you in a new country where traditions overlap like cheese slices on hamburgers? I feel like I'm lacking in verifiable traditions. I want to talk to someone who still has theirs.

For this, I drive down to chat with my friend Madeleine, a first-generation Haitian American, neuromuscular massage therapist, doula, and Witch. She's married to Theodora, the person who co-ran the coven that I engaged with in my early twenties. Tonight I sit on the powder blue couch in their cozy living room, staring at their shelves of stuffed animals, stationary, yarn, and collections of Tamora Pierce books. The walls are covered in photos of people smiling and hugging, and two competing Yankee candles perfume the air. We munch on Thai takeout, and I ask Madeleine about how she became interested Witch-craft.

"I was raised Roman Catholic," she says in her firm, kind voice. "The mystical things in Haitian culture were never talked about directly in our family. One time when I was a kid, I was watching *Paranormal Activity* with some friends and my mom turns to me and says, 'If that ever happens in your house, here's what you do. You get a little paper bag. You get some needles. You get some sesame seeds. You break the eyes off the needles, you put them in the bag with the sesame seeds,' blah-blah-blah. Basically you give the spirit an impossible task so it's too distracted to hurt you. I tried to ask her more about why she was telling me this, like, why did she think I might need this information. But she would just clam up. I don't know if this was from her own trauma, but she had this almost unhealthy distrust of people. I have a million stories like this."

"So your family didn't initiate you into anything?" I ask, a little surprised that she was left out of her own immediate family's heritage. "They wanted to keep you in the dark?"

"Basically. We were asked to participate, but nothing was explained. Like once a year, my grandpa would cleanse my dad's business. Did they explain to us, the kids, what was happening, and why we were doing it this way? No. You were just there because Grandpa wanted you there. That's the best I could get. My mom always told me, 'Don't ask other people about Vodou. Ask your family.' But then, when I did ask my family, they never had answers. If I lived on the East Coast, maybe I would have gone to Creole school and found a community to talk to. But even then, probably not, because Haitians never talk about this stuff in public."

"So how did you get into Witchcraft?" I ask, passing her some papaya salad, more curious than ever.

"I get to high school, and suddenly I can drive, and Barnes & Noble is the spot, right? And also, I'm reading a lot of fantasy books, and I knew the magic in these stories isn't real, but it has to come from somewhere. So, I start looking for information on magic and Vodou, and I find . . . well, I find what Barnes & Noble has."

"You find Silver RavenWolf," I chuckle between a mouthful of pad thai.

"I find Silver RavenWolf," Madeleine says, nodding. "And here's the thing. She was, like, 'Here are the books. This is number one, two, and three. You start here and you end there.' And I was, like, 'Cool, bitch. Say less! You have directions for me to follow and these other people aren't talking to me? I will listen.' Also, when you're coming from Catholicism, structure feels like a safety blanket. Then in college, I met another friend, and she's, like, 'Hey, let me show you this book by Cunningham. Let me show you this tarot deck, and this other thing.' We would get together and do readings, and go to witchy stores and do intentions. We became a group."

"Looking back," I prompt, "do you feel like you were still tapping into the same ultimate thing when you went looking for books on Vodou and you found books on Wicca? Or did it feel more confusing? Did any part of you feel like these books were signposts on the right road, or were you upset because you knew it wasn't at all what you were looking for?"

"It's interesting that you say 'signpost on the road,' because I did feel like I was looking for a path," she says, crossing her arms and giving the ceiling a pensive stare. "Some of it didn't feel right because the people in these stories—Wicca's stories—didn't look like me. But there were exceptions, which came about from Vodou's syncretic qualities. You know Celtic Brigid? There is a Brigid in Vodou—Maman Brigitte. In Haitian culture a lot of things bleed together.

"The thing is," she continues, "I think I found what I found as part of my experience being a Black kid in a predominantly white area, trying to shoehorn myself into something. I was doing that with everything in my life: body image issues, sexuality, my approach to my professional life. My attitude was always 'This could almost fit, I can make this work.' Now I realized that it was a phase of exploration. I ended up having conversations with my college friends about things that in theory should have been part of a closed practice. But I didn't always feel safe going to other Vodou practices to have those conversations. This is something about being Black and queer: just because someone looks like you, doesn't mean that they're safe for you. So I talked to the people I felt safe with, who were my college friends. I think that's the point of community and coming together—it's to have a container that helps you figure out what you are looking for. And what's funny is as time went on, my mom even opened up to some of them. She was a prophetic dreamer, and I had a friend who was a spirit medium, and they talked about a lot of stuff."

"Did you ever end up getting the information you wanted about Vodou?"

"Yes," Madeleine says emphatically, getting up to show me a long line of books on a shelf. "Some of them were hard to find, some are no longer in print because there's not enough interest. I also eventually connected with my uncle in Canada, who is much more open about everything. He's gay, and I think part of his affirming of his queerness is to also affirm the parts of our culture that the rest of our family wanted to hide. The last time I went to Haiti with my extended family a few years ago, we actually went to some ceremonies, and I was finally, like, 'Why don't we talk about this more, why did we never talk about this when I was a kid?' I found out my grandfather used to be oungan, a Vodou priest. My dad finally said, 'I don't know enough to feel like I could lead you through this. We didn't know enough, so we just told you no.'"

"So they weren't so much hiding it from you when you were a kid. It was that they were unsure about the traditions, too?"

"Yes," she says, sitting back down in her chair and giving a little sigh. "They didn't feel like it was safe to lead me through the details, because it is no small undertaking. My grandpa eventually told me, 'This is not an easy life, you know." Because to hold a title is not just to have gone through initiations. You also have to hold an entire community. You have to be responsible for ancestor veneration, ceremonies, being a container where people can feel safe enough to go through these rites and to have these experiences. Vodou has medicine, it has counseling, has community. Vodou has applications for people's biopsychosocial and spiritual well-being. You need to hold all of it. Because these things aren't actually separate."

"So you had these bonding experiences with Wiccans growing up—but you also have this strong tie to your Haitian and Vodou heritage. What does your practice look like now?"

"I use a very, very, very loose Wiccan framework," she says while carefully selecting an eggroll. "I have an altar and I have elemental representation, and I care about what direction things are facing. I rarely read tarot. In my head, I associate it with Wicca. But I do read oracle cards. I also never used to celebrate the sabbats, but now that I'm with Theodora, who follows the Wheel of the Year, I say Samhain instead of Halloween. At the same time, this has strengthened my awareness of the Vodou calendar because the second of November is also All Souls' Day. Overall, my practice is about communication with my ancestors, doing weekly offerings to the deities that I feel closest to on their days, and asking for help and guidance through deep meditation and prayer. I also never entirely let go of Catholicism; it's too much a part of my upbringing. But I had to release the Catholic expectation of what getting married was going to look like for me. That's also in line with letting go of adhering to a religion that has a very specific process and doctrine. Basically, my practice honors who I am in every facet. It's not in a box. It reflects me and I reflect it. It's a lot of different things."

"That is something I've learned is a trademark of Witchcraft," I say. "You can be a Witch and be a part of another religion. You can blend spiritualities. I imagine that's very liberating."

"Yeah! The real question for me becomes: What is a practice, and what is a religion? A practice is this living thing. I feel like religion in some ways—and I hate to say it—is dead. It's dead because it's not evolving. Religion implies an agreed-upon creed, and somebody is in charge.

If you're doing something because someone told you that's how it's supposed to be done, but it doesn't feel good to you, then you're still being led by someone else versus being led by your own self-direction and standing in your own power of growth, intelligence, understanding, and compassion. And that's what a spiritual practice is. It's self-directed.

"Spiritual practices are also, by nature, diasporic," she continues. "There's no one way to do it. If I went to Benin right now, I'd see things I'd recognize from Vodou and some things I don't, temple to temple, family to family. That's what it means for a tradition to be alive; it's constantly adapting and constantly changing. These practices, whether it's Witchcraft, Vodou, Lucumi, Candomblé, Hoodoo, whatever—they evolve with the populations."

"That actually brings me back to the idea of closed practices," I say, thoughtfully poking at my rice. "I respect the closed door, and why it's closed. But do you ever wonder if what's behind some of these closed doors is going to eventually get forgotten or lost?"

"That's the thing," she says, putting down her fork. "Like people go out and discover Reiki, for example. They feel an energy that calls them to it, and they're, like, 'I don't know what the fuck to do with this.' But at the beginning, when you start something, you don't have those questions, because you're still trying to find an answer to this bigger urge you're feeling. And then you grow—in theory, if you are still on this path of discovery—and you can say, 'Oh well, this served a purpose, but it's not what I thought it was, so I'm moving on.'

"With Vodou today, because there's no centralization, when people tell me they practice, I take everything they say with a grain of salt. Their life experience is going to influence how they interpret the traditions, and I have to remember just because someone looks like me, just because someone is Haitian like me, doesn't mean they're safe. For example, I can go to Haiti, but I can never take Theodora there and say, 'This is my spouse.' All of this to say even when someone is from the same place you are, it doesn't mean their space is for you. There are closed practices, but if they're closed and not evolving or not inclusive, then other spaces are going to have to be made."

"And they're being made," I realize aloud.

"That's exactly it," she says, putting her hands on the table. "They are being made."

DAY 71

Magic is a convenient word for a whole collection of techniques,
all of which involve the mind.
—MARGOT ADLER

Today a prowler tries to break into our house at four in the afternoon, with all the ninjalike grace of walking up to our front door and jiggling the handle (it was locked). He then strolled casually into the backyard, heard me yell, gave me a winning smile, jumped onto the compost bin, broke the lid, and leaped over our back fence while the chickens squawked in terror. This is an encore from an 11 a.m. appearance, where he peered into the window of our downstairs friend, Joanna. I'm not sure whether to be terrified or impressed.

"I wonder if PCP is making a comeback," I tell Justin jokingly, trying to dim the lightning bolts of adrenaline pulsing through my body.

"I cannot stand this city anymore," he says, fuming and stomping back inside the house after yelling at the neighbors to lock their doors, alerting them that a prowler was in the neighborhood trying door handles. Justin has lost his patience with Oakland since our garage was broken into last year and many of his woodworking tools were stolen (some of them sentimental items, inherited from his deceased grandfather). The reality of living in Oakland through the pandemic has become a sore spot in our relationship. Most of his friends moved away last year. Crime is rising. Rent refuses to descend. Anywhere we could go that reminds us why this city is actually a fun place to live is shuttered. I get an email once a day telling me that yet another beloved bar, club, concert hall, festival, or restaurant has been taken off life support.

I joke with Justin today because I don't know what else to do. We already have a front porch camera, dead bolts, and a fence. Basically, everything except a very big dog (which, if our renter's agreement didn't forbid, I would happily adopt). I have done all the nonmagical (aka "mundane") actions that I can do to keep myself safe. But I still feel an overwhelming sense of vulnerability, like our house is a dartboard waiting for a strike.

Then I remember I am a Witch now. I have power in situations I was previously asked to simply accept.

I go into my newly engorged home office library. Juliet Diaz's *Witchery* is already open. I flip the pages until I find a protection spell, and, to my surprise, I have all the ingredients I need already in the house. I smile.

I go into the kitchen and mix equal parts salt, dried basil, and cumin. Justin comes in and briefly asks if I'm making a steak rub before I yelp, "I don't tell you how to do your job!" and then head outside to encircle our property, methodically sprinkling the spices around the entire perimeter. As I process, I chant in my head, "You are protected, you are protected, you are protected . . ." and try to push out the idea of the neighbors seeing me and wondering what I'm doing. Maybe they will think I'm testing out an organic pesticide.

I eventually get downstairs to Joanna's half of the duplex. I've done all our shared bits of the property already (including the chicken coop, because why not). But now I'm standing before her front door. I feel like you can't just throw spices at people's front doors without their consent. It doesn't seem neighborly. More important, consent is a defining feature of ethical spellwork. This idea is repeated again and again, by old authors and new: if you cast a spell on or for someone without their consent—in other words, if you interrupt someone else's free will—you're technically performing baneful magic. *But what if it's simply protection, a benevolent intention, does that count?*

Joanna is home and sees me hesitating outside her front door holding a bowl of what is effectively potpourri. She interrupts my internal debate about her free will and my free will by popping her head out of the window and asking,

"Hi . . . are you . . . okay?"

I hesitate. Joanna, like Justin, is an open and confident atheist; someone who has already decided she doesn't care about being embraced by the divine, and of whom I am afraid to look dumb in front of for trying. But she is also my friend. I decide to explain what I'm doing.

"I know it's dumb, but it actually feels like it's helping, and since there isn't a lot else we can do, I don't know . . . I already did all our doors and windows, so then I thought about your door, which is kinda right in front and—"

She cuts me off. "I don't think it's dumb." She's smiling at me the way one might smile at a kindergartner showing off a particularly large fingerpainting. But then she pauses before she goes back inside and says, "Thank you."

DAY 72

Witchcraft tends to attract people who, by nature,
do not like to join groups.
—STARHAWK

Samhain is approaching, and I want to go big for my first Witch's New Year. This means I need to find a coven; one with a good reputation, but that also welcomes strangers. And also is taking Covid seriously. And also is meeting in person. And also on a day that doesn't conflict with what I'm referring to as "the secular Halloween party" Justin wants to have in our carport on Saturday. It is, admittedly, a tall order.

Margot Adler has a helpful list of groups and events that a prospective Witch can connect with in the back of *Drawing Down the Moon*. I punch each of them into my laptop and discover half of them no longer exist. I am greeted by a series of letters on websites that appear to have frozen in 1997, explaining something to the effect of "So long, and thanks for all the fish" in Papyrus and Comic Sans fonts.

There is a small occult shop about two hours away from me that is having a Samhain ceremony in their back room on October 31. I message the business asking if they are requiring any vaccine proof, or masks. The owner replies quickly with: "as per El Dorado County guidelines, we do not ask."

This opinion does not represent the majority of witchy event organizers, it's worth noting. The Aquarian Tabernacle Church (a global interfaith Wiccan fellowship) has a statement on its website that reads:

THERE IS NO TENET IN WICCA THAT WOULD EXEMPT YOU FROM GETTING A PROVEN LIFESAVING VACCINE, SUCH AS THE MRNA AND OTHER WIDELY ADMINISTERED VACCINES FOR THE COVID VIRUS, OR FROM WEARING A MASK. IT WOULD BE AN ABUSE OF OUR AUTHORITY TO SAY THERE IS ONE.

Finally, I see the Council of Magical Arts has an entire festival dedicated to Samhain, but it finished two days ago. I had no idea how much of paganism would be about planning. I had no idea I was this bad a planner.

I sigh. I worry I will not be able to attend anything and will be stuck at home again with my cardboard box.

I wish I could do something without any preparation, like just showing up at a church. But there is no All Are Welcome banner hanging off any neighborhood pagan churches. There aren't really any neighborhood pagan churches. You really have to work to get in here.

In the afternoon, after scouring more and more, I find a coven that seems almost too good to be true. Their crimson-and-cream website shouts "Welcome, Moonbeam" at me. They are having a Samhain event, outdoors. They require vaccination. They are only a half hour away. My teeth are practically chattering with excitement. This is it.

I send them their modest donation request to register for the Samhain ritual and await further instructions.

DAY 80

Tarot is (or should be) of special interest to magicians and
would-be magicians.
—LON MILO DuQUETTE

Lauren, one of my Witch mentors for a year and a day, comes over
tonight after discovering I have done no divination about my spiritual quest. Divination is one of the skills—and theoretically, perks—of
being a Witch. If you're having trouble understanding what comes next
in life, need help making a choice, or just want some reassurance you
are on the right path, you can commune with otherworldly forces for
answers to what—if you ascribe to the time laws of Einsteinian physics—
would otherwise remain shrouded in the unknowable future. There
are countless methods of divination in Witchcraft: reading tea leaves,
throwing runes, peering into a large crystal, pulling up a star chart, and
so on. But tarot cards are probably the most accessible and well known
to your average Jane. All you have to do, really, is know how to shuffle
and read the book that came with your deck, which conveniently tells
you what all the cards mean. This is not to say reading tarot takes no
skill. Like all forms of divination, every answer that appears can be inter-
preted in more than one way. I have never been a fan of divination for
this reason—whatever answer you get always seems to generate more
questions than the relief of answers. It's the art of interpretation that
makes a good Witch great.

I answer the door and Lauren is wearing a corduroy jumper, a bondage harness, and a deer antler the size of a dinner plate as a necklace. We
sit at the dining room table while Bird, my gray-and-white cat, dances

infinity symbols around her legs. I feed her homemade shakshuka and a gin cocktail.

I've had a tarot reading or two before: high school nights spent giggling over a candlelit card table; sitting on the carpet in Liza's sunny living room after a coven meeting, watching her tap her lips with her forefinger as her eyes dart from card to card like she's solving a complicated math problem. If you were looking to test whether psychics are real, you could argue a tarot reading from someone who doesn't know you might be more scientifically "pure." But a tarot reading from a Witch who *does* know you—your struggles, your strengths, all the wonderful ways you bullshit yourself—will probably be far more helpful for solving your actual problem. There was indeed an alchemy in those late-night teenage tarot sessions. The cards allowed us to transmute what would otherwise be interpersonal judgment and gossip into productive conversation and therapeutic advice. It didn't matter if we could read the future. It mattered that we now had a gentle and empowering way to tell someone their boyfriend sucked.

After dinner Lauren pulls out a small velvet bag the color of dried blood. She reaches inside and I half expect her to pull out the dark crystal itself. Instead, it's a Lisa Frank tarot deck. She invites me to shuffle the cards. A frenzy of pink unicorns, neon rainbows, and sunshine-yellow emojis whirs between my palms.

"You know I really don't like tarot," I begin, staring at my hands. "Every answer ends up being another question."

"Do you want to stop?" she asks.

"Well, no, but I—"

"Then ask a question to the cards," she says, shushing me. "And think about it as you shuffle."

I look at the candy-colored images careening in my hands. *Where am I now?* I think.

No, wait. That's not interesting. *What comes next?* That's what I really want. I want a flashlight. I want someone to tell me I'm on the right path, that my efforts will be worthwhile. I want someone to tell me, "Good job, keep going, the doubt will fade. This will get easy."

I feel like I never know when to actually stop shuffling tarot cards. It's another part of Witchcraft people gloss over. Like what "working with a deity" actually means in terms of technical steps.

But eventually I find I am setting them facedown in a neat pile on the table.

"Okay," Lauren says. "Now pull the top card."

I place my finger on the top card and find myself muttering aloud, "Please don't be the tower, please don't be the tower, please don't be—"

The tower.

I screech. Lauren laughs like someone just dropped a puppy into her lap.

"No, dude!" I scream. "That's the worst card! That's the *actual worst card*."

Like most people, I used to think death was the worst possible pull. But tarot readers are often eager to correct this assumption: Death doesn't mean you're going to die. It merely means you need to end something that is no longer serving you, and should prepare for rebirth and reinvention.

The tower gets none of death's happy framings. It is the actual shit card. It's less about endings, and more about calamities, signifying that something life altering, dangerous, and distinctly unexpected is on its way to you.

"Oh my god. Do I have cancer?" I ask, pushing back my chair and standing up, running my hands through my hair. This is the part where normally I'd say I don't believe in this. But the fact that I said the card's name before flipping it over—a one-in-seventy-eight chance—has me spooked.

"No, it doesn't mean you have cancer. Necessarily." She sighs, but she's still smiling. I want to ask her what is so funny about this. "The lightning-struck tower means you're about to come crashing down. It's about crisis, yes, but also liberation. Look at the image. It's a prison being cracked open."

I look down at the card. It shows a skyscraper-sized ice cream sundae, lightning bolts piercing the whipped cream on top. Two sunshine-yellow smiley faces fall down the sides of the fudge-streaked glass to their doom.

"You're about to be broken down and built up again," she says, tapping the card and giving me a half smile. "My guess is, it will hurt. But it will feel better afterward."

DAY 81

It's all in your head . . . you just have no idea how
big your head is.
—LON MILO DuQUETTE

"So what was with the screeching last night?" Justin asks me over dinner.

I explain that I pulled the impending danger card of the tarot deck. I also describe how I said aloud, "Please don't be the tower," right before flipping it over.

"Wait, so you *manifested* it?" He gives me a pointed look and draws out the word.

"Oooh, that's a very big word for an atheist!" I reply.

He gives me a big smile.

Justin continues to be supportive of my Witchcraft journey. He occasionally asks me if I'm doing spellwork anytime soon, because he enjoys the campfire-thick scent of burning herbs which inevitably fogs the house. He once told me he felt that atheism was the nearest cousin to neopaganism: they are both considered rebel spiritual paths, they both seek alternatives to the problems of mainstream religion, they both tend to appreciate the earth. Still, sometimes I wonder if this year would be easier if he was doing this journey with me. I have slight pangs of envy at couples who do crazy shit like believe in the same gods and pray together. There's an intimacy there I wonder if I'll ever attain. But also maybe I'm just afraid to do something alone. And I want the comfort of an exit buddy if this all goes to shit.

"Lauren thinks it's about my spiritual journey," I say, returning to the tarot reading last night. "That I'm about to break down parts of myself and build them back up again. But I'm nervous. The tower isn't about conscious reinvention. It's about crisis."

"Or . . ." Justin says, trailing on what he wants to say next.

I know what he wants to say. He's going to say that because I am so worried about something bad happening, something bad is going to happen.

"It becomes a self-fulfilling prophecy?" I finish his trailing sentence with a huff. His eyebrows rise and he waves his hands in the air as if to say, "You said it, not me."

But we mean different things. He thinks I mean that I'll start noticing misfortune. I am worried I'm going to create it by being unable to stop thinking about it.

It's not exactly helpful to be told something bad will happen without any further explanation of what the bad thing will be. Should I be stocking up on survival equipment? Pull my money out of the bank? Prepare my will? I am teeming with "brace for impact" energy and have nowhere to direct it. The best way out of this anxiety would be to say I don't believe in any of this. But that would mean giving up on my spiritual quest.

I wonder, in a spirituality where your words are spells, your thoughts affect your future, divination advises your fate, and the world is supposedly full of secret signals that can help or hinder you, how do you avoid living in total paranoia?

DAY 83

*I am in no way saying that prewritten or preworked spells aren't
"good," because magick can be found anywhere we make it;
however, harnessing the power of intuition in a controlled way
can open a level of depth and understanding that we miss by
relying fully on others' spellwork.*
—TEMPERANCE ALDEN

I'm still too freaked out about pulling the tower card last week with Lauren. So I start planning a protection spell.

It was a full moon yesterday, but I read somewhere that you really can take advantage of full moon energy for spellwork for about three days. Today is the waning day, which is great for banishing. I want to banish a potential crisis. Perfect.

This will be my first intentional, official esbat (or full moon rite), unlike what happened in the Ansel Adams wilderness, when I wanted to dance in the moonlight but was too put off by the sensation that something that might outrank me in the food chain was watching me from the depths of the forest. I'm nervous, but I have real motivation: I'm trying to protect myself from an apparently impending calamity.

I flip open Lisa Chamberlain's *Wicca Spellbook Starter Kit* and start looking for spells that attract protection and banish negative energy. They all center on burning candles in particular colors: orange for helping you cope with unexpected change, brown for grounding and centering, and black for clearing negative energy.*

I have none of these materials, so I run across the street to the

---

* Spellbook authors often try to clear up any confusion about the color black being synonymous with so-called black magic. In modern Witchcraft, black is a helpful color, associated with protection and the neutralization of negativity. If you want to refer to the type of magic that has cruel intentions, "baneful magic" is more accurate.

occult shop (once again, thanking fate that I live in NorCal and can basically step out of my house and trip over metaphysical trinketry) and purchase a black-and-brown candle. I think about getting orange, but the orange color chart in that store doesn't mention anything about balancing bad energy, just joy and communication. It's a hard call, but rather than trust Chamberlain, I trust the people actually selling me the candle. So instead of orange, I opt for a silver one, which according to their chart means protection. And also seems to match with my full moon theme.

As I walk home, I wonder if any other religion has this much optionality in their rituals. Everything is so fluid, so open to interpretation in Witchcraft. The number of options for what objects to use and how to use them continues to feel more complicated than empowering.

I get home and start decorating the altar. Once again, I'll be practicing in my office. On the cardboard box. It made the mistake of working last time.

I gather up all my altar items that represent the various elements and deities, and lay out everything on a white silk veil, borrowed once again from my old closet of dance costumes. In the center of the silk, I cluster the three taper candles inside one oversized votive, trying to get them to stay upright even though they keep slipping to the side.

I pour myself two shots of gin, take my hair down, and turn half the lights off.

I begin by aggressively sageing everything in my room like Mr. Clean. I know white sage is no longer the preferred smoke-cleansing method for modern Witches—it is considered a culturally appropriative practice, taken out of context from certain Native American rituals, and mainstream affinity for the herb has led to exploitive overharvesting, which is pretty ironic considering Witchcraft's commandment to save the earth. But I have this fatty j of sage sitting on my shelf that someone gave to me a decade ago, and throwing it away feels like an equally disrespectful act. I'm using it up until I can get a new roll of something local, or even start harvesting cooking sage from my own garden, which Liza tells me works just as well.

After I have cleansed myself and my altar (and once again by happenstance, my laptop, my books, my printer, my office junk drawer, and the veterinary records for my cats), I sit down cross-legged. The room feels dark and empty. I close my eyes for four breaths and try to bring myself into the moment, reviewing all five of my senses.

It feels too quiet. I have both windows open to try and get the light of the moon into my room. I feel off.

I haven't cast the circle yet, so I give myself permission to turn on my laptop and search "Wiccan ritual music playlists" on Spotify. After a few forays into sludgy goth rock, jolly Celtic Woman jigs, and something I can only describe as "Icelandic Elf Power Metal," I land on a playlist with the descriptor "calm music so I can do spellwork." Amazing. I press play. A soothing, trancelike minor key song wafts out of my laptop speakers.

I turn back to my altar and resume centering myself.

I stand up, cast the circle, and call the corners, the God, and the Goddess. I realize I don't have any water, so I pour some gin into the seashell representing the element.

The music is, much to my surprise, phenomenal. I find myself thinking about my invisible benefactor, another Witch somewhere in the world who spent hours collecting these harmonic, translucent songs and decided to share her bounty for no other reason than someone else might need it. I think about all the objects scattered in my house, now on my altar, that were freely given to me by Witches who thought maybe someday I might need them, not knowing when or why.

I am constantly amazed by how much Witches don't seem to like each other. They bicker online about everything. Twitter is an ocean of "um, actually" and "you forgot about." They bash each other's character and catapult judgments of "uninformed," "misguided," and "complete idiot," like archaeologists at war over a new theory about the development of agriculture. Evidence overwhelmingly suggests they hate each other. It is all the more amazing that they are constantly trading gifts and lending each other light and power. Truly, there has never been a better example of sisterhood.

I light the spell candles and struggle to get them to stand upright in the oversized votive. Some brown wax spills on the snow-white veil.

"Fuck!" I yell, watching the silk steam as wax infuses itself into the fabric. I need to get actual taper candleholders. No matter how many things I buy, I always seem to need something else.

I begin to perform my spells, starting with the one that uses the orange candle that I don't have. Instead, I just skip to the part where I confess to a piece of paper all my fears about calamity, and then stick them under the cluster of candles, in the hopes they will fly away into the sky. Next is the black candle spell, where I imagine a ball of energy with a black rim emanating off the candle, surrounding me in a globe of protection.

About twenty minutes have passed and my back is killing me now. I had my MRI a few days ago but won't see the results for a week or more. Sitting cross-legged for too long still hurts. So I decide to lie down on my back in front of my altar. I worry if this is disrespectful, but I tell myself I'm just trying to get into a deeper state of meditation. I think any gods and/or elements I have managed to actually summon will understand.

I see the light of the full moon out the window and close my eyes. I think about drawing it down to me, an aura of moonbeams surrounding my body, to aid me in my working, and to help calm me down.

Suddenly I feel a tightness in my chest. It's a little bit like what was happening in the attic back in August. I think my back must just be tense. I try to exhale fully and move my knees around to take pressure off the muscles. But it won't let go.

Trying to hold the image of moonbeams around me, I flip my body around and go into child's pose. I see the moonbeams start to fall away, and unbidden, I see a veil of cloudy, opaque black surrounding me. I'm not doing this. It's like a dream. And it doesn't feel like a good thing. *Black isn't bad*, I remind myself; *black is a shield. This is the shield I just asked for. Black is good.* But this doesn't feel good. This feels like a black hole, a void. This black feels bad. *Does fearing black make me racist?*

I open my eyes and sit upright again, focusing on the light of the three candles. I go back to chanting Lisa Chamberlain's orange candle spell words: "I am grounded, centered, and ready for new blessings. So let it be."

It doesn't make me feel better. The tightness in my chest has not yielded at all. I feel like I can't take a full breath, just like when I tried to meditate in August. It only gets worse the more I try. I wonder if I am having a panic attack.

I try clearing my mind, shaking my hands of excess energy. I turn my body back into child's pose and force my head to the floor in complete surrender. I try to imagine all the energy pouring out of me, into the floor; the black clouds, the moonbeams, all of it, I don't care anymore. I think about the earth swallowing everything, grounding me.

The tightness in my chest doesn't go away.

The more things I try that fail, the more I feel myself panic. I recognize I'm spiraling. This isn't working. I want to hit the emergency switch and get off the ride. Finally, I lean forward and blow the candles out with one huge gust of breath.

There's a moment where everything is dark. The music is still playing. I turn around and snap my laptop shut. Silence.

I get up and turn on my office lights, rapidly put everything on my altar away, trying to ignore the weird, dizzy panic I feel. I cross through the apartment and walk into the kitchen. I'm not hungry, but I eat a piece of toast anyway, hoping it will ground me. I curl up with my laptop on the couch and watch two episodes of trash TV until I feel sleepy, and then get in bed.

It still feels like a giant has my rib cage in his fist and is gently squeezing.

I think about talking to Justin. I don't know how to tell him what I'm feeling. So, I keep it to myself.

Eventually I fall asleep. At 3:04 a.m., I awake to lashing rain; a storm has arrived outside our window. I still feel like I'm trying to breathe through a straw.

What have I done? I think. *Oh fuck fuck fuck what have I done to myself?*

DAY 84

Have you ever met an energy healer, a psychic, or a witch who
seemed to be entirely out of their mind and out of touch with
this world? . . . [T]hey've fried themselves.
—MAT AURYN

"Have you ever had a spell hangover?" I ask Blanca. This is a term I learned accidentally after Googling "can you accidentally curse yourself." We're sitting on the couch in her living room, which looks like a tornado has run through it. Blanca moved last week, and half-unpacked boxes, clothes, books, and knickknacks are strewn everywhere. The fact that she's having me over at all, in the midst of her own chaos, is a favor, and I'm grateful.

"Oh, absolutely," she says, looking up at me from her tea, like I have just asked her if the sky is often blue. And I feel myself start to unclench.

Blanca is a friend of nearly twenty years and has been undertaking her own spiritual quest since leaving the Jehovah's Witnesses after high school. She found immense comfort in Wicca and other forms of neopaganism, specifically the Goddess, who was warm and welcoming after years of the cold judgment of Jehovah. She's the only other person I know who has struggled to seek the divine; like me, it didn't seem to click for her at first, when it was apparently clicking for everyone else who tried.

"I spent my whole life praying, hoping to hear something back from God," she tells me. "Then, the first time—*the very first time*—I reached out to Hecate, she answered me. And she laughed."

I want to ask her what she means. Was this a dream, a vision that came on after meditation, a deliberate invocation? I feel like I never know what people mean when they say they have connected with a deity. But I don't want to interrupt her flow.

Blanca has always had a healing job. Which is to say, jobs that take their toll on your emotions. First nursing school, then nonprofit education, then working the front desk for a transitional housing complex. "If I had a bad day, and I needed to drive home an hour, and I needed to keep it together, I would reach out for Hecate," she reflects to me. "I'd ask for her help to keep me stable and safe enough to get back to my house. Sure, I'll break down crying the minute I walk through that front door. But when I need strength to get through something, she's there for me, and she gets me through."

I know that Blanca has always had an altar in her house. Well, I call it an altar. It's a collection of crystals and candles and other sentimental objects, arranged on an old tapestry, with a massive vintage mirror presiding over the scene. It's here now, the first thing she set up in her new home. It frames her body perfectly from behind as she looks at me on the couch and says, "I actually don't really identify as a Witch."

"Really?" I say, staring pointedly at the scene behind her.

"I'm a pagan. But not a Witch," she corrects.

"But you practice magic," I reply delicately, curiously. "You have a connection—a relationship—with the goddess of magic. What is your definition of a Witch?"

"I think a Witch is a healer and a teacher. And I'm not public about anything anymore. I tried to go into covens, other communities. But they were too rigid, too full of hierarchy. I wanted the community I left behind when I left the church, you know? I still miss it. Nothing—I mean nothing—is like the community of Jehovah's Witnesses. It is so tight, and so powerful. You can go anywhere in the world and be treated like real family. But I didn't find that in Witchcraft. So now I just worship alone. And I don't do spells. Not anymore."

My eyebrows rise, and she continues, gesticulating into the air to emphasize her points.

"I think it's incredibly arrogant to assume you, this puny mortal, can command the will of the gods and change fate. I believe in opening yourself up to their will. Asking for guidance. Giving gratitude. I believe in receiving their messages. But this idea that you can *use* them, or talk to them as equals, is insane. Plus, have you met people who do a lot of spellwork?"

I think about this for a moment. "They are a little . . . different, yeah."

"Yeah. Everything has a price. You can't just change the course of the universe over and over again and not expect to pay a price," she says firmly, sipping her tea.

A few days ago, I might have scoffed at this. Not today.

Could all this anxiety I feel be nothing but the penalty for trying to practice magic?

Or was it that I couldn't decide what anything meant to me while I was in my sacred circle. Maybe I'm being punished for simply not having a pure heart and a focused mind.

Or did I do everything right? And this stress, this anvil on my chest, this anxiety is simply the toll I must pay, over and over again, if I want to change the course of creation in my favor.

DAY 91

You may perform rituals before realizing what you're actually doing.
—SCOTT CUNNINGHAM

I go out into the October morning glow to throw a few handfuls of treats to the chickens, and see something has gone into their coop and thrown half a week's worth of grain out of their feeders. It's scattered like a layer of sand on the floor of the run. I have never seen this before. My imagination sees a squirrel in front of the feeder, reaching in and digging out the food like a puppy in sand. But squirrels are normally too nervous to venture into the chicken run during the day, and their food is locked up behind rodent-proof wire fencing at night. I have no explanation.

Shaking my head, I head back upstairs, take my mucking shoes off and walk into the house. A few steps later I'm in the dining room and my bare foot meets a pad of cold, squishy carpet. I pause, circle back, tapping the carpet with my toes. It's sopping wet. I get on my knees and discover a trail of water, running from the bottom of a table where we have kept two emergency jugs of water. One of the jugs, for no reason I can see, has sprung a leak. This entire half of the dining room carpet is soaked. I pick up the offending, soggy-bottomed jug and try to find the crack but can't. Eventually I give up and throw it into the kitchen sink as if it will think about what it's done.

"Great job, buddy," I say to Bird as she strolls into the dining room with wide, innocent eyes to see what the noise is about.

"Why would you assume it's her?" Justin says, after I rouse him and tell him I need help moving half the dining room furniture around so the carpet can start to dry.

"Because cats chew on plastic stuff. I don't know. What else would it be?"

He goes into the kitchen and examines the jug. It's only a year old. Like me, he can't find bite marks. But we can both agree it's leaking, somehow, someway, because our carpet is on the verge of becoming a petri dish for a new form of penicillin.

I recall two nights ago when I was reading in the living room and heard what sounded like an animal peeing in the kitchen. Basil, my orange tabby, was staring at the refrigerator like there was a movie playing. Fearing some pipe had sprung a leak, I dug behind the fridge and discovered a small trail of trickling liquid. A water bottle from the top of a shelf, one that neither one of us could remember filling, had tipped over and started dripping over the counter. I cleaned it up immediately. But now this.

More burst pipes, I think sarcastically. *If water is trying to get my attention, I'd love for it to just tell me what it wants.*

As I mash wet towels into the carpet and haul the fan over, I think about how this time of year is indeed when the veils are supposed to be thinnest. Tricksters and spooks are afoot, whether it's humans driven to devilry or spirits bedeviling humans.

But I don't have time for this today. I don't have three hours to go to the occult shop and buy another five specifically colored candles and meditate in a cloud of incense and invoke the ancient deities that birthed the universe and commune with water spirits—or whatever is having fun at my expense. I have chores to do. I have work to finish. I am fed up.

I stop what I'm doing, get up, and march through the hallway, sopping towels in hand. I'm not thinking, I'm just moving. I draw my attention to all five senses at once. All the light gets brighter. My footsteps sound like drums. My skin feels like a baseline. I enter the bedroom and turn my face to the ceiling.

Hey. Knock it off. You had your fun. Now go away.

I don't say this aloud. It's more like it radiates off my body, a non-verbal soundwave. For once, I'm not thinking about Witchcraft. I'm just acting. Anger is helpful like that. My imagination glimpses a gray-white aura booming off my body, pushing the air out of the room, into four corners of the ceiling, out of the house, into the sky.

I realize I heard the words in my head in the command voice of a Bene Gesserit Witch. I just rewatched *Dune* on Wednesday. That's what I get for not thinking and just acting, I suppose.

I roll my eyes at myself, then turn around back down the hall and go to hang the wet towels outside.

The air feels clean and bright. I feel like I maybe have really done something. Or at least successfully convinced myself that I've done something. The rest of the day passes pleasantly and without incident. I have banished the tricksy spirit.

Hours pass.

At around 9 p.m., I'm standing in the kitchen washing dishes, and realize today is my father's birthday. He would have been seventy-one.

I remember how much he loved to play little pranks on us when we were kids.

My arms stop moving. I stare off into the middle distance of the sink. A few soap bubbles burst and reform together.

Justin comes in, sees me frozen with a sponge in my hand, and asks, "Are you okay?"

I burst into tears.

"Hey, whoa, hey . . . what?" he says, confused, pulling me away from the sink.

I blubber into his shoulder. I can't tell him. He wouldn't believe me. I don't believe me. But it's too personal this time, this little game of Witchcraft I'm playing. It's not cute anymore.

I whisper the only thing that feels true at the moment.

"I think I'm going crazy."

DAY 93

They gain the company of numerous spirits—sometimes in the form of the dead, with whom the witch holds necromantic discourse.
—CORY THOMAS HUTCHESON

It's Samhain. It's happening. Here we go. A few days ago, someone from the Temple of Luna finally got back to me with the instructions for tonight's ritual. It took a very long time. After the fifth day of radio silence after sending them registration funds, I started to wonder if I had been swindled. Perhaps this is the new Nigerian prince scam: criminal rings masquerading as moon priestesses, praying on the spiritual needs of lonely, jaded women.*

But eventually, the confirmation came.

The email is from a woman who signs herself "Priestess Ismene." She is warm and gracious. She is happy I will be joining. She outlines a list of seven items I must bring with me to the ritual: an offering for the goddess Hela; a Samhain-themed Craft for the altar; an object for my

---

* I realize that some people might call the moon priestesses who believe they *are* moon priestesses scammers, so the real difference here is intention.

ancestors; an unscented, contained candle (orange, black, or yellow preferably, but white will do); a drink (since we won't be sharing a chalice); a chair if I am unable to stand; and a jacket in case it gets cold. There is also a reminder that they do not observe "pagan standard time," and "the circle is cast promptly at 7:30."

I go about the house grabbing the various objects. I have a picture of my father as a young man, which I bring only after asking Ismene if we'll be able to take the items home afterward. I don't know if this is going to end in some kind of raging bonfire where I toss in everything that has brough me grief. Dad and I had a complicated relationship, but I have only two photos of him. I'm not burning one.

Next, I need to find an appropriate offering for Hela. After a lengthy internal debate about whether or not she'd prefer red wine, roses, ice-blue crystals, or red fruits, I settle on a bouquet of red roses. Seems easiest.

"Why don't you pick the roses outside in the garden?" Justin asks me later that day as I grab a commercial-perfect bouquet at the grocery store. "Aren't those more significant because you raised them?"

I have two potted tea roses in the backyard that recently started blooming. They do this often around November, when the temperatures descend from the burning heat of California's second summer and a few showers convince them it's safe to come out. I pity them. They think it's spring.

"I Googled it, and apparently she likes red roses. Most of the ones we have outside are pink. Plus, I want them, you know? Then it's like she can enjoy them in our garden. So it's not that I'm making the smaller sacrifice by not giving her *my* roses, it's that I want to encourage her to be around longer."

"Huh? Oh, okay, yeah," he says, rooting around on a shelf for light roast coffee. I think he has forgotten I'm taking about a Viking death goddess. I don't remind him.

Next up is the occult shop, where I try in vain to find a candle that is fragrance free. There is a row of pillar candles encased in glass—novena candles, the kind you usually find at pharmacies with a sticker of the

Virgin of Guadalupe wrapped around the cylinder. These are stickerless, however, the only colors are white, blue, and pink. I groan.

"Just get the white one," Justin whispers. "Didn't they say white was an okay color?"

"I don't wanna bring the cop-out color," I whisper. "That's like bringing a bag of chips to a potluck."

One of the store employees must see me staring, because he approaches me and asks, "Can I help you find anything?"

"Do you have any unscented black candles?" I ask.

"No," he replies.

"What about orange?"

"No."

"Yellow?"

He shakes his head and gestures to the wall of candles. "What you see is what we have." He says this in a tone that sounds more like, "Lady, what day do you think it is?"

I realize I have done the Witchcraft equivalent of showing up to a Christmas tree farm on December 24 and hammering the staff about why there are no more six-footers.

I buy the white candle and leave.

After the sun sets, I go into the bedroom and dress myself in black leggings, a black skirt, a black duster cardigan, my eleven-year-old fugg boots, a pentacle necklace, a moonstone necklace, black eyeliner, and a red-and-orange-gold shawl. I take my hair down. I don't know what you wear to a public Witchcraft ritual. With Liza's coven, we always wore jeans or the occasional spring dress. But this feels like a grander affair. I am meeting the largest group of professional Witches I have ever met in my life. I want to look the part. Without trying too hard.

I pack all my requisite items into two canvas bags and spike my "personal libation" thermos of sparkling apple juice with two shots of whiskey, despite the email's instructions to not bring hard alcohol. I appreciate that they don't want anyone getting sloppy. But I have a feeling I'm going to need something to loosen me up. Besides, we're not sharing the sacred chalice, so no one can snitch on me.

I get into my car and begin the thirty-minute drive to the address in question. I exit the freeway and enter a neighborhood of peeling, one-story tract houses. Teenagers are clustered like pods of mushrooms in front of waxed Mustangs and lifted 4x4 trucks. Heavy bass thumps from behind one or two kitchen screen doors. I park in front of someone's dead lawn and walk a few blocks to the house. One of the troops of teens stares at me as I walk past, eyeing my black clothes, the rose bouquet and autumn Craft supplies spilling out of my bags. Blessedly no one says anything.

I know I've reached the right house when all the lights are out, except for candles on the ground.

They light my path down a dark driveway, where a woman sits in front of a table draped in purple. She holds up a lantern. "Welcome," she says, smiling brightly.

"Hello," I say in return, and force myself to smile back. She asks my name and checks me off a list. She examines my vaccination card, writes down the dates of both my Moderna shots, and has me sign a waiver. She scans it with her eyes before whisking it away in a folder. It seems a bit dramatic, but nevertheless I tell her I'm glad they are requiring this; not everyone is. "Oh, we know," she says, nodding emphatically. "We know. Magic is science, and science is magic. We believe in both here." She then ushers me to the lightless porch behind her. A patch of the dark starts to move. I realize it's a woman, in a black tulle veil.

"May I cleanse you?" she asks, producing a burning bundle of herbs. I nod.

She waves it over me, and I resist the instinct to hold my arms out as if she's a TSA agent scanning me for metal.

After the smoke cleansing, I feel more in the mood. She grabs hold of my hand and leads me to the front stoop. The door opens, and I am inside a stranger's house.

It's dim and warm, orange and yellow, with veils draped over the living room space. The woman in the black tulle veil guides me down the hall. I obey silently.

At the end of the hall, there is another woman in a head-to-toe black veil, although this time I can see her black club dress, lacy goth boots, and fishnet tights underneath. She is holding a shallow blue bowl of water.

"Close your eyes," she tells me. "You'll feel a little coolness."

Once again, I obey. She gently sprinkles me with water.

"Open your eyes," she says, and smiles at me under her veil. She turns her body so I can step through the patio door.

The backyard is an oasis. It's lit everywhere with candles and torches. A car-sized bougainvillea is creating fireworks of pink flowers along one of the fence walls. The grass is green and smells freshly mowed. A Samhain altar glows in the corner, heaped with roses, pumpkins, skulls, crystals, photos of the dead, and candle flames. There's a large iron firepit, burning brightly, in the center of the scene.

A third woman in a black veil approaches, smiling at me as if she's been expecting me this whole time.

"Is this where I can place my ancestors, and my gifts for Hela?" I ask, gesturing to the altar.

"Yes," she replies. "You can put everything here. Just find any place that feels right."

I cannot see an inch of tablecloth through the thick landscape of objects on the altar, but after a few minutes, and some shuffling, I find a place for my feather and flower crown, my father's picture, and my candle. The altar is so crowded with roses I have to hide my bouquet in the back. I briefly lament not bringing the bones of a chicken carcass, just to be original. I'm pleased to see that most of the candles on the altar are white, however, except for one black pillar that has clearly seen more than one ritual. The owner probably takes it home for safekeeping and only brings it out when necessary. Smart.

After that, I try to look busy, stuffing my bags in a corner. I think I was expecting a small festival. There are only four other people in the backyard, talking in a tight circle.

One of the women in black approaches me, again with a smile. She hooks my arm through hers like an eighteenth-century gentleman and pulls me over toward the group.

"This is Diana," she says, introducing me to the cluster of people. I don't remember telling her my name. "She's new to our group."

The clique parts to make room for me. There is an awkward silence. Then a woman steps forward and offers her hand in greeting. She's petite, late forties, dressed in a sweater and jeans. The other two people, I realize, are men. One looks like a cross between Gandalf and a lumber-jack. The other looks like an off-duty construction worker in a T-shirt, black baseball cap, and paint-stained boots. I learn that each of the men are the husbands and boyfriends of the coven sisters. We make strained but polite small talk, as if we are all trying to make the best of a long elevator ride. Twenty minutes pass. I step away from the group to find my thermos. I take a swig.

Just then, another woman steps out of the house. She is tall and wide, dressed in a jet-black polyester Halloween dress with a thigh-high slit and a glittering black veil covering her body like a shroud. Her feet are bare. Her chest displays a tray of cleavage so perfect, and so ample, I catch myself staring at it like a drunk college freshman boy.

I take another swig and then hastily put the bottle down.

She strides into the garden with the confidence of a runway model, joyful, voice loud and proud. She instructs us to form a circle, and paces around the fire, looking each one of us in the eye. She welcomes us. She explains that this year, Hela didn't just want to be spoken to, she wanted to *arrive*. She is thrilled we have decided to join the ritual. With a quick wipe of her eye, she explains that this is the first public gathering they have held since Covid began. Whenever the inevitable night bird or dis-tant police siren attempts to interrupt her speech flow, she weaves the audio right in, like strands of a braid.

I want to be in her coven.

Although the backyard is a convincing liminal space, I consider the neighbors who share the fence border. I dare a few peeks between the wood panels. I don't see anyone. I wonder if there's a kid hovering in the dark window of the top floor of the house next door, livestreaming us to some private channel. I shuffle my hair to cover more of my face.

At Ismene's instruction, we breathe together, ground our energy, and sway while holding hands in a circle. Eventually we raise our eyes to the sky, everyone turns east, and we begin calling the corners. Ismene beseeches the guardians of the east with a lovely poem, and then everyone in the group shouts, "Come to us. Come to us. Be here now!" I jump. But by the time we get to the west, I know the words, and am joining in.

Once the circle is cast, she passes around a bowl of "bones of a sycamore tree older than you, older than your parents, older than many of your ancestors who have already passed," and tells us to summon our grief. This could be for a person, a situation, a relationship—whatever we want to let go of. We will then cast the bones into the fire, one at a time. After each casting, we will all recite, "It is gone, it is gone, it is gone, gone, gone." You can say nothing aloud, if you wish. But not casting your bone into the fire doesn't appear to be an option.

For some reason, this makes me like Ismene even more. (She has never told me her name. I'm just assuming she's the one in charge.)

I stare down at the pale bone-branch in my hand. Everyone is silent. The logs crackle in the firepit.

I try to summon my grief.

The first thing that comes to my mind is, of course, my father. He is the largest grief I have known so far (one moment while I knock on all the wood in my house). He left the family when I was four, and we saw each other in random spurts for most of my childhood. He was an addict and fell in and out of prison. I remember being nine, watching his head peek out of a van as it drove away after a supervised visit, gripping my big sister's palm so tight my fingers went numb. When I was nineteen, just after he had successfully achieved sobriety, remarried, and we had begun to exchange a few tentative emails, he suddenly died of heart failure. No warning, no goodbye. Not even enough time for his new wife to call 911.

I had no idea how to process his death. When I told other people who had lost their fathers—their *real* fathers—they gave me a look of knowing sympathy that made me feel like a thief. I didn't know how to describe the loss I was feeling. How do you mourn something you never had?

That was over a decade ago. But if I think about it too hard, it still gets to me, like a wound that never finished healing, because it still isn't sure if it's allowed to exist.

Eventually, my father attained a kind of starry perfection in my mind. I clung to any scraps of information anyone told me about him, and my brain filled in the rest of the blanks with love and wonder. Ultimately, it made me feel better to think of him as a good person who turned into a bad person because of circumstance. He left very little to this world, and I am one of his three remaining descendants. My mother, despite her frustrations, always insisted that he loved us, his children. And so because of this, I resolved to be worthy of his invisible love. If guardian angels are real, I decided he's mine.

I don't want to throw my grief for him into the fire. Yes, it makes me sad to think about him. But I have almost no memories of actually being with him. If I throw away my sorrow, I don't know what else I have to remember him by. With a sinking feeling, I realize how pathetic and self-indulgent that is. But it's too true to pretend it's not what's going on.

Then I realize something else. I feel a tingling at the top of my scalp.

It's the idea of him that is holding me back from Witchcraft.

I have felt his legacy like a weight draped on my shoulders. He was a man filled with regrets for his mistakes. And so I feel a pressure to be everything he wasn't. He abandoned his family, so I can never walk away from anyone, no matter what they do. I'm terrified of drugs, or losing control, or risking any addictive behavior—anything that feels too good is dangerous. I have felt an intense pressure my entire life to be strait-laced, morally perfect, and painstakingly loyal because I have to prove I'm better than him, that I won't make the same mistakes. Because that's what I think he would have wanted. Because I am his legacy. And I can fix it.

Dad was, above all things, religious. He was a staunch Christian for his entire life. Christ helped him achieve sobriety, more than once. He was reading the Bible the night before he died. Becoming a Witch is the only rebellious thing I have ever done against his memory. If he found out, it would cause a rift between us, a rift I cannot afford, a rejection I could not stand because there has never been any acceptance to balance it. I never enjoyed the empowering teenage tradition of rebelling against your father. It's no fun rebelling against someone who rebelled against you first.

His family is the same way: evangelical, devout, and estranged. Although I barely see them, I feel like I can't afford to lose them by making any un-Christian choices. And yet, even now, I almost never approach them, because I have assumed they would never approve of me even in a pre-Witchcraft state. But I'm still too afraid to go all in and risk losing their approval entirely. Sometimes it's easier to remain in limbo; Schrödinger's family acceptance.

And this is why I am at war with myself, going into the world of Witchcraft. It's not my scientific skepticism; I wish it were just that. I'm realizing now that it's my father's judgment. If he is my guardian angel, he is watching me. And I can't disappoint him.

But he isn't real, a voice says from the back of my mind, cautiously but clearly, like a prisoner peering her eyes through a crack in a door. *He is a dead man. There is no guardian angel. You have made all of this up in your own head.* I stare at the tree-bone.

I realize the paternal approval, my answers to questions like, "Why did you do leave?" A heartfelt conversation of closure—none of it is ever coming. Neither is the disapproval I'm worried he might levy on my spiritual quest. All the skin on my body suddenly feels painfully bright, like I'm getting a sunburn.

You can't get disapproval from a dead man. You can't get anything from a dead man. He is never going to come down and tell me he loves me, that I'm perfect, that I've redeemed us both and can relax now. He's also never going to tell me he doesn't approve of me. He's never going to tell me he's disappointed in me. He never asked me to be his legacy. He's never going to tell me anything about anything, ever.

He's dead. I'm alive.

I can do whatever I want.

But I don't want to do whatever I want. I want his approval, another voice in my head says.

You can't get approval from a dead man, says the epiphany.

But if I throw his judgment into the fire, who else will watch over me? Diana, he's dead.

Eventually, the person to my right tosses their stick in, signaling that it is my turn. I look up from the tree-bone, and step forward toward the fire. Everyone is silent. I feel like I'm on stage.

I look down at the twig again and say aloud, "The judgment of my father and my father's family." On the last syllable, my voice cracks. *Oh shit*, I think, *don't lose it. Not here. No one else is crying. People are casting their dead brothers in here and not crying.* I take a deep breath and push the tears back down. Then everyone around me shouts, "It is gone, it is gone, it is gone gone gone," and it's impossible. Hot tears dribble down my cheeks. I force my face not to move as one last reach for dignity.

I spent three years paying an old man in a quiet room $150 an hour to watch me cry and never got to this place therapeutically.

The ritual goes on, and I feel like a set of invisible chain links have just loosened over my body, so I can now step forward into a bright and terrifyingly blank future, one not defined by the perceived judgment of a dead man. For the first time in my life, I have rebelled. I have to—I *get* to—reinvent what I think is a virtue, what I believe is right or wrong, in a way that doesn't concern him. There is no one to decide what part of my spiritual journey is bad except me. This is freedom. But there's a loneliness, a bittersweetness, too. I am keenly aware I just exorcised a guardian angel out of my life, possibly the only one I ever had. I feel like a wine barrel that has been emptied out all at once.

Priestess Ismene guides us in a moving meditation, down, down, down into the center of the earth, past the warmth, into a blue-white land of ice. There, Hela, the protector of the dead, will see us if we approach respectfully and tell us anything we may need to know.

After what feels like a half hour of circling the fire and chanting and visualizing myself at the icy gates of Hela's realm, without any preamble, in real life, another woman steps out of the house. She is in an elaborate black dress and headpiece, her face a swirling mask of stark white makeup. The black-veiled sisters rush to her and hold her limbs, guiding her to a chair surrounded by candles. They cluster at her feet.

This year, Hela wanted to arrive, I remember Ismene's voice from earlier.

As the rest of us circle the fire, Priestess Ismene peels a person off and brings him to Hela's feet. I try to maintain my meditative state, but I can't help casting a side-eye. I wanna make sure nothing weird is about to happen.

Nothing does. After a few minutes at the feet of the Goddess, the man rises, is led away by Ismene, and replaced by another.

I consider bolting right then. I drank two sips of whiskey and apple juice an hour ago; I could drive home. But instead, I keep circling the fire, chanting. I am terrified of meeting Hela, because I think I'm going to cry like a baby. No one else has cried so far in this entire group.

Eventually, Priestess Ismene approaches me. I follow her, docile as a drugged lamb. *Just breathe*, I think. *Just breathe, just breathe, just breathe.* I am deposited at the feet of Hela, where I kneel, my knees dampening in the backyard grass. I look up into her white face. She looks me dead in the eye and smiles.

"*I'm sorr-ghhaee*," I keen, and fall forward onto the ground. I don't know if I'm apologizing for letting my father go, or for knowing I was going to cry. It feels like both. I don't want to look up because I'm pretty sure everyone circling the fire is staring at me. I am sobbing. I cannot stop.

Hela reaches down, grabs my face with both hands, and turns it upward toward her. Her palms are warm. I want to pull back. I want a box of tissues. I am ugly crying here, okay? I'm pretty sure there's some snot running onto her hand.

Hela looks into my eyes, concerned, silent. She leans forward, gets six inches from my face, cocks her head, and smiles again. She takes her palm off my left cheek and places it on the bare skin of my chest. It is disarming, almost violating. For a moment it's the only thing I can feel. I'm shaking like a fucking leaf. *This will be over soon*, I think, *everything is temporary.*

Still not breaking eye contact, she takes one grand breath, and I realize I'm supposed to follow her example. I inhale with her, and exhale. The sound of our breath merges, a great whooshing, like wind between sails. The fire reflects off the white of her face. We do this for a few minutes. Eventually I stop crying. She has not stopped smiling at me.

I have the sensation that she has absorbed my suffering. Or at least told me, as politely as possible, it's time to stop crying now.

Ismene approaches, bends and gently takes my arm as I stand, and slowly leads me away. I do my best not to meet anyone's eyes and rejoin the chanting circle as if I didn't just completely lose my shit in the lawn a few feet away. I don't cry again for the rest of the evening.

After about an hour, things start to wind down, and we do a proper "grounding," where you touch the earth to discharge any excess energy raised. With relief, I close my eyes, and kowtow into the grass. A few minutes later, the priestess officially ends the ritual, and I open my eyes.

Right in front of my nose there is a very bizarrely shaped dead plant, sticking upright. Its limbs are thin as needles, about three inches high. It's so wildly different from the green blades of grass surrounding it I don't know how I didn't see it when I knelt down. It's too perfect, too symmetrical, and it reminds me of something. Possibly a wine bottle opener with its arms in the air.

Then I realize it looks like a rune. At first, I think I'm imagining things. I don't know that much about runes. But no. I am not making this up. It's as clear as if someone laid a three-pronged white rake on a green carpet.

After I get home, I lie in bed and Google "three-pronged fork rune."

The rune is called Algiz. It is exactly the shape of the plant I saw in the grass. I read that it is the ultimate rune of protection and a bridge to the divine. At first I roll my eyes, because every symbol and stone in Witchcraft seems to symbolize protection and a bridge to the divine. Then I read something else.

Algiz is the symbol for divine guardianship. It signals the presence of a guardian angel.

NOVEMBER

〉〉🌒●🌘(((

DAY 96

I am still facing a white wall of static where there should be
visions, knowledge, information.
—AUGUSTEN BURROUGHS

"I have a herniated disk?" I almost shout this at my computer, which is currently displaying the face of a doctor.

"Two, actually," she replies calmly. "But only one is pressing on the nerve in your back."

I cannot believe this.

"But I go backpacking!" I tell her, stammering. "I—I walk. I ride a stationary bike! I even dance sometimes. How can I have a herniated disk?"

As far as I know, herniated disks aren't something you can "power through." They cause that kind of DEFCON 1 pain; pain that makes you collapse on stairs or vomit uncontrollably. I just have a pinch that won't go away.

My doctor skates past my confusion. "They can manifest in different ways."

"Do they ever . . . go back in?"

"Not really," she says, almost offhandedly, as if we're on a TV baking show and she's frosting a cake, except the cake is my body and the frosting is a promise of low-grade chronic pain for the rest of my life.

"I'm referring you to an orthospine doctor," she says. "They can advise you further."

DAY 99

Morning thought: Witchcraft has swung too far into capitalistic self-help culture and needs to come back to its gravitational pull: being in service to the earth and land we inhabit.
—BRITTON BOYD, @ARCHAICHONEY

I make an appointment with the orthospine doctor. In the meantime, I try to distract myself, to remind myself that millions of people live with far worse conditions and thrive. I am already pondering the idea of trying to fix myself with a spell, but after what happened at the end of October, I am nervous to attempt to wield magic again. I still don't know entirely what I did wrong, why I felt so awful after trying to protect myself from the tower. Maybe I didn't ground myself well enough, despite several attempts? Or I was selfish for asking for protection without sacrifice, and felt the price? Did I give myself a panic attack? The ghost of my dad is having a holly jolly time haunting me?

I need a distraction from metaphysics, from the murky speculation parts of Witchcraft. I don't want to hide in a dark office with my books and candles. So today, at exactly 10 a.m., I park my car across from the Abigail Blau Low Income Senior Home, strap a KN95 on my face, and walk up the ramp to meet their volunteer coordinator. I'm pretty nervous for someone who has decided to spend the next two hours working for free. But I'm also excited. I have been bereft of coworkers since March 2020, when the pandemic started and I began working from home. Today I'm actually going to be working alongside other people.

Unlike other religions, Wicca doesn't have any commandment around charity. A cursory image search of modern Witchcraft could easily lead one to believe the entire endeavor is little more than crystal shopping and a veneration of bath time. There is no codified equivalent the likes of Proverbs 19:17, or Islam's pillar of zakat, or Buddhism's concept of dāna.

This is despite just about every Witch from Raymond Buckland to Juliet Diaz writing about the Witch's *imperative* to help heal the earth and serve all her creatures. It's an informal rule (just like all the rest of them), but it is repeated across the decades with regularity. With the open question of how precisely one can go about this, my dear Cunningham has some suggestions. Environmentalist efforts head the list. You could donate to ecological organizations, volunteer for trash pickups in your area, and protest developments that poison the earth. Starhawk is probably the most remarkable Witch on that front, having battled 1,742 timber logging Caterpillar RD6 tractors with her bare hands.

I don't think I can take down an RD6, but I'm sure I could be doing more tangible "earth-saving" work than agonizing about whether or not I'm a bad person for buying sauerkraut in a plastic container.

To give back to the earth, the first option that occurred to me was to donate money. It's easy, efficient. I could just set up a recurring donation to one of a number of environmental charities, pat myself on the back, and get back to buying candles. However, I quickly reject this option. It's not that I don't have a few bucks I could spare. It's that every week, a thick tower of letters reminds me of every canvasser I ever handed five dollars to over the course of a decade while running to the train or waiting at a stoplight. The letters contain things like address labels I didn't ask for, tote bags I don't need, and greeting cards I do not want. Giving money to the Sierra Club seems to have only encouraged them to chop down a literal forest in my name.

I want to actually perform acts of service, practicing helping others simply for the sake of it. Maybe it's just my residual American Puritanism talking, but I still think service is a virtue. I can't remember the last time I went out and just helped somebody for no reason. Cunningham emphasizes that even good ol'-fashioned feeding the hungry counts as service to the earth, because you are helping her creatures.

I found a registry of volunteer opportunities online, and went digging around through it, trying to find something that felt right. An hour went by. Then two. The options were overwhelming. Why was this so hard? Why wasn't there some magic button I could press to connect me with a place that would satisfy all my desires to be a good person? Nothing restrains a rushed call to altruism like bureaucracy. The food bank's shifts were full for the next two months, 30 percent of everything else was closed "to protect the health and safety of our volunteers and clients in these unprecedented times," and everything else was Christian.

After filling out several forms, I eventually got connected with an organization in my neighborhood that could make use of me, my semi-broken back, and my two hands. It's a low-income senior home that needs help organizing and distributing groceries to its residents.

Today I'm here for my first shift. I step inside the building, and it smells like someone hasn't opened a window since 1982. Especially with Covid, I feel the urge to break one, to get the light of day in here. But instead, I follow around the volunteer coordinator as she explains what we'll be doing. I notice she's wearing a modest golden crucifix necklace. I am mildly resentful at her freedom to wear a religious symbol so openly, so without fear. I stared at my pentacle necklace as I walked out the front door, and almost put it on. I am here on a religious errand, after all, a spiritual call to serve. Shouldn't I help to correct Witchcraft's image as Satan worshipping at worst, or self-serving therapy quest at best? But in a senior home, I was afraid the stereotypes of yesteryear might persist, and it would be a matter of time before some elderly man pointed at my chest and screamed "she-devil!" at me as I sorted boxes of cabbage.

As the morning progresses, I lift several pounds of produce and dairy that remind me I have a herniated disk, but I try to hide it. At one point, an ancient Chinese woman comes downstairs, says something to me in Mandarin, grabs a box that I'm pretty sure is half her body weight, and throws it onto the table like it's a teddy bear. I briefly wonder what I'm doing here.

Near the end of the day, a plump blond woman comes downstairs and gives everyone in the rec room a boisterous hello. She asks the staff how their kids are doing, waves to the janitor as he walks down the hall. She strolls up to my table and starts to bag her groceries. I try not to stare at her chest as she stands in front of my station of frozen peas and chicken nuggets, introduces herself, and asks sweetly, "Well hello, dear, are you new?"

She's wearing a pentacle necklace.

DAY 102

When this card appears, it usually means you've ignored or denied something that's rotten and needs to be blown apart. You're probably surprised, but you shouldn't be.
—SKYE ALEXANDER

Tonight, Justin and I have an argument. An explosive argument. It begins as little smoke burps and then grows into a red, fuming monster before my eyes.

I want fast resolution. He wants space. We're both spitting lava. Eventually I leave him to sleep upstairs, despite the fact that I really don't want to. Something about "never going to bed angry" with your partner is ringing in my ears. It feels like someone left a pot of milk out to rot in the sun and then poured it into my solar plexus.

We have been coworkers, roommates, lovers, and co-pet parents since March 2020, the very weekend Covid lockdowns began. In 2021 he began talking about wanting to move back to Seattle. Most of his friends and family are there, and everyone he knew in Oakland fled in 2020 like it was on fire.*

But I don't want to move, because *my* friends and family are here in the Bay Area. Sure, I like cedar trees and ennui and coffee as much as the next writer, but there is nothing for my heart in Seattle. I continuously sweep the topic of moving under the rug whenever he brings it up.

But today I can't sweep anymore. He is bursting, and I am forced out of denial. He says he wants to leave, and he's going to, with or without me. I am terrified and furious.

At 2 a.m., I stare at the wall, conscious of the empty space in the bed beside me, power cycling through my thoughts.

What makes it harder is that I don't have any ammunition with which to defend Oakland. In many ways, it's a proud and beautiful city, powered by immigrants, tech, and progressive politics. But it's also kind of evolving into a weird, barbecue-scented, cyberpunk dystopia. Last week, someone shot a two-year-old in a car seat; collateral damage between two gangs on the 880 freeway. The tech-induced housing crisis, spilling over from what San Francisco's limited geography can't contain, isn't so much bad as comical. You can drive through downtown with a Frankenstein shantytown of tarps and pallets to your left, and a glossy, five-thousand-dollar-a-month luxury apartment skyscraper to your right. Homeless people have smartphones, but they don't always have access to toilets.

Petty crime is a fact of life. "Oakland sapphires" glitter on every street corner, broken window glass from cars whose owners left so much as a dust speck on their back seat while running an errand. I've seen a homeless man masturbate while groups of children walk by. Twice. We've had four shootings within a one-block radius of our house in two years. I've slammed my body to the ground of my bedroom as a gunman shot past my front yard. I've had my mail stolen more times than I can count. When I vent about this to other locals, I am told "that's just the Town" with a smirk, with a smile, with an almost-wagging finger, as if I

---

* Which it *technically* wasn't. It was just really, really, really (really) smoky.

should not be so soft, so prudish, so *suburban*. As if the joy of living in Oakland is getting to brag about living somewhere that never lets you unclench. If I'm generous, I can imagine many of Oakland's petty criminals feel like Robin Hoods, snatching iPhones and wallets and French bulldogs at gunpoint to get back at the elites who have gentrified their families' neighborhoods. But at the end of the day, I still don't enjoy paying this much rent to feel this guarded.

Of course, it isn't all bad. Oakland is the kind of place where you can walk into any building wearing Technicolor leggings, paint-stained combat boots, and a vintage leather jacket and be taken more seriously than a man in a tailored suit. I love our little urban farmhouse with its fruit trees and chicken coop. Lake Merritt sparkles down the road, a giant yard party every weekend, where people sell homemade jerk chicken and gather for drum circles and free outdoor yoga classes. Two days ago, I saw a guy in a wheelchair and four rough-looking teenagers dancing in the street together. Walk around the lake and you can hear every language on earth swirling overhead—diversity isn't just a buzzword here, it's a reality. The people are political, passionate, Promethean. This is the city that gave America the Black Panthers. There is a strong sense of community. Sideshow cars will stop in order to let public transit buses through the four-point intersections they take over at 2 a.m. Older folks will chat with you breezily at the grocery store, giving you the benefit of the doubt that maybe you've been neighbors for thirty years and didn't just move here from Minnesota to take a job at Salesforce. I have been given free crystals and bags of kettle corn by the vendors on Lakeshore. There's a redwood forest—an actual redwood forest—ten minutes from my apartment. Above all, my closest friends and family are a short drive away.

Covid is the real culprit in this fight between Justin and me, I think. It must be. We haven't been able to enjoy any of the perks of paying big-city rent, because we've been trapped inside for a year and a half. If I could just convince him of that, maybe this would all go away and we can go back to normal.

But this is also not the first time in my life someone has told me they can't live here anymore. My twenties are haunted with friends and lovers flying away to transplant themselves in other diverse, prosperous, interesting cities, cities gentler on both the soul and the wallet. Everyone I have met after college was born somewhere else, and half of them have already moved on. The Bay Area is not a safe place to grow roots. Sometimes it feels like no one really lives here. I feel like I'm trying to live in a waiting room.

No, I think. *A tower. A tower that's been struck by lightning.*

DAY 103

Think of yourself as a paper package. The look and feel of the wrapping paper is affected by everything inside this package, both spiritually and physically.
—JULIET DIAZ

Today I'm doing my twice-daily routine of physical therapy stretches and strengthening exercises. In the middle of a figure-four stretch, I feel a sudden tug in my low back. Something inside of me burns molten hot, then freezes up like a glacier.

I lie on the floor gasping. The entire left side of my butt and hip is frozen. I cannot move an inch without everything seizing.

I lie there like a turtle on my back for twenty minutes before getting up, dragging myself to the bathroom, then running to my phone and making an emergency appointment with the physical therapist.

DAY 105

Often, those who practice magical healing are seen as different
from the rest of the community . . . [T]hey fill in where medical
practices seem to miss.
—CORY THOMAS HUTCHESON

"I can't turn over in bed," I tell the physical therapist under the fluorescent lights of her office. "I've been taking ibuprofen like Tic Tacs. I can't sit down in my office chair. Any chair." I have been practicing what I'll say to her all morning, and I say it now: "I am scared something is wrong. Really wrong."

She looks at me piteously. "You're not supposed to do the exercises if they hurt."

"But then I wouldn't do them at all," I say, genuinely confused. She's looking at me like I'm the idiot.

She lays me down on the table and gently palpates my seized muscles. She suggests I go back to the orthospine doctor for a cortisol shot and another MRI. I blanch. My previous insurance plan ended, so I can't go back to the same doctor who referred me here, let alone get imaging, without paying thousands out of pocket. I could start over with a new doctor, but that would also be hundreds upon hundreds. I am already paying for the physical therapy out of pocket because they don't take insurance. To complicate the decision, I had a previous doctor caution me against a cortisol shot, telling me I was too young for that kind of treatment, and the risks of tissue damage weren't worth the gain. Maybe he was wrong. But consulting yet another doctor for a second opinion would be hundreds more for possibly the same recommendation. I suddenly feel exhausted. Pain is exhausting, and the decisions around managing it don't feel empowering. The doubt of accuracy is just a drain on an already depleted well of energy.

I ask her simply, "What if I can't get a cortisol shot?"

"Then we can just try scaling things back," she says.

I drive home, stressed, feeling powerless. I mull over my options. My imagination directs seven different one-act plays where I call my physical therapist a hack.

Witchcraft has been used for centuries by people who lacked (or had been prohibited from accessing) Western medicine. And it's more than herbal remedies. Books have been written about the power of belief, the power of prayer. There are countless documented stories about faith healers achieving miracles. I feel like I need a miracle.

So I reach for Silver RavenWolf's *Solitary Witch: The Ultimate Book of Shadows for the New Generation*, the encyclopedic guide to magic that has a spell for virtually every problem under the sun. (Or any fixed point in the universe, probably).

My fear of practicing magic again is gone. This injury has been with me, with varying degrees of severity, for over a year. I have tried chiropractors, a neuromuscular massage therapist, an acupuncturist, an orthospine doctor, and a physical therapist. What I haven't tried is magic. I especially haven't tried magic when I'm this motivated for it to work, because I feel like I'm out of normal options. *You're up, RavenWolf,* I think to the book as I flip through the pages. *Let's make me a believer.*

I eventually find something called the "Nine Sisters Chant."

RavenWolf files it under "healing," but mentions it's a useful all-purpose banishment spell. I read and then reread the directions and see that I'm supposed to recite the chant nine times, three times a day, for twenty-one days. This is a tougher regiment than the fifty pelvic tilts and forty clamshells that the physical therapist told me I needed to do twice a day. But I resolve to do it. And although my mind is swimming with doubt, I'm trying to muster all my will to believe in it. RavenWolf writes that "magick has always been around to help solve our problems . . . all we have to do is provide the faith."

I take a big breath and prop the book up on my bed to begin reciting. I close my eyes.

I suddenly realize I don't actually know where this spell comes from. I stop, open my eyes, pick up my phone, and Google the title, just to make sure it is not some appropriated Algonquin incantation that's going to bring the souls of a thousand betrayed indigenous warriors into my bedroom.

The Nine Sisters Chant is Anglo-Saxon. Good enough.

I turn back to Siler RavenWolf's book and stand over it. I take a few deep breaths, hold my hands over my L4 and L5 vertebrae, and recite aloud:

Nine were Noththe's Sisters,
then the nine became the eight,
and the eight became the seven,
and the seven became the six,
and the six became the five,
and the five became the four,
and the four became the three,
and the three became the two,
and the two became the one,
and the one became the none.

I don't really know how to pronounce "Noththe." RavenWolf doesn't say so, and neither does Google, so I end up approximating it with "noth-ith."

I am trying to stay focused on my back, but Justin is all over my mind. Every time I open my eyes something in our bedroom is there to remind me of him, of the fight we are still in. I've been distracting myself all day, but now, as I'm trying to be calm, to ask my brain to focus, all my repressed thoughts are being served up like a buffet. His face bleeds into my back.

Everything hurts.

I keep chanting.

DAY 106

As we move into winter, we fully embody living death and sleep.
—TEMPERANCE ALDEN

I feel like I am regressing. I have given up on physical therapy. Every motion is like trying to move through the stabbing of twenty ice picks. The therapist told me to stop doing her exercises if they hurt. So I stop.

According to Temperance Alden in *Year of the Witch*, autumn is the time for healing, reflecting, and rest. So I let go my dreams of pretending nothing is wrong with me, of working through the pain. I come home that afternoon, lay myself onto the couch very, very slowly, and embrace the idea of becoming lazy as fuck. 'Tis the season.

Justin is supportive of this choice. He buys me a heating pad and makes me baked ziti. After hours of talking over the past few days, we have resolved our argument, at least for the sake of making peace. We tell each other that we love each other, we are committed to finding a middle path.

There is a simmering tension at the bottom of this peace, though, because neither one of us knows what a middle path actually looks like in a scenario where two people want to live in two completely different geographic locations. I am not prepared to break up with him. There is no pain greater than when you are forced to part with someone you love before you are ready. Also, I can't afford to live in our current apartment by myself.

The bottom line is my partner has told me he is critically unhappy where he is and has been so for a long time. To ask him to stay, to keep trying to love a place he's been out of love with for years, is not a fair ask. If I got down on my knees and begged him, he might. But that would not make me feel like a good partner.

I either have to let him go or go with him.

DAY 109

*Approach [a spell] with anxiety, and you're likely to get mixed
results or no results at all.*
—LISA CHAMBERLAIN

It is now day five into my twenty-one days of reciting the Nine Sisters Chant. And I have been chanting. Three times a day, I stop what I'm doing and perform my recitations with all the fervor of an honors high school student trying to get into Yale. I have tried to schedule the chanting throughout my day: one round in the morning while I brew my tea, one in the afternoon after lunch, and one in the evening before bed. But I inevitably get distracted, and they all tend to get pushed back to nightfall. I resent trying to go to sleep and then remembering I have to get up and finish two rounds of chanting. I resent the lengthy interruptions to my day. I resent Silver RavenWolf.

Today it occurs to me that bringing this resentful energy into my banishment spell is probably counter to the entire endeavor. I like to think I'm getting better at taming my mind and commanding my thoughts, but I'm still having some trouble focusing. Sometimes I get distracted from the fact that I'm performing a banishment, and start to visualize myself feeling normal, being happy. While reciting a banishment chant. This causes me to panic and go back to just focusing on the pain, trying not to wonder if I've made things worse. Yesterday I was half asleep in bed, reciting first thing in the morning to get it out of the way, when Bird came onto the bed for some morning cuddles, and it took me until line five, with my hand on her head, to realize I was technically in the process of banishing my cat.

Perhaps this is why it is not yet working.

Or perhaps singing to your back is not a way to produce effective anti-inflammatory healing.

Witchcraft is never very helpful with providing any kind of certainty about what's actually working versus what's a coincidence.

DAY 111

Hanging on to pain, resentment, anger, and fear will keep
you from embodying your authentic self, your truth, in all its
brilliance . . . [F]ree yourself from your own haunting.
—JULIET DIAZ

I am thinking today about why I'm having so much trouble staying focused on healing, on believing this can work. The truth is, it's more than skepticism. I have always resented self-care. And today's Witchcraft is strongly centered on self-care. This has been driving me nuts from day one.

I am aware this probably says more about me than anything else.

I come across a *Slate* article where Haleigh Schiafo, cofounder of Babe Coven and a self-described "makeup witchcraft" teacher in Brooklyn, explains exactly why modern Witchcraft is so steeped in self-care, and that this is exactly what's supposed to be happening. "Magic and witchcraft are first and foremost about honoring your own power, divinity, and strength," she says. "Those who turn to witchcraft are tired of a patriarchal system, and in magic they find a place that welcomes self-love, female empowerment, support, and growth."

The opposite of patriarchy is when the oppressed embrace their own power and refuse to be told they are less than. Which, I guess, means doing all the things the patriarchy hates. Like loving yourself.

Fine, I think. *But it's still annoying.*

I don't really know why every time I see a recommendation to take a break and breathe I get irritated. Maybe because I feel like people are trying to make relaxation profitable. Maybe because I feel like if I rest, something will fall apart, and so I resent people who actually feel like they can. Maybe because I'm afraid if I start self-pampering, I will lose the armor of restraint and industriousness that I have tried to coat myself in on the assumption that it makes me a good person (you don't have to be raised Christian to be subject to the American Puritan mind-set). Maybe it's just the messaging format that drives me crazy. Think about it. All those affirmations and calls for a little selfish behavior aren't targeted at you, they're sprayed at random. Your worst middle school bully is also looking at that Instagram post reminding them they are a powerful goddess who deserves a big, fluffy bath.

In the 1700s, Witchcraft was about reciting the Lord's Prayer backward and hexing your neighbor's butter churn. In the 1940s, it was about cursing Nazis and quibbling with Gerald Gardner about the most historically accurate location to put the bell on the altar. Today it's therapy.

I hated my body so much, I ignored it so much that I hurt it. And now my back is screaming at me, begging me for healing, to stop and *listen*.

Later that night, alone in my office, I try to put this epiphany into practice.

I have been reading Mat Auryn's *Psychic Witch*, and he speaks a lot about the mind-body connection, with entire chapters on meditation techniques and strategies for physical relaxation and the importance of unclenching muscles. These exercises are for the greater goal of opening one's connection to the divine flow of the universe, so that we may receive its messages. I'm just trying to see if I can use it as free Percocet.

I lie down and perform one of Auryn's exercises, imagining a white, minty-green ball of light at my feet, visualizing it rising up the length of my body, my muscles relaxing as it glides past. I do notice a drop in physical tension. When the imaginary ball hits my hips, I keep it there. According to Auryn, I'm supposed to let it rise all over, but I decide to keep it where I need it. I imagine the mint-chip-ice-cream-colored light seeping into my skin, soothing everything. I imagine the muscles surrounding my hip unclenching.

It still hurts. I ask my mind to accept the sensation, and stay on target with the orb. With each exhale, I imagine pain leaving, and with each inhale, relaxation entering.

Finally, I do something Auryn suggests. I tell myself: "At the end of these four breaths, you will no longer be in pain."

Four, three, two, one.

I don't know what chemical seems to drench my brain at one, but something hits. Relief courses out of my head and down into my tailbone. It's real. There is a lasting quiet in my left hip, for the first time in weeks. *I can't believe it*, I think. *All I had to do was this?* My pulse quickens. I am positively giddy, but trying to remain calm, lest I break this magic moment.

I feel like I have been granted mercy. In this state, I imagine my body not as an enemy, but as a victim of my own neglect.

"Okay. I hear you. I hear you. I'm not going to hurt you anymore," I speak softly to my insides. "We are going to do things that feel good. I am going to listen to you from now on. I am going to listen to you when you talk to me. I'm not going to force you to do anything. I love you. I understand you need care now, and I'm going to give it to you."

Some minutes go by where I sit in a glossy pink cloud of epiphany and oxytocin.

Eventually, I open my eyes and stand up. I take a step.

My hip spasms, and I catch myself against the doorframe, trying not to cry out.

Or maybe fuck self-help.

〉〉●((

DAY 119

Even the best of books, however, often did little to replace a
powerful or knowledgeable teacher.
—CORY THOMAS HUTCHESON

"You know, when I was fourteen, I dislocated something in my ankle, and I went to a curandero. Have you thought about that?"

I was talking to my brother-in-law—a medical doctor at one of Oakland's top hospitals—about my back issue. I'm using him as a free second opinion on what I should do next. He patiently listens to everything I've tried so far, and then tells me the story of his miracle recovery by a traditional Latin American body-and-spirit healer. "My mom could take you, if you like."

As a white person in America, I don't usually have access to curanderos. And they are sometimes referred to as "witch doctors." I am writing a book about Witchcraft. I add all this up in my mind.

"Yes. Yes, I would like that very much," I reply.

So today I am in the car with Pearl, a sixty-five-year-old retired Nicaraguan American social worker, driving down the freeway, on my way to meet the curandero. Pearl is a generous woman, a true matriarch who has always treated me as warmly as if I was one of her own daughters. She's excited to be my guide today. I trust her.

"I really appreciate this. I have never been to a curandero," I tell Pearl, feeling nervous. My back is a wall of stiff stone. She had to get out and close the driver door for me, because I still can't lean to the left.

"Oh . . . this is not a curandero. He told you this was a curandero?" Pearl says to me in her softly accented English. "We're going to a sobador."

I am taken aback. "What is a . . . sobador?" We're already twenty minutes down the freeway.

"Like a massager, a body worker. Not really a curandero." She says this in a tone that is polite, but also suggests she is not in the business of ferrying white girls to indigenous shamans just because of a backache. She goes on to tell me that she has had knee issues for years, and the sobador has helped her manage the pain. One time he fixed a shoulder she pulled out on vacation, in one session.

What could go wrong.

We exit onto an unassuming street of single-story tract houses with dry lawns, the pavement pockmarked with holes. I pull up to the sobador's house and peek out my car window. A pink-and-white shrine to a life-sized statue of the Virgin of Guadalupe takes up 80 percent of the front yard, novena candles and fake roses pooled around her feet. I am buoyed.

The garage is open, and Pearl and I walk into the concrete box. A Latin American man who looks like he ran out of fucks in 1985 is sitting in a faded armchair, looking me up and down, assessing my gait, as a laundry machine hums on spin cycle behind him. There is a medical bed to his right, with a pee pad and two flies circling. My confidence plummets like a stone in water.

Pearl takes the lead. She knows I speak very little Spanish, but through Californian osmosis have learned to understand some. She tells him about my back pain. She tells him all the things I've already tried. The sobador nods at her, his eyes darting from her face to my body.

Finally, he rises out of his chair with surprising speed, straps a Covid mask to his face, and gestures for me to lie down on the table. Pearl quickly pulls out a scarf from her purse and puts it over the bed and the pee pad (which I'm happy to discover seems to have no smell). I lie facedown.

The sobador's fingers palpate my back like an iron garden tiller. He says something to Pearl, then grabs my back leg.

No no no no no. Something inside of me says. I try to exhale and relax. *It will hurt more if you don't relax.*

He yanks my entire left leg up and back, and lightning shoots through me. A sound escapes my throat like a Victorian child who has just seen a ghost.

Before I can even feel embarrassed, he has my other leg in his hands.

No no no no no, the voice in my head says. But it's already over. I am dizzy, sobbing, my tears wetting Pearl's scarf. My back feels like the surface of the sun. A pair of women are above me whispering soothing Spanish sounds, butterflies swirling behind my head. I feel something wet and menthol on my back. "I know, baby," Pearl says, switching to English, rubbing my upper back as I heave in breaths. "Your hip was out, and he put it back in. He had to put it back in."

I realize I need to get up. I do not want to be the dramatic, soft white girl, weeping in the garage of a man who I'm sure has tended more injuries than an inner-city ER. I pull myself up off the table, shaking, and face my healer. He is back in the armchair; his expression is unreadable. "It will hurt for a few days," he says in thickly accented English, "then feel better." I ask him how much to pay him. He waves his hand as if he doesn't know. I consider that I have been impolite. "Twenty," whispers Pearl to my shoulder. "And eight for the Aspercreme." There is suddenly a woman in the doorway; I assume one of the butterflies. She smiles at me, wearing a pink floral apron, her hair in a neat black bun at her neck. I remember the carefully tended Guadalupe shrine in the front yard. I hand her forty dollars. "You will feel better," she says to me, beaming.

Pearl and I walk out to the car, and I suddenly start to chuckle. She starts chuckling, too. Within ten seconds, we are practically falling down on the sidewalk. I am in so much pain, but I cannot stop laughing. I feel like I've been dosed. The word "endorphins" flashes through my mind.

"Did you hear that noise I made?" I stammer.

"This is how it goes," she says, a huge smile on her face. "You should have heard me the first time. You're gonna be okay, honey. Just give it a few days."

DECEMBER

> ） ） ● （ （

DAY 124

Because evergreens retain their needles even during the cold winter months, they symbolize the triumph of life over death.
—SKYE ALEXANDER

There's an irony about the time of year known in America as "the holidays." It is a season we have earmarked for joy, generosity, and rest—the planning for which is stressful, expensive, and exhausting. Indeed, the holidays are beautiful. As long as you believe that pain is beauty.

With all that said, I love Christmastime. What is not to love about twinkly lights, the citrus-snap scent of pine trees, bow-topped presents being passed to and fro, and a succession of excuses to eat cake? The best part about Christmas is that you don't have to be a Christian to enjoy it. American consumerism is more welcoming than any actual religion. In fact, according to a Pew poll taken in 2013, 81 percent of non-Christians in this country look forward to the "most wonderful time of the year," further proving Jesus really only has to have something to do with it if you want him to.

My absolute favorite part of Christmas (as every liberal arts college sophomore can't wait to tell you) is that it's inherently pagan. Every yuletide tradition we have in this country is basically an ancient European rite, preserved over the centuries under a pathetically thin veil of Christian dominion. From hauling evergreen trees into our living rooms, to drinking spiced cider, to the very melodies of the famous carols—paganism does not need to be brought *into* Christmas. You just have to dust a little Puritanism off the surface and it's right there.

At the same time, as I plan for the holidays, I can't really figure out what to put on my Christmas tree that is in fact "authentically pagan," while at the same time being readily available to a middle-class twenty-first-century American woman. There's also the issue of which Witchcraft version of Christmas I want to celebrate. There are more than a few, including modern neopagan yule, and the celebration from which it was derived, ancient Nordic Jól.

Wicca's Yule is celebrated at the beginning of astronomical winter, usually December 21. Nordic Jól is celebrated for either eight full weeks or twelve days, most often starting on the solstice, but this really depends on whom you ask. While down a research rabbit hole, I discover a Nordic neopagan group called the Asatru Folk Assembly that starts their Jól feasts on the solstice. I try and see if they have any public rituals I could join, as it's about time I connected with my German neopagan roots. I begin reading through their website, and after a few minutes realize a small, quiet voice in my head is trying to alert me that something here is wrong, although I can't quite put my finger on precisely what it is. I start from scratch. I open a new tab and Google "Asatru Folk Assembly." The second hit is an article from the Southern Poverty Law Center, classifying them as a white supremacist hate group. I close the browser and erase my history.

This is the trouble with a lot of the northern European branches of neopaganism. Germany has spent the better portion of its post-WWII years dismantling its military, opening its arms to the world's immigrants, and hosting more vegan dinner parties than the entire University of California education system combined. Racial diversity in Nordic countries climbs year after year, as they simultaneously smash global records on social prosperity and individual happiness. And yet there are branches of neopaganism that weaponize the idea of "connecting with our roots," to justify an agenda that includes phrases like "blood purity." They complain that it's not fair that other racial groups get to take pride in their heritage, but when white people do it, they're called Nazis. (They leave out the inconvenient fact that historically, when white people do it, they tend to act like Nazis.)

I default to thinking of Witches and neopagans as the liberalist of all liberals. The Witchcraft I'm most familiar with was born on a tie-dye carpet at Woodstock and fed pure hash resin until it could graduate from Sarah Lawrence to make a living in Portland selling discount crystals to runaway trans kids. But the truth is Witches are found across the political spectrum, sometimes even hurling spells at each other.

The most recent example is during the 2016 presidential election, when the likes of blogger Dakota Hendrix, author-magician Michael M. Hughes, and even Lana Del Ray led movements to bind, hex, and otherwise thwart Donald Trump. In response, the "Witches for Trump" Facebook page began gathering a small amount of steam, crafting magical counterattack movements against those threatening their beloved leader. Occultists David Griffin and Leslie McQuade of the Hermetic Order of the Golden Dawn—a modern Thelemite group based on Aleister Crowley's original nineteenth-century secret society—hopped in to help. Griffin called it a "magic war." I suspect most American voters were unaware that a patriotic reenactment of the Battle of Hogwarts was happening right under their noses during this time, but I imagine it was quite thrilling to have been involved.

According to history of religions professor Egil Asprem of Stockholm University, neopagans use rituals to create collective effervescence to bond over simmering distrust in the establishment. That distrust of the establishment is, I'd wager, something shared by Witches on both the left and the right of the political spectrum—possibly the main factor that got them practicing magic in the first place. Witches are symbols of rebellion. They connect with forgotten powers, follow their inner voice, and fight anyone who might oppress them. The only real difference seems to be in whom you think your oppressor is.

I should mention that numerous Nordic neopagans—often preferring to call themselves capital-H Heathens—are working to fight the white supremacy in their midst, vigorously declaring to anyone who will listen that while their traditions come from Europe, they are open to all of the earth's people, and racism is firmly against their code of ethics. I admire their tenacity. In the winter of the Omicron variant, however, none of them are meeting up.

According to the Nordic Heathens, Jól is also a time when the veil between the worlds is thin and the dead are celebrated. *How many times a year do I have to commune with dead people*, I wonder. I have very little interest in doing that again. I have accepted that my evangelical ghost dad has seen his daughter trying to become a Witch and said he loves her anyway. There is absolutely no reason to reopen that conversation.

I decide to keep it simple. I look up traditional Jól tree decorations: holly, which was sacred to the Druids; mistletoe, believed to bring about fertility; oak logs for blessings of strength and longevity; wassail—a boozy mulled cider—to wish good health for your neighbors; the entrails of one's enemies.

I linger on that last one.

"So what are you going to do?" Kim, the middle child of my three-sister family, asks me when I bring this up on a post-Thanksgiving family walk later that week. We are ambling up the hill to gawk at the seasonally bedazzled Oakland Mormon temple.

"I don't know. Roger Dewan is in New York," I say thoughtfully, thinking of my fifth-grade bully, the closest thing to a mortal enemy I may have ever had. "And I think he's a model now or something. People would notice if he's gone."

"What about the entrails of a possum, or a raccoon?" she suggests helpfully.

I consider this seriously for a moment. I have a soft spot for the pudgy trash pandas that roam our backyard after dusk. Justin, on the other hand, hates them. He squirts them with a hose at any chance. One morning I stopped him from putting a rock in front of their den door while they were asleep inside—a mom and four young pups. (He did it at night, after they were out.)

I consider asking if he would be willing to eviscerate one of them and then string its intestines on an eighty-dollar noble fir. According to his DNA results, he is at least 10 percent Swedish.

As I research this problem later that night, I realize that while a lot of people like to cite the "fact" that Vikings decorated their Jól evergreens with entrails, no one can actually find any original citation that it happened.

I give myself permission to go with traditional German nuts and apples instead.

DAY 125

Proof is a tremendously comforting thing.
—MARY ROACH

Yesterday was the last day of my Nine Sisters Chant banishment spell.

Now the million-dollar question: Did it work?

Sort of. My pain is not exactly "banished," but my back does feel better. I can close my own car door now, and don't want to scream every time I try to sit in a chair. Whether this is due to the sobador or the Nine Sisters Chant, or just the plain old passing of time, is not entirely clear.

Silver RavenWolf didn't promise me miracles. She adheres to the idea that you can't just pick up a book, robotically recite what is there, and expect magic to happen. Your heart has to be in it; you have to believe. If this is true, certainly, the Nine Sisters Chant failed. If I am being totally honest with myself, despite genuine effort, I could not, three times a day, stop what I was doing and summon my inner Indiana Jones in *The Last Crusade*, hand clasped over chest, so empowered with righteous belief I could step into a chasm of air—or believe I could cure muscle pain by uttering words.

The idea that you have to believe in magic in order for it to work is repeated by the vast majority of my recent Witchcraft authors, but in fact this is a profoundly new concept. In eighteenth-century Witchcraft legends, a hapless fool can summon otherworldly power without even meaning to. You repeat a limerick backward on a dare, or accidentally recite a few words from a found grimoire, or light a black flame candle in a shack on Halloween next to Allison Watts all the while swearing up and down you don't believe in Witches and poof—you're suddenly knee-deep in magic. This is not true today. Today your heart has to be along for the ride. This is unfair.

Really what I'm doing is circling the drain on the larger question I've been grappling with since July: *Does* my belief in my spiritual journey really matter in order for it to be effective? Can I practice magic while having doubt?

Belief is a very tricky thing. Because it is a feeling, it can't be measured objectively. Any experiment where it is a variable can't be put through the rigors of the scientific method. If you operate under the assumption that the strength of a Witch's magic is fueled by belief in herself, this makes magic impossible to prove.

In *The Triumph of the Moon*, historian Ronald Hutton writes about "cunning folk" healers in rural England, and how a patient's belief in their Witch healer was critical to their successful outcome. The actual methods these healers employed varied wildly. They specialized in ailments like rashes, wounds, bleeding, nervous system issues, and emotional upsets. According to Hutton, in the mid-1900s, their success rate seemed to be total. The singular failure case that could be found by researcher Theo Brown, who spent years tracking these stories, was of the treatment of a skeptical journalist. Brown concluded from this "that any element of doubt, distraction, or lack of genuine need on the part of the patient was fatal to the process, which is why it could not be subjected to scientific testing."

Anyone who has heard of the placebo effect probably doesn't think this is such a wild story. But this is where things get even more interesting.

In her book *Cure*, Jo Marchant writes that the placebo effect doesn't necessarily depend on the individual's belief at all. A 2021 study by physician-researchers at Beth Israel Deaconess Medical Center found that sufferers of IBS taking a so-called honest placebo (basically, where the patient knows they are taking a pill that has all the medicinal prowess of a gumdrop) still reported meaningful clinical improvement of their symptoms. There are other studies like this. In other words: there's a growing body of evidence that shows you don't even have to believe in the placebo for the placebo to work. You can know you're taking a pill that is supposed to do nothing and still experience something. This is mind-blowing to me.

So, despite what RavenWolf and Cunningham and a zillion other Witches would argue, I believe there is potential value in me chanting a banishment spell over my back, regardless of the level of doubt in my heart.

Because here's the real epiphany: stopping everything I was doing three times a day to force myself to ponder my choices about my back was pretty potent mind work. Devout Muslims pray to God five times a day. I often thought this was the mark of a fanatic. However, praying to my back three times a day led to increased gratitude for my health and increased respect for, and self-acceptance of, my physical limitations.

I think that if you stopped everything you were doing several times a day to focus on just one thing—God, your back, the tone-deaf teenager next door learning how to play the violin—it will force you into a more positive relationship with that thing. I don't need the scientific method to understand that.

DAY 130

*Even if you don't understand all the symbols in the cards, your
subconscious will recognize them.*
—SKYE ALEXANDER

I'm trying to plan an off-season trip to Salem, Massachusetts, around
February next year, when the crowds will be thin and there will be a
small festival I can attend. Even though the Witches of the notorious
Salem witch trials weren't really Witches, Salem is the undisputed home
of modern Witchcraft in America, so it would be an oversight to not visit
during my year and a day.

Today I discover a pretty phenomenal deal on a plane ticket. I'm
hesitating to buy it, because the tickets for the festival haven't gone on
sale yet, and buying a plane ticket for an event for which you don't have
an actual pass feels like a big gamble during Covid. In-person events are
still being canceled left and right.

But the deal is good. Really good. "All eShakti dresses are $35 this
week only" good.

I sit in front of my computer, wavering back and forth. I have notorious decision paralysis. Then I remember I'm a Witch. I now have agency
where I previously had to exercise patience. There are a million ways of
querying the universe about what the future holds, and what I should do
now to best meet it.

I go to my bookshelf and grab my tarot deck in its little velvet purse.
I have *The Modern Witch Tarot Deck* by Lisa Sterle—it was one of my
newer best-selling books about Witchcraft that turned out to not be a
book at all. I briefly consider the idea that I'm being disrespectful, to
use tarot for something so mundane. In *The Dabbler's Guide to Witchcraft*, however, Fire Lyte consistently encourages readers to use magic
for small, realistic, achievable goals. This whole time I have been trying

to talk to the moon and reverse chronic pain that has defied medical specialists. Why not try something a little more practical? I might not be able to feel the cosmic energy coming off an oregano plant. But maybe I can figure out if I should take advantage of an airline sale.

Skye Alexander's best-selling book, *The Modern Witchcraft Book of Tarot*, has a simple spread for yes/no questions. You are to shuffle the cards while thinking about your question, and then begin stacking them face up. When you uncover an ace, you stop, and start stacking a new pile. If you get to thirteen cards in a pile without uncovering an ace, move on to another pile. At the end, if you get two or three aces turned up in your stacks, your answer is yes. If you get zero or one ace, it's no, or "at least not right now."

I pull the cards out of the bag, sit on the ground in my closet-office, and begin to shuffle, asking the universe whether or not I should give Priceline my credit card information.

I start flipping the cards over onto the rolling office chair I am using as an impromptu divination table. The seat periodically wobbles, and I have to grab hold of it to keep it centered in front of me.

An ace appears on my fourth flip. I start a new pile.

An ace appears on my thirteenth flip.

I start a new pile.

An ace appears as the thirteenth card, again. I lean back from the chair.

"Well, damn." The fact that an ace came up on my thirteenth flip, twice, is not lost on me, even if I don't know what it means.

I turn back to my computer, whip out my credit card, and buy the ticket. I truly am feeling more confident about the purchase.

A moment passes. It's about eight o'clock at night. I think about what other plans I have this evening. Nothing.

I look again at the deck of cards on the seat. It seems the communication channels are very clear tonight.

Twenty minutes later I'm sitting crossed-legged on my floor in a cloud of cedar incense, a mug of tea on one hand and my Witchcraft playlist roaring on Spotify, flipping cards onto the office chair like a blackjack dealer. The cats have abandonded their usual post at my closed door.

This mania is not unfamiliar. When I was twenty-two, I won eighty dollars at a slot machine in one of the cheaper downtown casinos in Reno. I sat staring, wide-eyed, as the little machine went berserk in my face like Yosemite Sam with his pants on fire, sirens blaring and golden coins falling. My friend came up behind me, grabbed my arm, and said, "We need to leave, now."

I protested, holding tight to the machine. "No, we need to keep playing! I only gave it ten dollars!"

"This is precisely why we are leaving," he said. "I do not like the look in your eye."

This is how I feel now. I ask a question, any question, watch the pretty cards flutter between my fingers, and get an answer. It's intoxicating. And it's free.

After asking about my career, my family, my love life, my family members' love lives, I murmur a question I'm a little more afraid to get an answer to.

"Should I move to Seattle. Should I move to Seattle, should I move . . ."

In the middle of a cut, a card shoots out of the deck and lands facedown on the scratchy gray rug. I recall a snippet of text while flipping through Alexander's book a few moments ago, about the significance of dropped cards. "It might cut to the heart of the matter in the simplest terms," she says. "It serves as a signal: pay attention."

I eye the card on the floor like it's a ticking bomb. Then I bend forward, grab it firmly on one end, and pull.

The ace of wands beams back at me, upright: a single, god-sized hand, emerging from an iridescent cloud and haloed by sparks of light. The hand's elegant fingers are thrusting a wand triumphantly into the sky, entwined by lush green leaves.

I have not memorized any tarot card meanings, but I feel positive just looking at this one. Possibly because it features leaves and sparkles. (Possibly because it's just not the fucking tower again.)

I flip through Alexander's book for the meaning. "This ace symbolizes a new beginning, one full of passion and rich with promise . . . It can mean loyalty, commitment, and a strong sense of purpose—perhaps of a creative nature—in an existing partnership."

Then I read this—and I wish I were making this quote up: "I think of this as the 'go for it' card.'"

I let the book fall between my palms and stare at the far wall.

I have to admit this is probably the closest I've ever felt like I'm talking to fate in a language that needs no additional interpretation. These are not the opaque prophecies of a swamp sorceress, or a four-line magazine column designed to apply to the lives of everyone born between July 22 and August 21. This is as clear and direct a divination answer I think you can get.

Then again, the skeptic in me just wonders if I'm pulling a story together out of loose threads.

It is, technically, my day job.

DAY 133

You'd better not hope for too much.
—THORN MOONEY

Today I get an email declaring the festival I was supposed to attend in Salem—the one for which I just bought a plane ticket—has been canceled due to Covid.

I glare at my tarot cards in the corner.

)　)　)　●　(　(　(

DAY 135

Hanging above us in the stars in an illustrated fabric of what it
means to be human.
—LISA MARIE BASILE

Lauren and I are talking about astrology today. Which is to say, we are arguing.

I have a grudge against astrology, and I've been avoiding it, despite the fact that it's a wildly popular part of modern Witchcraft.

This is because, as a teen, I used to be really, really into astrology.

The astrology most Americans are familiar with today was introduced to the Western world about a hundred years ago by English theosophist William Frederick Allen—pen name, Alan Leo.* Leo saw a business opportunity in recasting an ancient science to suit the occultism trend raging through England's upper class. Thus he went about simplifying seventeen centuries' worth of Central Asian divinatory knowledge to produce what his audience wanted: a mirror into which they could gaze at themselves. It's worth noting that he did this at the protestations of many of his contemporaries. Nonetheless, he effectively created the easily digestible sun-sign astrology most of us bump into today next to the scented candles at Urban Outfitters—an astrology that's less about divining the fate of the heir to throne or timing a war campaign, and more about telling you about yourself.

The reason I don't like astrology now is not because I am an adult. (Or because I'm a Leo, and Alan Leo ruined it for the rest of us.) It's because at some point I realized I was using astrology as a permission slip to stereotype everyone I knew, including myself. Generally speaking, making assumptions about someone based on information they have not

---

* Yes, he took his sun sign as his last name. Cue all your Leo jokes here.

given you is at best, rude, and at worst, dangerous. But I enjoyed being told who I was, because it was easier than engaging in the never-ending, self-indulgent process of *discovering* who I was, based on things like trauma, privilege, genetics, and upbringing. Liberating myself from the personality box I had let astrology put me into was probably my first real experience with self-actualization. I don't want to go back into that box. Which is why today I am insisting to Lauren that astrology is directly antithetical to modern Witchcraft's philosophies of self-discovery and self-empowerment.

"For a group of people so intent on rebellion, on breaking out of what society tells them they must be, why do Witches seem so eager to build personality cages for themselves out of star charts?" I nearly shout at her. "How can a spirituality so intent on self-discovery be so wrapped up in a science that gives everyone a birth-based blueprint telling them who they are?"

"Your relationship to the cosmos and its effect on your life is information to inform your knowledge of self, and your spellcraft," Lauren replies in a heated voice over Zoom. "Knowing yourself is the best way to become the best version of yourself. And besides, your sun sign is just a small part of your entire chart, which should all be taken into context."

"Okay, but that's not how astrology is being used today," I fire back. "It is bullshit. Surely bullshit. I will have no part of it."

DAY 138

Real psychics make you mad.
—FIRE LYTE

So today I'm getting my astrological chart read.

Meg has interceded between Lauren and me and has graciously recommended a high-quality Witch-astrologer I might consult with. I concede I need to at least try talking to a professional before I write off astrology completely.

I email the astrologer the time, date, and location of my birth, send her three hundred dollars via PayPal, and a day later we meet over Zoom for an hour discussion of my entire life. I tell her the premise of my book, and am open about my skepticism of Witchcraft and my inflamed history with astrology. For reasons I cannot imagine, she requests to remain anonymous.

I start by asking her the heart of what I want to know, which is if I actually have to care about astrology in order to be a successful Witch.

"What do you think is the role of astrology in a Witch's practice?"

"You'll find very mixed opinions about astrology in the magical community," she says thoughtfully. "Some people swear by it, some people think it's nonsense. Some use the sun and moon and that's it. Every practice is different—both Witchcraft and astrology are very decentralized, very disorganized. Ordo Templi Orientis and other ceremonial magicians still use structured astrology heavily. But most Witches don't focus on the intricacies of the outer and inner planets. That's just the flow of eclectic spaces."

"I have heard that before the Victorians, astrology was used more to divine events rather than to infer someone's personality," I ask. "Do you have any opinions about this? Do you feel astrology is better suited to divination versus psychology?"

"I think both are valid and both are interesting," she replies. "Ancient astrologers were using natal charts more to determine whether you would have good fortune—not so much if you would be loud, or quiet, or things like that. They also had more emphasis on the inner planets. Possibly because the outer planets hadn't been discovered yet."

I skate past the part where I want to ask if she thinks the outer planets still had meaning if they hadn't been discovered yet, and instead try to phrase my ultimate concern with astrology as politely as possible.

"I feel like today, astrology is being used as permission to stereotype others rather than for self-determination. What do you think about how astrology is being used today?"

"I absolutely hate when people judge others based on their sun sign," she says emphatically. I think she's actually happy I asked. "Especially since most people who don't like astrology don't relate to their sun sign. Each person has all the signs in their chart, in different houses and planets. Melting astrology down to this single solar reading, you miss the higher qualities of each sign. For example, for you"—she glances down at some papers just out of view of the screen—"your sun sign is in your ninth house, which is your education house, so you probably have a high opinion of education, and have high ideals, and you're very dignified and value communication. You also have Saturn in your first house, so you're probably really sarcastic. But someone could see you're a solar Leo and would never inquire into any of that."

"I am sarcastic," I reply.

"Right. And the other thing is, some people just hate being told who they are. They hate the idea of predetermination, or fate. And some astrologers really go overboard. I often have to tell people, you know, 'That guy's not an asshole because he's a Pisces. He's just an asshole.' It's kind of like being so obsessed with magic you start to think everything is an omen. It's not. Like, sometimes a crow is just a crow.

"I do think astrology helps to fuel spellwork," she continues. "If I wanted to do a love spell I would pay attention to Venus. I might even do it in the hour and the day or even the minute of Venus. All points of time have astrological correlations. For example, if you are trying to pitch a book, you might want to wait until Mercury is in retrograde, and then do it on Wednesday."

I admit I write this down.

Then we get to the meat of our conversation, where she tells me about me. I will confess that despite myself, I am a little bit excited to hear what she has to say. It's the same feeling as when a friend dares you to walk up to a mirror and say "bloody Mary" three times. You know it's not real, *you know* nothing is going to happen. But at the end of the third "Mary" your blood pressure still gives the tiniest little spike.

The reading takes a solid hour, and she is nothing if not thorough. Some things ring uncannily true: my Sagittarius rising means I'm probably a physically big person (I'm tall, I'm wide, and I have huge hair). Apparently, the position of Pisces means my spirituality is tied up in my career, and a Virgo midheaven means I'm hardworking and would make a great writer. Then there are other goodies: my Venus is in Gemini, so I'm "incredibly charming and clever." A certain Aquarius position means I love helping people simply for the sake of it. At one point she says my moon is exalted and I beam like an idiot, despite having no idea what that actually means.

I want to say that much of her assessments could be inferred simply by Googling me, asking our mutual friend about the book I'm writing, and good ol'-fashioned telling me what I want to hear. But the thing is, I don't think she is swindling me. Her tone is earnest rather than unctuous, and the papers she keeps flipping through look like my sister's old calculus homework. She says some things that aren't flattering about my childhood. She calls me indecisive, accuses me of vacillating between extremes. She tells me the position of Lilith in Virgo means I am controlling, and have a desire to gain approval from others, and Chiron in Cancer means that deep down, I desire more than anything just to be loved and nurtured, but this very fact repulses me. I wonder if she ever considers how much her personal bias, or what she knows about her client beforehand, affects her reading. But, like tarot, that's probably only a bad thing if you're trying to prove astrology is a psychic art, rather than a therapeutic one.

Which is why I want to get away from personality traits. I want to ask her about what's going to happen to me in the great shadow of the future.

She's suddenly hesitant. She tells me she rarely does divinations for others, usually only for herself. I tell her I'm not expecting anything grand. But I really am curious, "for research's sake" and encourage her to proceed.

She studies her papers. There're a few beats of silence while her eyes run back and forth. Then she begins.

"In January, your tenth house in Virgo will be activated and Mercury will be your ruler."

I blink into the camera.

She takes a breath and clarifies. "You'll probably spend the first part of 2022 writing, because your career house will be activated. In August, your eleventh house then goes into the realm of Venus: this is the realm of friendships, partnerships, and love. You might be going out with friends a lot more, spending money, going on dates, and overall being consumed by romance. Or you'll just be making a ton of money."

I write this down, too.

She finishes with: "Also, pretty soon this year, Venus will go into retrograde, which usually means you'll be breaking up with your boyfriend."

"Sorry—what?" I pip.

"Or you will change banks," she says smoothly, still looking at her papers.

"I can't break up with my boyfriend, I had a tarot card just tell me to move with him to Seattle," I say.

"That's why I give people options," she replies, undeterred. "There are so many ways a planetary movement or placement can manifest itself, or you can use the energy of a particular astrological event. Venus rules both love and money. So it just means something eventful is going to happen with love or money. Or love and money."

"Right," I say, because I don't know what else to say. This is the trouble with divination and prophecy: whatever answer you get from the fates usually obfuscates more than it reveals. It's only in hindsight that you can see how the puzzle pieces fit together.

At the end of our three-hour call, I concede I don't think I am being had for a pigeon. I think she is taking her role seriously and is giving me her best effort. I respect and appreciate this.

Still, I can't see myself using this as a tool in my everyday Craft. There's too much imprecision in astrology, too many different ways to read things. Witchcraft has enough uncertainty in it already. I don't feel the urge to add the many moods of Mars into the mix unless I absolutely have to.

DAY 141

The ways of the old country were lost to me.
—LORRAINE MONTEAGUT

The day is bright, trees shaking off silver glitter from last night's rain. I strap on my hiking boots, step outside, and breathe in the freshly washed air. Today I am going foraging for toyon, a native plant that also goes by the name of California holly.

If I were in ancient Europe, I'd be collecting apples, mistletoe, and sweet chestnuts to decorate my sacred evergreen. But I'm not in ancient Europe. I'm in twenty-first-century California. This complicates what a traditional Yule is going to look like for me. Wicca implores me to honor the earth—not the earth as it was a thousand years ago in a snowy cave in the hinterlands of what will become Brandenburg, but the earth here and now. The anthroplogist in me—and the inner child who wants nothing more than to feel like she knows precisely where she comes from— would love nothing more than to re-create my ancestors' traditions. But it feels less artificial to embrace a more intuitive Wheel of the Year practice as Temperance Alden describes in her book *Year of the Witch*. I will celebrate Yule as modern California offers it.

I pull up to the trailhead and set off, armed with an empty bag and an app that will help me identify plants. As a child, I remember the adults around me telling me never to eat the red berries that grew in ample profusion across the fences of our school. But turns out there are three kinds of red berries that grow in this part of California at this time of year: toyon, firethorn, and cotoneaster. Toyon is native, medicinal, and apparently makes a tasty jam. Firethorn, while not exactly tasty, is technically edible. And cotoneaster is poisonous. The best part is the berries are, as far as I can tell after studying several photographs, completely identical. It's the saw-toothed edges of toyon's leaves, and the telltale thorns along the branches of firethorn, that assure the difference among the three.

No one is on the trail, and my boots slop in the uphill mud. The sky is cornflower blue, the grass leprechaun green. This is Christmas in California. Bright, clear, sunny, and not a drop of snow in sight. I normally lament our lack of frozen flurries, sung about with such love in all the carols you hear your whole life growing up. But today I simply appreciate the scene before me.

I am an avid hiker—my first book was a prankish-but-practical guidebook on how to get started hiking and backpacking. But this is the first time I have ever actually attempted to identify and really interact with the plants around me on a hike. I flash my little app at everything in sight, learning the names of plants that have made up the backdrop for most of my life. It's like seeing someone's face every day for twenty years, and then finally asking their name: coastal oak, woodfern, cheatgrass, Italian thistle. Everything is beaming up at me with dewdrops on their cheeks.

I stop in front of a little shrub, about hip height: Pacific madrone. Its leaves are emerald green and smooth, each with a long white vein running through. It's particularly captivating.

I glance up the trail left, then right. No one is around.

I haven't tried this since August, when I followed Thea Sabin's exercise to feel the energy of individual objects, especially plants, and failed to commune with my beloved oregano.

I put my hands in front of the madrone, a few inches away. I close my eyes, then open them, and look left and right again, just to be sure. I don't want someone coming up on me posing like an extra in a Depression-era musical, warming their hands up against a New York City trash can involuntarily played by a plant. I close my eyes again, taking a few deep breaths, and try to clear my mind. I open all my senses, feeling the cold on my cheeks and fingers, and the scent of the freshly churned mud and wet leaves gets more pronounced.

A few moments pass with my hands outstretched.

I don't feel anything.

I open my eyes to make sure my hands are in the right place and try again.

Nope, I just don't feel anything. It's the oregano all over again. I don't get it. The midst of a forest is my happy place. But alas. The plants just don't want to talk to me like this.

I put my hands back by my side, feeling a little disappointed.

I try and shake off my failure, carrying myself up the hill. After a few minutes, I see a small tree on the hillside, bunches of holly-red berries clinging to its branches, upturned toward the sky. The app confirms my hunch: toyon. I beam. I feel like a nine-year-old who has found her first painted egg on Easter.

I stand underneath the toyon's boughs, arms outstretched, and realize I can't reach a single berry.

I hike for another forty-five minutes. I find five or six more toyons but they are all growing out of reach. At one point I step off the trail and gently climb uphill, to try and reach one that seems promising, but I end up sliding downhill in the mud and almost landing on my ass. As I slide, my low back gives one sharp spasm, a warning. I remember my promise to listen, to be kind to it, to love it even when I feel like it's holding me back. I decide to leave the toyon be.

I am not upset, however, because I have noticed a few other things: bay laurels are growing here in profusion. They have fragrant, white clusters of berries emerging from galaxy-swirls of leaves.

I reach my hands into a thicket of bay branches, and it occurs to me I am about to break one of the most sacred tenants of backpacking and hiking: leave no trace. This is the commandment of all responsible outdoor stewards. It means the obvious things like picking up your trash. But it also means not picking up anything that was already there. Like, for example, harvesting wild plants.

I am about to commit a massive violation of a moral code I literally wrote a book about. On the other hand, this stuff grows like mad. There's a tree every thirty feet or so. Nothing will be harmed if I take a few handfuls. Right? The term "ethical wild harvesting" flashes into my head.

I look left and right up the trail again, just to ensure I don't have to explain myself to anyone.

The hand-sized blossom comes free after some wrenching (I realize I should have brought some scissors), and its spicey aroma blooms around me in a cloud.

"Thank you!" I whisper to the tree once I've grabbed some handfuls and placed them into my plastic shopping bag. I head back downhill and get into my car.

On the way home, I see a shrub on the side of the freeway on-ramp, about ten feet tall, and covered in a galactic number of luscious red berries. I all but swerve into traffic to pull over.

I get out of my car, doubling back on foot. I whip out my phone. "Firethorn" says the app. Not toyon, but it's nonnative, plentiful, and edible. Just like me. It will work.

I reach my hands into the shrub and unthread the octopus tentacles of red berries. At first I worry about the drivers on the road who can see me, but after a few minutes it becomes impossible: I can't harvest without being seen. So I just go for it, grabbing fistfuls of berry bunches and shoving them into my bag, bright red dots flying everywhere.

Yule is abundance.

DAY 143

The distinction between the magical and the mundane is an illusion.
—THORN MOONEY

It's the night before the solstice. I've spent all day in front of the computer, and I have cabin fever. At 5:15 p.m., dusk has almost faded into full black, but I get into my car anyway and drive down to a bike path near some wetlands. It's a place not too far from the road where you can look out over brackish bay water and see where the lights of civilization kiss the sky.

By the time I get out of my car, it's already night. The air is black and blue, flat lines of clouds, and reflections of the city's distant life. Wind messes with my hair, pylon tower lights flash red in the darkness, miles in the distance, like titans playing with strings of artificial stars. I'm alone.

As I walk, my thoughts start to burble up from the back of my mind.

I realize why most Witchcraft ceremonies still make me uncomfortable. It's not that I feel like a grown-up playing make-believe. I'm ready to buy in. I believe in the power of the mind, the power of prayer and spellwork to focus the mind to bring about a goal, even if that goal can only affect yourself. Basically, I'm ready to believe more in the law of attraction than anything else at this point.* It's the awkwardness—no, the arrogance—of summoning the elements and deities of the universe that I can't get over. I still think maybe it's some vestigial bit of me just wanting to surrender to a higher power rather than *be* a higher power, as Witchcraft seems to encourage. But, semantics matter. Commanding the very element of earth—"come to us, come to us, be here now"—feels extraordinarily presumptuous. The elements, the gods, are here all the time. They were here before us, they will be here after us—how can we summon them? They are here all the time.

I stop walking.

They are here all the time.

I glance down both sides of the trail. It's opaque and gloomy. I'm on a dirt road that stretches between two wide planes of marsh water. I see no one, and even if there was someone there, they probably wouldn't see me.

Okay, why not. I'm not going to try and commune with the pickleweed. The rejection of the Pacific madrone on my last hike is still fresh. I'm going to try to talk to elements again, which I haven't tried since September.

---

* The New Age philosophy adopted by many (but not all) Witches that asserts whatever you focus your thoughts on is what you will attract into your life.

I think about the four elements. I think about drawing them near to me, summoning them, like Nancy on the beach in act three of *The Craft*. But with less crazy eyes.

It still doesn't feel right. It's like picking up a phone and hearing dead air on the other end.

They are here all the time.

I can't summon something that's always here.

I look out into the mottled gray expanse of the marshland. I feel like I'm on a dark alien planet. I think about the sci-fi concept of terraforming, about the electricity that powers the lights twinkling in the office complex miles away, that flows through the electricity towers ahead in the distance. They blink like low-hanging thoughts. I think about connection and interdependence.

It occurs to me that the energy in my body is the same as the energy in the red power lights, just a different current. What's inside the office lights is inside me. It's also what's in the stars a million miles away. The water in my blood is the same stuff rushing in the creek next to me. The wind that is outside of me is also inside of me. I pull it in and push it out; it is the same breath being used by the frogs, the birds, the people breaking into cars downtown, pumping through the HVAC systems of the condos down the road. I pick up my hand and stare at it, thick, heavy, cold. I am earth. This is earth. I am the dirt I am walking on. I am conscious earth.

They are here all the time.

Something, finally, clicks.

Bliss floods me, like a drug, like a wave. I take a great, heaving breath. All the atoms in my body remember what it was like to be inside the core of a star right before it went supernova. Before I know it, I am staring at my hand, crying. I am crying because my hand is a miracle. It's like I have never seen it before. My hand is all five elements made flesh. I am a miracle. Everything is a fucking miracle. It is urgent. It is overwhelming.

I briefly wonder if this is what a good acid trip feels like.

I know this isn't news, from whenever or wherever you are reading this. You take one high school physics class where you learn we are all made up of the same protons and electrons and neutrons, and that matter is never really created or destroyed, just constantly recycling into different forms. I learned it.

But I have never *felt* it.

I understand, without having to ask anyone, that this is the flow of the universe that Witches plug into, work with, manipulate.

I walk back to the car, giddy, high. "I am not a woman, I'm a god" by Halsey comes onto the radio, and I turn the volume up to ten, singing at the top of my lungs. My eyelids flood every time I reach a stoplight.

DAY 144

The purpose of ritual is to change the mind of the human being.
It's a sacred drama in which you are the audience as well as the
participant, and the purpose of it is to activate parts of the mind
that are not activated by everyday activity.
—SHARON DEVLIN AS QUOTED BY MARGOT ADLER

Today is Yule. I'm standing in my apartment's tiny kitchen, using every available inch of counter space to make wassail according to Timothy Roderick's recipe in *Wicca: A Year and a Day*. The back window is steamed up with the scent of buttered apples and hot beer. I try to incorporate some kitchen witchery into my working, thinking very methodically about every action, every lemon squeeze and sprinkling of spice. But each time I try and really infuse them with the love and merriment of Yule, that emotion quickly devolves into fear that what I'm making is, well, disgusting. Then I worry I will become a version of Tita in *Like Water for Chocolate*, when she poisons everyone at her sister's wedding with fits of sorrow and vomiting because of her negative emotions while baking the wedding cake. Despite meditating regularly, I'm still having trouble controlling my mind.

Eventually I turn on the news to distract myself.

Nearly everything is shut down as the Omicron variant runs rampant through the country. I am feeling moderately secure since getting my booster, but it doesn't much matter, as all public rituals have been called off. Turns out a postvaccine world, much to the chagrin of many, does not mean a "you can relax now" world. Meg has taken some pity on me and agreed to host a small ritual at her house with whoever else might be vaccinated and willing. "I'm a third-degree Gardnerian initiate. If I can't lead a Yule ritual for a bunch of new Witches, what's the fucking point?" she tells me over Zoom one evening last week. I ask if we have to be naked. She shoots me a look that implies questions like this aren't cute anymore.

I sent out a handful of invites to friends who had expressed cautious curiosity about my spiritual journey. Three people replied.

Tonight we gather in a basement apartment for my first traditional, official Gardnerian Wiccan ritual, my Crock-Pot of wassail steaming among the potluck buffet in Meg's kitchen.

The coffee table has been transformed into a large altar, laden with all the sacred objects I recognize from my books—the bell, the statue of the Goddess, the statue of the God, the athame, the candles—all in their proper spots. I feel sheepish about our group size, recognizing Meg has gone to great effort for a relatively small turnout. The air in the room is stiff, even though we are all friends, like we're about to have our first orgy and no one quite knows where to start.

Meg knows where to start. She announces she will be aspecting the Goddess, for lack of anyone else. She and her husband cast the circle, call the corners, lead us in various processions around the table, kiss our cheeks, anoint us with oil, direct us on what to sing. The ceremony is complex, but the two of them are obvious pros. I feel less like I'm in a holy trance and more like I'm in a dance class, trying to learn the steps. At one point the anointing oil spills on the table, on Meg's athame, and she mutters, "Shit," and lifts up her dress to wipe the blade on the bare flesh of her thigh. She gives me a quick, nervous glance. I think she's worried I'm judging her. I think about reminding her so far I've been working on a box of old T-shirts.

Later, in the midst of the ritual, as we are discussing one of the mysteries of life in the universe, I find myself spacing out in front of a chair leg. Meg interrupts whatever she was saying, projects her voice down to my end of the table, and says, "Diana, where did you just go?" My head snaps up to her, like a child caught daydreaming in class. "I don't know, I'm sorry," I say. I feel genuinely guilty, fearing I have disrespected her. She nods, looking at me curiously, but not wholly offended.

The ritual ends. I am left feeling more impressed with the fanfare of it all than anything else. I can't believe how long it must have taken to memorize all these steps. This is the grand ritual I wanted initially when I started back in July. But I don't feel the way I want to feel, the way I think I should feel. Maybe it's because the ritual is between worlds, but the people inside of it aren't. Some spaces are easier to engage with when you don't have to worry about the people on the inside remembering what you did once you're outside again. I'm still afraid of what being religious will make people think of me. Even among my friends who volunteered to do the same thing. I wonder if this fear will ever go away. I had no idea it was this deeply established in my personality until I tried to fight it.

We sit around the living room for a few hours, sipping bubbles and nibbling cheeses. It is good to be in a room with people I care about, recalling inside jokes and catching up on gossip. A year and a half of Covid has made these gatherings feel so much more precious than before. I feel warm.

As our party, such as it is, winds down, my friend Brandon announces he has a series of runes to give away. Brandon has been a Heathen neo-pagan since high school, basically as long as I've known him. He made his own rune set by harvesting a branch from a living white oak on our friend Melody's property, after praying underneath it and asking for permission. He carved each seashell-sized piece by hand, and colored in the characters with a paint made of cadmium and his own blood and spit. It took weeks. They were then consecrated with yet more blood on a Wednesday (Odin's day) under a full moon. He had this set for years, occasionally producing it at parties the same way a Witch might offer to read some tarot. Then on a recent hiking trip, he lost one of the pieces.

The set is now incomplete, unusable, unstable. Now, he has to recycle the rest of the pieces, which is accomplished by giving them away.

He offers me the mouth of the simple cotton bag with Mjölnir embroidered on it. I reach inside and pull out a wooden circle the size of a hair tie. It's emblazoned with a fire-engine red fishhook.

"That's Laguz. It's the rune of creativity, flow, and dreams," he tells me. "Its element is water, and it's directly associated with the feminine and birth. It is the primordial water that meets the seed for growth."

My mind flashes to a memory of standing on a dirt road under a billowing black sky between two marsh seas, crying at the existence of my hand.

He is searching my face, trying to figure out if he's just delivered bad news or good.

"Makes sense," I reply, taking a sip of wassail and not meeting his eyes. I'm not ready to talk about what happened. I don't know how to describe the realization that I am a star, and also a river, and shit, and a light bulb and a kitten, without sounding like I am either in need of or have been abusing some powerful medication.

DAY 147

God, how do normal people live without a direct connection to
the underworld?
—AUGUSTEN BURROUGHS

Little things keep happening.

At Yule a few days ago, we sang a rather classic neopagan Witch song at the beginning of the ritual: "The earth the air the fire the water, return, return, return, return." Today I click thoughtlessly on an episode of *PEN15*, a TV show I haven't seen in a year. Within fifteen minutes, I watch as one of the lead characters puts on a set of headphones and—

guess what song starts playing. It doesn't even make sense in the scene. She could be listening to Britney Spears or the Wu-Tang Clan with equal applicability.

This could be written off as coincidence. But it's the quantity of coincidences like this that's remarkable. Like it's probably not just luck that the song I'm listening to on the radio in the car ends exactly when I turn into my driveway the last five times I've pulled into it. Or that I keep checking my phone precisely when the minute and hour hands meet up, or that I will be thinking about my upcoming Boston trip on a walk, and then someone wearing a Boston sweatshirt will turn a corner and start walking toward me. I was out running errands yesterday when for no reason, Pink's "Get the Party Started" got stuck in my head.* Forty minutes later I go into a grocery store, and the ambient radio was playing "Get the Party Started."

These moments feel so special. So powerful. So *witchy*.

I don't necessarily think it's divine intervention (if it is, I certainly don't know what it means) so much as my subconscious suddenly helping me out. Like a butler orchestrating little pleasantries throughout my day.

But there are also a hundred moments like this that could happen, all day, each day, that don't.

What about every time I try to change the stoplight from red to green, and it doesn't work? What about every stubbed toe I don't see coming? It's easy to read into the moments of synchronicity. But ultimately, it's hard to know if more "witchy coincidences" are occurring, or I'm just paying more attention to what's going on in the moment, reading more into the normal amounts of coincidence that occurred before I started this journey.

There must be some ratio of wins (moments of inexplicable coincidence or light premonition) versus misses that I could measure to prove if I'm really more in tune with the world. But how would I count the misses? You can't count a scenario that doesn't exist.

---

* I have nothing against Pink, to be clear. But this is a song I haven't intentionally listened to since high school.

If I indulge the idea that I'm orchestrating all these coincidences—I am plugged into the divine flow of the universe—I'm not so much impressed with myself as terrified. For example, sometimes when I'm driving across a bridge, I start wondering if this is the precise moment when that 9.0 earthquake they've been saying will hit California before 2030 will arrive. Then I worry I am in the process of manifesting it, and the only thing that calms me down is the idea that that would be impossible, because I'm simply not that powerful yet.

I know Witchcraft isn't about repression, but perhaps some thoughts are worth repressing.

DAY 152

I've noticed that when someone first starts on their path it is often the subtleties of the holidays that are overlooked in an effort to become "advanced" more quickly.
—TEMPERANCE ALDEN

Justin is in Seattle with family (stranded, to be precise, after four flight cancellations in a row due to Covid-related staffing shortages and a blizzard that seems to have gotten lost on its way to Idaho). I have spent the last four days of Yule inside alone. I wake up at 8 a.m., then roll over and wake up again at 9:30 a.m., then roll over and finally at 10:30 a.m. realize I should get out of bed before the atoms in my body start merging with the atoms in the mattress. I put on socks, feed the animals, plop a few spoonfuls of whipped cream into a cup of chai, do twenty minutes of yin yoga in front of the Christmas tree, and then more or less get back in bed around noon for lack of anything else to do. Occasionally I get up to do a load of laundry or to purchase more whipped cream.

I didn't actually plan to be in bed all day. I wanted to do some version of the twelve days of Jól, starting on December 25, by lighting a traditional oak wood fire in the backyard firepit every night and drinking ale with friends into the wee hours. This is in keeping with ancient European traditions. According to the Norwegian sagas, it was mandatory that a farmer brew enough Yule ale for at least three of his neighboring farmer friends to enjoy with him. If he didn't have three friends, he still had to make enough beer as if he did, and then, presumably, drink it all himself. If he didn't brew any beer, he had to pay a fine. Yule in ancient Norway was basically government-mandated alcoholism.

Unfortunately, I have not been brewing my own ale since October, because I didn't know about this tradition until December 1. My "fine" is going to an upscale grocery store and spending half my bank account on imported German Christmas ale—the closest I can find to Scandinavian—and then promptly remembering that half my friends are either sober or stranded in airports. I hate drinking alone, so the bottles are sitting on the kitchen counter, rather offended at their unlucky lot to be cast into the home of an idiot Witch trying to run a twelve-day Yule party during Covid.

Joanna takes some pity on me tonight and huddles with me by the firepit during a break in the rain. We pull up the folding chairs in the backyard, find a few semidry logs, and begin to try and light a fire. Yule tradition also holds that you should cut down your own oak log and anoint it with wassail to serve in the Yule fire, but I had to pass on this since I don't think a park ranger would turn a blind eye to me chopping up an oak tree on state property, even if I did invoke the First Amendment.

The problem tonight is that it has been raining, so all the firewood I purchased is soaking wet. This, I maintain, is not my fault. I didn't think I would need to put a tarp over my firewood. I live in California. The trees spontaneously combust and corporations stole all the water. I have no idea why or even how it is raining right now.

I rustle a few hexane fuel tabs from my backpacking kit to try and start the fire under the logs, but it's still no use. We give up, sit outside in the rain-scented dark, and decide to immolate some clove cigarettes. In one last attempt to produce some semblance of a real pagan Yule, I offer her a bottle of one of the fancy German Christmas ales. I explain that I bought enough for myself and two neighboring farmers.

She coolly observes the overelaborate, royal blue label, shouting gilded promises of authentic 1512 flavor, and politely declines.

"But it's traditional," I say, nudging the nose of the bottle toward her.

"I have a new religion, too, and it says I can only drink tequila," she says, taking a sip from her glass.

JANUARY

))) ● (((

DAY 161

Many of us today were not born into unbroken lines of these old
ways of herbs and charms, but it's never too late to heed the call.
—REBECCA BEYER

Today I decided to begin planting my garden. In most parts of the country, especially the lands of Wicca's ancestors, it is far too early for such things. Everything is still hibernating under a thick frosting of ice. But in Northern California, where I actually live, it's the perfect time for several brassicas. More important, I am not yet ready to let go of the idea of myself as a green Witch. I don't care if I got rejected by an oregano bush and a madrone tree. I love nature. This is going to be my niche, goddammit.

I step outside into the sun, armed with a trowel and gloves. The garden is a mess. Abandoned tomatoes wither on metal cyclones. Crisp brown leaves cling to pots begging to be pruned. Emerald green grass—gorgeous really—has completely colonized one of the beds.

No matter where I've lived, I have always tried to have some kind of garden. I enjoy crowding every living room bookshelf and apartment windowsill with herbs and lettuces, peace lilies and orchids. The catch is, I'm not actually that good at growing anything. Only a few things take off. More often than not, my lettuce would be destroyed by aphids and my bell peppers would grow a single, inch-long fruit and promptly die from the effort. I once killed an *ivy*.

Because she is a good friend, Joanna tries to tell me I am a good gardener. She points out several plants bursting to life outside as proof.

"That's the thing," I said one day as we stood over a bed staring at a patch of fava beans. "I didn't even plant those; they are left over from last year."

"I don't remember you planting fava beans last year," she says.

"I know," I reply. "It's because they all died."

Last year I was blessed with three volunteer tomatoes that simply appeared in a pot of basil. My orchids are notoriously healthy, as are my supposedly difficult-to-grow roses. "My secret," I once drunkenly told a friend at a party as they complimented my array of flowers, "is that I forget they exist."

Basically, everything I ignore tends to do very well. Everything I pour my attention onto tends to die. I have been trying for years not to take this personally.

The reason I am planting arugula today is because some came up last year around this time, despite me doing nothing. It grew three feet and decorated all my salads before dying off in May. I consider that maybe it's not that I kill things with love. Maybe I have been relying too much on what a book or website is recommending, rather than taking cues from the earth around me.

To that tune, I'm making a point to get to know the land spirits in my yard, something Lorraine Monteagut writes beautifully about in *Brujas* and Temperance Alden recommends in *The Year of the Witch*. Alden suggests I sit down and imagine myself floating over the property, seeing where the sun and shadows hit, sensing where there is strength and sickness: "Can you identify the primary land spirit?" she asks me. This is the spirit in charge of balancing the rest of the area.

This is going to be tricky, because in our backyard is a forty-foot date palm tree. Its gigantic, muppet-head top looms over the roof, peeking into all the neighbors' windows. It's the first thing people comment on whenever they come over, and it might as well have its own zip code. Currently two distinct families of pigeons and a squirrel's nest occupy the base of the canopy. We can hear them bicker about the rising cost of rent, and screaming at each other to turn the music down. I believe it was planted in the 1960s, when America was fetishizing all things tropical. During windstorms, it drops canoe-sized palm fronds that stab the garden beds and make the chickens go berserk. It clearly is the plant in charge, but Temperance Alden says the primary land spirit in your yard might not be the biggest thing. So I attempt to ignore the date palm, and observe the other, smaller bushes, herbs, and trees that surround it, like worshippers: the plums, the pomelo, the magnolia. I think about how much someone must have loved this place in the past, to plant so many wonderful things. That person is no longer here, but I get to enjoy them. What a gift.

It's inevitable that I think about what was here before the date palm, what this place looked like when it wasn't a garden. Who was walking around. Who was tending to the plant life.

The other name for Oakland is Ohlone land, specifically Huichin Ohlone. That was the indigenous tribe that lived here before the Europeans came—my ancestors. I have known this for a couple of years. I try to stay up to date on their current initiatives. They've been in a yearslong battle to get federal recognition, build a longhouse, and reclaim one of their largest graveyards, on which—and this is not a tossed-out script from *Captain Planet*, I swear—a gigantic shopping center is currently implanted (and named after the graveyard!). Last year I started paying them "Shuumi," an optional tax that nonnatives can pay to help fund the Ohlone's rebuilding initiatives. They have a calculator for it on their website. I have no idea what the formula is, but last year I input the square footage of my rental, pulled out my credit card, and paid the annual eighty-three dollars it determined I owe. At first it felt like a lot. Then it seemed a rather polite figure, considering what we're talking about.[*]

It's at this point, mulling on my connection to the land on which I live, that I usually start to feel guilty. It used to feel like a duty, or at least an easy default. I think everyone is tired of white guilt, but I don't know how I'm supposed to think about this stuff and not feel guilty. Witchcraft implores us to connect with our ancestral roots, and our land. But Americans are transplants. Some of our ancestors were brought over here by force, some forced others out to make room for themselves. My successful existence here is the direct product of injustice, the blood and violence of Manifest Destiny. If I didn't feel any guilt around this, I think something would be wrong with me.

Lorraine Monteagut says, "We can commune with them, those ancestors who turned the earth and put their struggle and pain and joy into the underground network, through our service to the land . . . we owe it to the land to pay back what we've taken."

I find my way back to the date palm. It stands before me. Silently. Like a tree.

I reach my hands out and touch its surface—gently, as if it were a human body. I am surprised to feel that it's warm. It's still cool out, probably not over sixty-five degrees. But the flesh of the tree is warmer than the air. I circle it, tracing my hands over the scratchy surface. I allow that new way of seeing the world to enter my brain, or rather, I allow my brain to tune in to that way of seeing the world. It's getting easier. I see the air floating through the barren treetops of the plum trees, the vibrant green of the succulents. Everything seems to be flowing to and from the palm tree. This is obviously the primary spirit. I think it is happy. I think it has seen some shit (it has been in Oakland since at least the 1960s). I think it is tolerating me on a semipleasant basis.

Eventually I stop groping the tree and get to work on the garden bed.

I take last year's dead vines over to the compost, starting a new pile. I love compost. It's the process by which you can turn the dregs of death

---

[*] Genocide. What we're talking about is genocide.

into the soil that creates new life. No candles, no coven, no god needed. It's a satisfyingly accessible form of magic.

I churn it around, happy to discover the brown mess smells good, not bad. This means it's ready. I shovel up some of the bottom layers and take it over to one of the planter beds, mixing it with the spent soil.

Eventually I ditch the shovel, get down on my hands and knees, and stick my hands into the earth. It's easier to work this way. The dirt feels rich and moist, yielding under my fingers. I take my gloves off; I don't care how much I'll have to scrub my fingernails later. It feels good to be bent over a pile of dirt, listening to the chickens peep, while light filters through the treetops. I try to erase all negative thoughts from my mind while I plant. For once, it's not hard.

Why do I drive four hours and hike thirty miles to the middle of nowhere to find this feeling? This is available to me, anytime. I just have to go outside, stick my hands into the dirt, and open my eyes.

While putting the arugula seeds in the new bed, I hear a crunch. I turn and I see that my elbow has accidentally knocked a leaf off a neighboring cactus. Curious, I lift the broken leaf to my nose. It smells brightly of green bell pepper.

For the first time since living here, I wonder if this ornamental succulent that's been in my backyard is edible or medicinal. I realize I don't even know what this plant is. I take it inside, wash the sticky mess off my hands, and use an app to look it up on my phone. It's called soap aloe, and it's from South Africa. It has several medicinal uses, but nowhere can I find any recipes. Most websites will tell you the edible and medicinal uses for a plant the same way a high school textbook will explain the use of the guillotine during the French Revolution: for legal reasons, specifics are omitted. I wish I had a grandmother to teach me what to do with this. But my grandmother wouldn't know. My great-great-grandmothers wouldn't know. The Ohlone grandmothers probably wouldn't even know. All the grandmothers who would know are in South Africa.

I stare at the plant, broken off at the edge, its wet, colorless blood shimmering in the sun. It's a foreigner, but it has a remarkable ability to grow.

DAY 170

*They encouraged the practitioners to empower themselves with
incantation within a ceremonial setting, so that they came to
feel themselves combining with the divine forces concerned
and becoming part of them . . . [I]t did not matter to this work
whether or not the entities concerned had any actual existence.*
—RONALD HUTTON

It's January. I'm over halfway done with my year and a day of trying to be a
Witch. And I still haven't formally made a relationship with the Goddess.
Some Witches say you can just dive into spellwork without this preamble, as
I have done. But old-school writers like Raymond Buckland and Starhawk
suggest it's better first to get to know the elements and deities before you
start to practice the Craft. So far, I've been avoiding the Goddess in a way
that's starting to make me feel like a poser in this whole endeavor.

Enough is enough. Today I'm going to knock on her door.

Adoration—worshipping and communing with a deity simply for
the sake of it—is not talked about a lot in modern Witchcraft. A handful
of people chat about the wonder of connecting with the divine for its
own sake, but it's hardly the dominant conversation. My hunch—and
I can't totally prove this—is because it's a bit too much like the joy of
prayer. And we can't be seen relating to the evangelicals.

I want to do a ritual solely to make a connection with the queen of
Witches herself. Not to ask her for anything. Just to chat. So I know what
she feels like. (So I can ask her for things later.)

I'm not sure what I'm more afraid of: if I reach out to her she will
be there and I'll have to wonder if I'm delusional (again), or she won't
be there and I'll have another oregano-flavored rejection on my hands.

It's a full moon today, which I honestly didn't plan for, but feels like
a positive sign. I begin my preparations in the morning for once, and not

just an hour beforehand. I'm trying to decide between two rituals, one from Gerald Gardner's book and one from Timothy Roderick's. Eventually I opt to combine them.

In Wicca, all the world's goddesses are believed to be aspects of the ultimate Goddess. Picking a specific face to connect with, however, can often be an easy entry. Roderick suggests I research some goddesses, and then simply pick one I like.

I spend an hour reading the bios of Hecate, Astarte, Asherah, Ishtar, Guadalupe, Brigid, Quan Yin, and more, like I'm swiping through profiles on a dating site. Wicca tells me that basically anyone is up for grabs, as long as I feel authentically called to her. But also, these goddesses are very old, and sometimes their domains and symbols start to overlap. Tracking their similarities and influences through the centuries could be its own series. Sometimes its very clear which culture "owns" a goddess. Sometimes it's not.

As I research, my eyes keep going back to a particular passage about the goddess Isis in Roderick's book: "In mythic terms, Isis is your very body and spirit . . . when you tap into her spiritual energies, you also evoke your ability to become one with the natural world, with both sky and earth, life and death." According to Roderick, Isis presides over the full cycle of life and death, as well as healing and magic. She is referred to as the mother of all gods, and is represented by all elements, directions, and powers. She seems to be the very embodiment of "as above, so below." Her worship in the ancient world extended for thousands of years from ancient Egypt and then into the Greek and Roman empires.[*] Her largeness, her inherent universality, feels very welcoming.

And I like that she has a husband (Osiris). She's not a man-hating virgin, or a man-hating wife. She is one half of an exceedingly rare mythological couple: where both parties seem to actually like each other. And if she welcomed everyone from Britain to Sudan to worship her, she'd probably let me.

---

[*] Many hobby historians say Isis eventually turned into the Virgin Mary. Or Mary Magdalene. Honestly it depends whom you ask. There is someone online with an argument for how every biblical Mary is actually a prehistoric goddess hiding under downcast eyes and a blue veil.

I begin by going for a walk. This is to get me in touch with nature, and also to try and see the moon as it rises. In her classic poem invocation "The Charge of the Goddess," Doreen Valiente encourages Witches to invoke the Goddess while naked in some secret forest grove. I can't even get naked at home if I want the windows open and I don't want the neighbors to see me. I'm also not about to drive into the Oakland hills, strip my clothes off, and light a bunch of candles. At best I will get laughed at. At worst, robbed, assaulted, and arrested for indecent exposure. If I want to get any direct moonlight tonight, this little walk is going to be how.

I stroll down the shores of Lake Merritt at sunset, joggers, dog walkers, picnickers, panhandlers filtering by. One side of the sky is a meringue of blush, peach, flame, and amber, diffusing into a cool, soothing violet on the other. The lake is a clean mirror of it all. I feel like I'm walking in an oil painting.

I wonder if it really is *that* beautiful, or if it's just in my head. Since my encounter with the elements at the marsh in December, everything has taken on a permanent posthigh glow. It is absolutely impossible not to be intoxicated by the beauty of the natural world whenever I leave my house. I feel like I'm looking at the world through a Thomas Kinkade Instagram filter. It makes me feel like something about this Witchcraft journey is working.

For my walk, I have tuned into another "witchy" Spotify playlist, in an attempt to get into the mood. Sizzling harmonies and ambient synthesizers flood my ears. It's very mystical. Very exotic. But it's also, I realize after a few minutes, a little depressing. Everything is in D minor and feels like it belongs on the playlist for a Vulcan mind meld.

I am meeting the Goddess tonight. This should be a joyous occasion. I pull out my phone and try to think of the happiest music I know.

Soca.*

---

* Seriously. I don't care who you are, or where you come from. If you are having a bad day, turn on "Like Ah Boss" by Machel Montano and I challenge you—no I *dare* you—to be upset about literally anything.

So it passes that I walk home with my mood buoyed by ecstatic cowbells and bouncy guitar chords. The massive moon begins to rise in the bluebell-colored sky, while a song that could have served as the late-nineties Six Flags commercial anthem blasts into my ears. I feel great.

Once home, I begin gathering my materials to summon Isis. I carefully extract a bottle of wine off the back shelf in the dining room, one I've been hanging on to for about six years for a special occasion. I also grab the little plastic cow that decorates our front steps, rub my arms in lily lotion, and dot my wrists with my best perfume—an expensive, heady blend of gardenias and jasmine. I grab my oldest and thickest white candle, a loaf of bread, and whip up an Isis essential oil blend I found online to put in my diffuser. I enrobe my cardboard box in my white silk veil and begin to make a simple altar with all my objects. I pour a glass of wine for Isis and have trouble placing it somewhere where it won't tip over on the cardboard box's uneven surface, but eventually find a place. After a few minutes, Bird comes into my office and begins enthusiastically hopping all over my work.

I scoop up her soft little body and toss her out of the room so I can get back to business. My lily lotion, the incense, and the essential oils create a bizarre perfume of flowers and cedar trees. The witchy playlist is going. I read Doreen Valiente's "The Charge of the Goddess" three times—it really is pure poetry.

After I cast the circle and call the directions, Bird begins pawing at the door. I ignore her. Then she starts mewling. It's heartbreaking. I've already had to open the circle to run into the other room twice, once to get my smoke-cleansing herbs and then again to get the Starhawk book I forgot. How many openings can a sacred circle take before it's just like "fuck it, dude. You don't have your shit together, I'm out"?

I sit down and bump into the chair behind me, then I stand up to go get yet another book I forgot about and end up knocking over a wineglass. I catch it before the ruby liquid spills and puff out an exasperated sigh. All the while, Bird is still whining in the other room.

Finally I yield and open the door. Isis isn't Bastet, but she's still Egyptian. She probably likes cats. I also think any supreme Goddess force of the universe has to have a sense of levity.

Thrilled, Bird runs in and immediately lies down in front of the altar. I give her scritches, and she purrs. I shrug at the wall across from the altar, like I'm looking at a friend across a dinner table and saying, "Cats, man. What are you gonna do?"

Eventually, after jumping up onto my desk, turning on the printer, and hopping all over the altar, she gets bored and leaves the room. I gently click the door closed behind her, then sit back down in front of my goddess altar. I am alone, trying to think about what to do next. I feel nervous. I recall Timothy Roderick saying I should chant.

I close my eyes, take a deep breath, and murmur, "I-sis," over and over . . . The music changes, and I blend my voice with it. At about the seventh or eighth recitation something happens. A sense of calm overtakes me.

The song changes, begins to develop a beat. I sway back and forth. I have given up on staying still for meditation, instead practicing acceptance of the fact that I am a creature of motion, and movement is a perfect way to connect to the divine according to virtually all Wiccan ritual writers. I let myself sway. I keep chanting. Minutes go by. The perfume floods my lungs.

I focus solely on the idea that Isis is the Goddess of all matter. Isis is everything, is me.

Isis is everything, is me.

Isis is everything, is me.

I run my fingertips over my thighs. I try to visualize everything in the world, connecting, like I did in December at the marsh. I still struggle to describe the profundity, the bliss of opening up to this epiphany. But right now the feeling is more focused. I let myself marinate in it. For some reason, in my mind's eye, I start to see a white-rainbow orb, rushing up and down. I reach out and try to sense everything around me in the process of living and dying at once. I think about how the Goddess is inside of me, outside of me. Everywhere. My fingertips are still on my thighs. *This is what the Goddess feels like.*

I have a sudden urge to take my clothes off. I'm not going to do it.

I am still afraid the neighbor kid might see through my window. But I suddenly understand why Witches always seem to be getting naked. It's like an itch: you need to feel more of the world on you.

Something else happens in this self-induced trance. I am happy. No, I am ecstatic. Waves of ecstasy are rolling through me as I imagine the earth recycling itself, like I am on a low dose of MDMA. I periodically feel overwhelmed, and I have to lean forward and exhale hard. For a few breaths, I feel like I can't inhale, and I worry about the anxiety from my previous meditations coming back to attack me. But then I remember my taproot and imagine the excess energy my body can't hold pouring out of me into the earth. Then I continue chanting and swaying back and forth, and everything feels amazing again. I am the bottom of a pail, breaking open.

In my half trance, I reach inwards towards myself, and grab my lower belly. I hate my belly. But the belly is sacred to Isis, and so I trace mine. Lovingly. *Isis is everything, is me.* My belly is the Goddess's belly. In this moment, this realization is more fulfilling than any time a man has ever called me beautiful.

A rainbow-white winged goddess appears in my imagination. I see her fly toward me and enter my body, like a ghost merging with my flesh. I don't know how much time passes.

Eventually, I come back down to earth. I open my eyes. I nibble a bit of the bread, drink a sip of wine. I understand now why cakes and ale are considered the finishing touch of traditional rituals. The acts of eating and drinking do help me get out of my head and back into the 3D meat of my body. I lean forward and pet the forehead of the plastic cow sitting on my altar. I feel a little sheepish, like waking up after a night of hard drinking and trying to remember if I said anything stupid.

Bird appears in the doorway again, mewing, and I take this as my sign to wrap it up.

I come into the bedroom and check my phone and am shocked to see almost two hours have passed. It felt like twenty minutes.

I had no idea I was capable of feeling this good without the help of another human. I had no idea this level of joy was this accessible to me on my own. In Witchcraft, people talk about shadow work, justice, self-help, blood, crystals, astral projection, telepathy, astrology, will-power. Rarely do I hear anyone talk about bliss.

I have no idea how I'm going to tell anyone about this.

I have to figure out when I can do this again.

DAY 171

Take time to ask Isis what it would mean to live life through her energy and listen for her answer. Spend the day honoring this goddess by fulfilling another person's desire.
—TIMOTHY RODERICK

I am continuing to develop my connection to Isis today by performing one of Timothy Roderick's suggested exercises: fulfilling another person's desire.

The person closest to me on a daily basis is Justin. So last night, after my ritual, I approached him in the dining room. He was in the process of fitting a synthesizer into a wooden case. Tools, screws, and computer parts were strewn all over the table.

"Tomorrow I'd like to spend the day fulfilling your desires," I announced.

He froze, screwdriver in hand, then looked up at me from under his eyebrows.

"What?"

"It's part of my getting to know the Goddess," I said. "Nothing complicated. I just want to spend the day focusing on you, and helping you get what you want."

His eyes darted left to right.

"Is this like a . . . sex thing?" he asked.

"Not unless you want it to be," I said wryly.

"I don't think I like this," he said, putting down the screwdriver and standing up.

This was the wrong approach. Justin has a special issue with being doted upon. He is an excellent builder, inventor, giver. But ask him if you can massage his shoulders and he basically starts crying.

The secret, I've learned, is that I just shouldn't ask what he wants. I should just do it. That's what the best givers do anyway. They are like butlers. They don't just deliver, they anticipate. The issue then lies with me: I am classically bad at anticipating what people need. I have a great and terrible desire in me to help others feel better. But it does not always translate. I have been told I am particularly bad at talking to people with depression, and I tend to offer advice when someone just wants to vent.

I consider that I have betrayed the premise of service by telling Justin my intentions. But I can't unsay what has already been said aloud.

"I don't want to make it complicated," I reassured him, backtracking out of the room. "Tomorrow I will be putting you first. That's all. You don't have to do anything!"

This morning I am off to a bad start, sleeping in late with Bird nuzzled under my chin. By the time I get up he has already made himself coffee. I feed the animals, check the water dishes, and make sure everything is clean in the chicken coop. These are my normal morning tasks, however. Nothing special.

I begin planning the day. I want to bake him molasses cookies (his favorite), and order delivery from one of his favorite restaurants. I'd prefer to take him out, but Omicron is still peaking. Trying to have a great night out during a pandemic is like trying to throw a bachelorette party in a nunnery.

"I'm gonna do your laundry!" I announce, his hamper in hand, heading down the hall.

"Ah no—no no," he says, rising from his desk and snatching the basket from my hands. "But you *did* remind me that I need to do laundry, which *is* an act of service. Thank you." He pats me on the head and goes into the laundry room with his basket. I stand in the hallway, pursing my lips.

For lack of anything better to do, I basically spend the day cleaning. I vacuum all the floors. I clean the litter box and haul out the trash and recycling. I change our bedsheets and tidy up the clutter on the side tables in the living room. I do every dish that touches the bottom of the kitchen sink.

But this still feels like normal stuff, stuff I'd do anyway, stuff he would do, too. I'm just doing it all in one day because I've decided it's part of my new religion.

What can I do to fulfill his *desires*? Sex seems obvious. But Justin won't go near me if he thinks I'm only doing it out of obligation.

After work, I suggest we drive to his favorite thrift stop. He says he doesn't need anything. "Come oooooon," I say. "Let's just look around." He finds two giant cabinets for his new collection of Goodwill VHS tapes. I buy them. Even though I secretly hate his new collection of Goodwill VHS tapes. I finally feel like I've done an act of service.

In the evening, while waiting for the Ethiopian delivery to arrive, I reflect on my day.

The lesson I'm taking away is that fulfilling desire isn't the same thing as being quietly supportive of life. I never should have told Justin what I was doing, but I wanted his consent. Not because I thought I was doing anything potentially he'd disagree with. But because I don't trust myself to know what he wants.

I think what I realize is I need to be less afraid of my intuition. I have made mistakes in the past. And so now I'm desperate to always be told what someone needs. But what I'm really afraid of is rejection—it hurts to have your offerings of comfort rejected. The greatest gift you can give someone is sensing what they want and then giving it to them, without burdening them to ask.

Aren't I supposed to be semipsychic now?

No. Maybe that's not it at all.

Isis does not run around begging Osiris to give her tasks. She simply waits, relatively secure in the fact that she commands the entire universe. When asked for help, she helps, because she has the resources to do so. She does not go looking for problems to solve; she does not need to prove her worth through constant service. She does not feel a buzzing urge to anticipate. She trusts other people to tell her what they need. That's first. The second part is her ability to give.

DAY 175

Each of us, and everything seen, is her body, mind, and spirit.
—TIMOTHY RODERICK

Today I post how much I weigh on Instagram.
I do it to prove I'm no longer afraid of the Goddess's body; my body.
She's your body, too, by the way.

FEBRUARY

DAY 191

*If you live in the north, the idea that this is a fertility festival
may be a bit of a reach for you.*
—THEA SABIN

"If you hit black ice, you'll feel your brake pad vibrate; that means lay off. Just find a safe place to coast until you get traction."

Liza, who moved to Boston a few years ago, is giving me some tips on driving here mid-February. I'm visiting for a few days before heading to Salem, America's "Witch City," and also to celebrate some of the residual days around Imbolc, the Year of the Wheel festival that heralds the dawn of spring. Granted, the festival I wanted to attend was canceled due to Covid, but my tarot cards told me I should be here anyway, so here I am.

There is an irony in my decision to fly away from the lush, emerald hills of Northern California and into the chapped tundra of a New England winter in the name of celebrating a holiday about new life. Since my arrival, the temperature has not risen over twenty degrees. The sun hangs low, suffusing Boston's red bricks and iron gates in eerie orange light. Every time I step outside, I feel like I'm getting bitch-slapped by Frosty the Snowman. This is not a safe place for anything green.

And I need to learn what every New England and Midwestern teenager has learned about driving in the snow by the time they graduate from high school—within twenty-four hours.

"Driving here can be pretty intense," Liza says to me from the driver's seat, like a patient tutor. "Just make sure you go slow, and leave lots of room between yourself and the cars in front of you."

"I think we just ran a red light," I say, craning my neck over my shoulder to look behind us.

"We did?" Liza glances back in her rearview, the teacher voice abandoned. "Eh," she says with a shrug. "It's Boston."

"It's very pretty," I say, looking at the cumulous pillars of steam puffing out of brick buildings, and the he-man-sized snow piles heaped on every street corner. "Just intimidating."

I wanted to make a to-do of going somewhere special to celebrate Imbolc. Like Mabon and Lughnasadh, I've noticed it tends to receive very little fanfare—probably because it does not coincide with any major American holiday, the way Samhain coincides with Halloween or Yule with Christmas.

This is not for lack of trying. Imbolc is one of the four major "greater sabbats" originally described in the 1940s by Gerald Gardner, which he adapted from Ireland's Cross-Quarter holidays. According to historian Ronald Hutton, Imbolc was a famous Gaelic holiday before being Christianized into St. Brigid's Day and Candlemas. The story, as far as I've gathered, is that one February day in roughly the fifth century CE, the Catholic Roman invaders watched with concerned curiosity as the Irish pagans once again headed out into their fields and began piling up bonfire wood. They asked around and discovered this time they were set to worship a milky-breasted fertility goddess with flaming red hair. In a sweaty panic, the Romans transmuted the goddess into an abbess, allowing the pilgrims to carry out the critical business of getting drunk and lighting things on fire. Candlemas is also the day where (and I'm still a little fuzzy here) Saint Luke says you can finally take down the rest of your Christmas decorations.

By whatever name you prefer, Imbolc is meant to acknowledge that yes, we are deep inside the icebox of winter—but the return of spring is just around the corner. It is a good time to thank one's hearth (or, perhaps, your HVAC system) for getting you through the worst of the cold. There is a fiery, life-breathing goddess walking about in the snow now, ensuring the baby lambs will get their milk and something will be turning green soon. Chin up.

Later that night, Liza and I retire to her apartment with a pizza that I'm certain contains more saturated fat than exists in the entire city of San Francisco, and a case of Bennington chocolate stout. Her girlfriend greets me like an old friend.

She asks what I'm in town for, and I mention my disappointment that the larger Imbolc gathering I was hoping to attend was canceled; yet another group Witchcraft opportunity called off due to Covid.

"Let's do something here!" Liza exclaims.

"It's not even Imbolc anymore," I reply, waving her down from the ceiling. "It was last week! Seriously, I don't want to put you out." I remember the elaborate rituals she used to host with Theodora when she lived in California. They were their own Wiccan summer camps, complete with music, a buffet lunch, and an art project about our feelings.

"What the hell am I doing with all this stuff in my house if I can't use it for a situation like this?" she says, throwing open her hand-painted living room bureau doors to reveal a tidy apothecary of herbs, incense, candles, and yarn.

She picks up her family's grimoire that sits reverently on a small bookshelf in the corner of the compact living room, decoupaged by her mother in a print of faded leaves and lilies. "St. Brigid's day is about new beginnings," she says, reading from the pages. "Think about the parts of your life you want to ignite fire into, where you want to invoke passion and creativity, whether it's your family life, your career, your spirituality, or your relationship." With this last one, she gives her girlfriend's arm a squeeze and a loving glance.

Before I know it, she's handing me two sticks of cinnamon, a dried orange wheel, and a long string of searing red yarn. "Cinnamon is for purification, orange is for creativity, and red is for igniting your inner fire. As you wrap the thread around the four points of cinnamon, think about where you want to bring passion and growth into your life."

I think for a moment, staring at the objects in my hand, then begin wrapping dutifully. Within about a minute, I realize I'm doing mine completely wrong. Liza's looks like a four-pointed star—a St. Brigid's cross, with an orange in the center—which I'm realizing was probably the point. Meanwhile I have created something that looks like a St. Andrew's cross bound over an orange and held together with red tape.

"I think I did it wrong," I say, showing her my art project like she's my teacher and I'm failing second grade. She looks over and I can see a flash of something cross her face, but she quickly represses it. Liza is a master craftsman, a double-degreed professional costumer for city operas and ballet companies.

"Hey now, you made a totem with four points," she says reassuringly. "You just made it your way."

"It looks like a Martha Stewart bondage spell." I chuckle.

She puts her work down and looks me in the eye. "There is no correct way to do this, to do any of this, Diana. That's not the point of Witchcraft. You do it your way, the way you're inspired to. That's what makes it powerful. Haven't you learned that yet?"

DAY 193

Even those of us who do not occupy the Puritans' high spiritual plane are susceptible to what Mather termed the "diseases of astonishment"... We hope to locate the secret powers we didn't know we had.
—STACY SCHIFF

Today I drive to the Boston airport to pick up my sister Kim, who will be joining me on my journey to Salem. Kim is three years older than me, four inches shorter, and roughly five points hotter. Imagine if Lara Croft and Matilda Wormwood had a baby, but the baby grew up on Backstreet Boys and then got really into permaculture. Kim was a gifted honors student who composed her own piano solos, belted Christina Aguilera in the shower, and nursed a hobby obsession with the Freemasons and the Knights Templar through most of her early twenties. She's a passionate environmentalist and has a mixed relationship with the occult. In high school, I would wake up occasionally to the sound of her screaming. I'd get out of bed, open the door to her room, and chase out the "ghosts" that terrorized her while she was half asleep. Because of this, I was surprised when she responded with an exuberant yes after I asked if she'd like to pack her bags for a six-hour flight to one of the most haunted cities in America.

Pulling up to the arrivals lane, it takes me a moment to recognize her. She has dyed her chestnut hair blond and is wearing a pale, knee-length puffer coat I have never seen before. In other words, she looks like every other woman walking down Congress Street. "Who gave you the dress code before you left? And why didn't you tell me?" I say as she ducks into the rental car. I gesture to my wide knit gloves and hip-length vintage leather jacket—objects that have marked me as a clueless outsider from day one. "I don't know," she replies, looking confused, eyes darting like she's done something wrong. "It just made sense with the weather?"

We drive away from the light of Boston, a pebble in a slingshot shooting into the dark. My car flies down the freeway between skeleton forests, until the snowglobe of Salem's light starts growing on the horizon. We exit the freeway into a scene of immaculate white picket fences and stately colonial manors with candles flickering in each window. The winter-frosted glass of nineteenth-century streetlights gives the entire place a vintage Christmas undertone. I quickly realize that if you were in Salem, you might not know unless someone told you. The main drag of Essex Street, which has back-to-back metaphysical shops and tours that promise paranormal encounters, is the only giveaway. At every other angle, it is a tidy New England harbor town, full of crisp, salty air, wide houses, historical plaques, and charming redbrick sidewalks. Even the snow seems cleaner here.

Three hundred years ago, this was not so. As I learn in the fantastic history *The Witches* by Stacy Schiff, Salem in the winter of 1692 was a small outpost of feverish Puritans, swirling in darkness. The primeval forests that surrounded their soggy colony would regularly catapult their way rabid dogs, moaning cats, dagger-wielding Native Americans, and the French. News from Mother England was so delayed the colonists would sometimes spend months not knowing which (if any) politician was in charge of their safety or success. They spent the bone-numbing winters of the Little Ice Age huddled inside their kitchens, peering at each other through hearth smoke, spying through dim panes of leaded glass. Of their religion, they were fanatical, obsessive, zealous. Today we would certainly call them a cult. No one could do anything—court a lover, rebuff a suitor, argue for a raise, fight a land dispute—without quoting scripture. Puritan children, especially girls, were to do their chores, read the Bible, and sleep. The only fun permitted seems to be gossiping about which neighbors weren't performing the aforementioned tasks well enough. From under what Schiff calls this "Bible black" sky, America would receive its first brush with what we today call mass hysteria, and what the Puritans called Witchcraft.

People often look to Tituba, the woman enslaved by the town minister, Samuel Parris, when examining the ins and outs of what made the Salem colonists behave so irrationally with each other. She was the first person to actually confess to Witchcraft in public. However, according to the *Morbid: Salem Witch Trials* podcast that Kim turned on for our drive north, it's often left out that Tituba confessed to Witchcraft only after being brutally beaten by Minister Parris into doing so.

Like most people subjected to slavery, Tituba did not have great records kept about her existence. She was originally from Barbados, and historians suspect she was either Arawak-Guiana, Kalina, African, or some blend of the above. To the American Puritan, Tituba's herbal lore and folktales might read as Witchcraft (by the same token, to Tituba, the Puritans might read as hell-demons). But the Salem witch trials are not the result of some cultural miscommunication between a Black woman from Barbados and Puritan zealots from England. Tituba, like everyone else in Salem, was a Christian (at least outwardly). She could recite Scripture on a dime and was a devout prayer. The trouble with Tituba is that when she did "confess" in the farcical court of 1692 Salem, she illustrated a tale of Witchery so dazzling, so theatrical, so exciting it might as well have been *Godzilla*. Afterward, everyone in town was suddenly visited by more Witchcraft, not less. According to Schiff, people got on the stand and described tales that you and I might normally associate with a low-grade acid trip. This was the fuel needed for the trials to take off in full force. I wonder, if Samuel Parris had not beaten poor Tituba into confessing an explanation for why his daughters were suddenly screaming at him and bashing their Bibles against the wall, would the whole historical episode have simply fizzled out like a dud firework? Perhaps the home of modern Witchcraft would not be in Salem at all. New Orleans seems eager for the job. Maybe Taos.

But of course, that's not where the story ends. After Tituba "confesses," she is tossed in jail and forgotten, the Puritans lose their minds like a group of teenage boys lost on an island without a conch shell, start killing each other in the name of Christ, and now, three hundred years later, I have to fly to Salem to see all their houses.

Kim and I enter our Airbnb, the top floor of a two-hundred-year-old carriage house. Immediately we are greeted by an antique portrait of a watery-eyed Victorian child gazing at us from the prison of a peeling frame. Without any discussion, we walk across the room and turn it around to face the wall. The kitchen comes preloaded with eighteen kinds of tea, and you could roll a marble down the warped wooden floor of the living room. Kim's door wiggles in its frame, and there's an odd tapping in the ceiling, which I say is squirrels, and she says is spirits. We have arrived in Witch country.

On the podcast on the way up, I also learned that Giles Corey—the Salem man most famous for crying "more weight" as he was pressed to death *and* who was able to pass his lands to his children because of his refusal to confess—apparently cursed both the sheriff and the town of Salem with his dying breath. For three hundred years since, every Salem sheriff has died while in office or been forced out of his post due to heart or blood ailments.

One imagines that after just the first hundred years of this, even Richard Dawkins would pause before applying for the job. Yet, undeterred sheriffs continue to roll up, clutch their chests, and keel over.

Most historians agree that the Salem witch trials were not about punishing people who practiced magic. We should see this historical episode as an allegory for scapegoating, the dangers of ergot poisoning, greed, racism, rough winters, or as Stacy Schiff puts it, simply the "stubborn calcified knot of vexed small-town relations." My favorite interpretation is that the Salem witch trials are what happens when you give middle-school-age girls nothing else to play with but a King James Bible. At least some adults were using this opportunity to grab land rights and kill off their more unpleasant neighbors. It's a fantastic example of how you can weaponize a child's need to be heard.

I do not think anyone accused of Witchcraft in 1692 was actually practicing any. Most people don't. Most *Witches* don't.

And yet from it, a curse emerged.

They say magic is within us, without us; everywhere.

It's almost as if enough people insist Witchcraft is present—if it is invoked—it doesn't matter who is calling, or what year, or why. It will appear.

DAY 194

Witchcraft is not for sale.
—STARHAWK

One thing is for certain: Witchcraft is for sale in Salem. Kim and I head out to take on the bustle of downtown, and quickly discover it's a whole different landscape than the sleepy winter harbor village we drove into last night. Essex Street is basically a strip mall for occultism. We have many pleasant encounters with Witch shopkeepers, and dutifully purchase a few crystals and herb bundles. Then, in one store, I see a wicker platter labeled Tituba's Sage and Copal Smudge Sticks. I recall that Tituba was beaten by her enslaver into confessing to Witchcraft, forgotten by the children she used to sing to sleep, and left to rot in prison for a year before anyone remembered to come get her. I put the smudge stick back and leave the store.

Later in the afternoon, we walk to Proctor's Ledge, the recently discovered actual site of the Witch hangings. It's on a corner intersection about a mile from Essex Street, next to an auto shop and a CVS. Kim and I stand across the street next to the auto shop, facing the ledge.

"Can we sit for a moment and have some silence with them?" Kim asks. An SUV careens down the hill in front of us and splashes some slush onto our boots. There are two small buttresses that flank the wall of names on the ledge. We look both ways, cross the street, and each plop down on one. A few moments pass. I kick the snow, trying to think of what to say.

"Can you imagine how it must have felt. The injustice," Kim says thoughtfully. A set of tires hiss in the snow as another car passes a few feet behind our backs.

I try to imagine.

I think about the five-year-old girl who was chained up in a cell, all alone. I think about Giles Corey, and what it must be like to feel your insides squeezed out over three days. I think about Tituba and wonder how she passed the time in prison. And then I think about how many people have been hanged in this country for simply being Black. Salem has built an entire *economy* around the unjust deaths of twenty people. I think about how the Historical Marker Project still struggles to get memorials up at the physical (known) sites of lynchings during America's Jim Crow era. Perhaps because, if they were successful, about 25 percent of the American countryside would vanish under a coral reef of plaques. It would be too hard to see past them and enjoy the parts of American history we'd prefer to associate ourselves with.

I sit and stare at the names etched into the stone ledge. I imagine bodies hanging from a robust tree, uprooted long ago, hovering above my head. The skinny limbs of young elms are here now. Their winter-dead fingers reach toward the sky, backlit by the milky blue of evening.

I don't really know what I can do for you, I think to the swinging ghosts. *But if there is anything, I'd like to try. Let me know.*

I exhale, and blink.

All the light bulbs under the names turn on.

DAY 196

Witchcraft is not a step backward; a retreat into a more superstition-filled time. Far from it. It is a step forward.
—RAYMOND BUCKLAND

Kim and I decide to repair back to Boston for the day. We aren't done with Salem, of course. There is always one more amazing piece of history we've yet to gape at: the church where the currier accused the furrier in 1693; the house where Mrs. Horace Dunkinharvard slapped her stableboy in 1782. The sidewalk pebbles have their own historical plaques. At this point I'm fairly convinced that all the buildings in Massachusetts are haunted. The ones in Boston just stay open later.

After a day of oohing and aahing at the Boston Public Library, eating my first-ever lobster roll, sloshing through the Boston Common and attempting (unsuccessfully) to break into a succession of Gothic revival churches older than the United States, we are sitting in a bar called Durty Nelly's in the North End. The ceiling is low. Badges and stickers coat the back wall like scales on an armadillo. The bartender looks like he just graduated from Eagle Scouts, and in the back, a silver-haired Irishman has been given a guitar and is pounding out cheerful hymns about alcoholism and labor rights. The city's mask mandate has just been lifted. For the first time in two years, I am inside a room with strangers, listening to live music, with nothing covering my face. I sip the foam off my Guinness and it tastes like cream. I feel like I'm having an affair.

I ask Kim how she likes Salem. She stares at her whiskey a few moments and finally says, "The thing I can't get over, is that . . . none of this is actually real."

"What do you mean?" I try not to shout in her ear over the Irishman.

"It was all invented in the 1970s. I was hoping to find something . . ."

"Actually old?" I say.

"Yes!" she says. "But it all just feels fake."

I think for a moment. This was my issue when I first started. I was hoping to fall headfirst into the secrets of ancient grimoires, the kind of books that, as Ronald Hutton describes, "were thought not merely to contain information but possess powers of their own." I wanted that old-school, *Penny Dreadful* Witchcraft. I never found it, because Wicca was effectively invented in the 1940s. Kim is of course having the same problem. Like me, she believes in historical legitimacy. The older something is, the better. We went into the "oldest shop in Salem," and had to restrain our surprise when the affable proprietor admitted it was founded in 1978.

Six months ago, I had no answer to this. Today I surprise myself by saying, "It's because it doesn't matter how old something is. That's not what makes Witchcraft legitimate."

She gives me a blank look.

"When Wicca was getting started, a lot of people tried to prove that it was this long-forgotten, Stone Age, pre-Christian religion. They tried to back it up with universal customs and cave paintings. But they never got very far, except to people who already wanted to believe they were correct. And that's actually better. I mean, look at the Puritans: here is a group of people playing a seventeen-hundred-year game of telephone with God. What do they do? They go insane and start killing each other. I spent a long time wishing I could reach back through the veils of time and grab some undiscovered Celtic artifact, or unburn some book in Alexandria, and then everything I was doing would be so much clearer, so much more defensible. Magic would open up for me and I could stop doubting because I had this unquestionable, ancient thing that meant everything I was doing wasn't a fantasy or a trick I was playing on my own mind. But if I found that old book, and started using it, I'd really just be playing the same game of telephone the Puritans were playing. Possibly with similar consequences."

"Okay, but . . ." She pauses like she's trying to figure out how to say something politely. "How are you writing your book? Not to be mean, but what are you even doing if you don't know what's real?"

I freeze. I feel like someone who has just been caught cheating on a test. I stare at the thick, brown dark of my Guinness. Then I surprise myself by saying, "The history will never be perfect, and we'll never know what really happened or how people really used to practice magic. No one will ever agree on these things. So I'm trying not to see Witchcraft as a path home to the past. Not anymore. I think it might actually be a path to the future."

DAY 203

There may be witches out there who find the idea of cursing distasteful, and plenty of non-witches who feel the same.
—CORY THOMAS HUTCHESON

"**I** got robbed."

My mom's voice comes over the scratchy Bluetooth in my car. It's been about a week since I came home from Boston. I feel the blood run out of my body and have to remind myself to focus on the road.

"What? Are you okay? Where? What happened? Are you okay?" My tongue trips over itself, asking every question at once.

"I wasn't home, they just broke in and stole a bunch of things. Including"—her voice cracks—"the rings you guys gave me when you were kids."

I yell, *"Fuck!"* in front of my mother. The rings are small birthstone baubles we kids created for our mom at an after-school camp. But our family has very few real heirlooms, and we had come to think of these as such. It's the kind of thing that's worth absolutely nothing to a stranger, but everything to the person they stole it from.

She tells me she's already filed a police report, and her landlord is fixing the damage to her door. The weight of the injustice hangs around our conversation like a heavy curtain.

"Can you hex them?" she says as a joke to lighten the mood. "Aren't you doing that now?"

"No, not really," I sigh. "It's . . . complicated."

That's the quickest way to unpack the ongoing controversy behind hexing in the Witchcraft community. The Wiccan idea that any energy I put into the world, whether positive or negative, will be returned back to me three times, has a buffet of arguments for and against it that I've yet to fully digest and turn into a personal opinion. According to Meg, one of my mentors, Wicca's original prohibition on baneful magic was a midcentury effort to appear neighborly to the English Christians who would characterize any magic at all as evil. Today's Witches are less worried about following Wicca's rules (really, it's only rule) and also less concerned with appearing palatable to the Christian gaze. They have embraced the idea that balancing the scales of justice sometimes requires help . . . and ruthlessness.

Almost every other Witchcraft system besides Wicca supports the use of an occasional, well-deserved curse. But I remain hesitant to try one myself. I can't help but believe in the rule of three. Call it a lifetime growing up around suburban NorCal hippies who got starry-eyed talking about Buddhism, but the idea of karma makes a lot of sense to me. Emma, my friend who originally introduced me to Wicca, told me that she once tried to hex a rapist in high school—a noble cause to be sure. As a result, she had a streak of bad luck for a month: car trouble, illnesses, and a parade of slipups at school. She's never hexed anybody since.

"You can do a lot with positive magic," she told me. "You can focus on protecting and healing the victim, without raining hell on the perp, knowing that all that nastiness is just gonna get back on you, too."

I have been thinking about so-called baneful magic since day one of this Witchcraft journey. Would I ever feel called to do it? Can I call myself a real Witch if I never once touch the dark side? What would happen if I tried?

On the phone, I listen to my mom spiral, blaming herself, asking if she should have had a camera, a different lock on the door. She eventually asks if it was her fault.

"Of course it wasn't your fault," I insist. The moon starts rising on the edge of the freeway. It looks like a trickster, like a bat signal, like a dare.

I think it was mine.

Fifteen minutes later I pull my car into the driveway, race into the house and start yanking books off the shelf in my office, flipping through glossaries in a mad search for anything to help me recover a stolen item. Time feels critical. The thief could still be nearby with the rings.

"Why is everything a fucking *bath*?" I yell, throwing another book on the floor and running my hands through my hair. I don't need self-love. I need *help*.

Eventually I turn to the internet, where people have more vindictive concerns than what's covered in the white-light Wiccan primers that grace my bookshelf. The problem with the internet, however, is that page, after page, after page, is a hex. And only a hex. People seem far more concerned with punishing the people who wronged them than with actually getting their stuff back.

I think about the difference between vengeance and justice. As I surf through pages of angry spells, I arrive at the conclusion that I don't want to hex the thieves who robbed my mother.* It's for two reasons: the first is, it wouldn't feel nice, because I'd be too worried about the negative energy returning to me. The law of attraction probably applies in this case, and if any part of me still believes that doing baneful magic will have a baneful effect on me, I'm not convinced I won't just create the very thing I'm afraid of. I don't have enough time to convince myself otherwise.

The second reason is that I don't actually care about bringing fire and brimstone down on the thieves, who I can only assume are not having a great life. Anyone who is robbing children's jewelry from middle-class homes in rural Sonoma County is not exactly sitting on top of Maslow's hierarchy of needs. Don't get me wrong, it's not that I pity them. This is not a turn-the-other-cheek sentiment. I just assume they are already suffering, and their suffering doesn't actually solve the problem. Arguably, it has created the problem. I care more about getting back what was stolen than about putting on some dramatic Broadway show for two crusty thieves, titled *You Messed with the Wrong Sorceress, Buddy*.

Unable to find precisely what spell I need, I begin to wonder if I can cobble one together myself. "Can you just . . . make up spells? Yes. Yes you can." I read Fire Lyte's words while flipping through *The Dabbler's Guide*

---

* This assumes of course that if I wanted to, I could.

to Witchcraft. Scores of Witches agree on this point, all but declaring that DIY spells are often more effective than prewritten ones. I've never done it before, but how hard can it be?

I run to the occult shop and gather as many items as I can. They are all out of jumbo hex-reversing candles, which is a bummer, but have all the other herbs, candles, and colors I think I need.

Next I come home and take a shower. I try to imagine all the negativity running off my body, from head to toe. As I soap up, I indulge a little belief crisis—how on earth can something this tangible actually work? According to Fire Lyte, magic is most effective when it's "reasonable, clearly defined, and possible." Which is to say, paired with realistic mundane action. Magic can't make you jump off a roof and fly. It operates on the margins of what's already possible according to the laws of time and physics. In other words, it's less about supernatural powers, and more an extra boost of luck.

My mom already did what mundane actions she can. I have no further mundane actions I can take from two counties away. I am basically asking for a miracle, operating way outside the edges of magical odds. Belief seems more important now than ever. I imagine all my doubt running down the drain. *Fake it till you make it*, I think, watching the soap swirl.

I get out of the shower and lay all my collected materials out on the floor of my office: a scarf my mom gave me operating as an altar cloth, three candles for the missing rings, and a hawk feather that my mother gave me, to represent both strength and her. I place this at the top of the makeshift altar, so it looks like the light of the candles, which represent the rings, is flowing toward her. I pile crystals around the base of the candles: citrine and quartz that was given to me by a benevolent stranger in front of Lake Merritt a long time ago. I still am not sure I believe in crystals. But I feel like I need every advantage here. If nothing else, they represent altruism, despite man's baser instincts of selfishness. That feels relevant.

I spend twenty minutes casting the circle, calling the elements, invoking the deities, acknowledging the land spirits, meditating, dropping my taproot into the earth, and doing everything else I've learned to try and open my Witch eye and tap into the magical flow of the universe. I remember that the elements are in me; I am the elements. I think about Isis, all-powerful Isis, who is everything. I am Isis. Isis is me. I am everything, I am a part of everything. I try to *see* the interconnectedness of the universe, the pulsing flow of all the atoms. *I am not begging it. I am going to nudge it. Just a little.*

I open my eyes and try to light the first candle. The wick catches, then immediately sizzles out. I've stuffed too much cumin and juniper and basil around the top, so it won't light. Grumbling, I dig around my office drawers for a tool to flick out the excess herbs while some Bulgarian priestess wails over Spotify. Eventually I find a dull pair of scissors and remove bits of herbs from around the candle wick. I try lighting it again. It catches. I proceed.

I have some liturgy I've copied ahead of time from the hodgepodge of spells I found online. I try to invoke Hermes, the messenger, the runner, the fetcher. I have never in my life tried praying to Hermes; I just read online that he's the best man for jobs like this, so I try to introduce myself and ask nicely. I visualize the rings returning to my mom. Every time I start to think *what in the holy bejesus fuck are you doing, Diana,* I remind myself that I am asking myself to experience a mystery, and in order to do that I need to shut off part of my thinking brain. I am sending out a message into the network of the atoms of the world. The gods are just metaphors for what I'm trying to embody; what I'm trying to accomplish with the hidden powers of my mind. We never know what we're capable of until we try.

Eventually I just start chanting, "Return to her, return to her." I'm lost in the details of the spell I tried to create. I can't tell if I'm arguing with Hermes, or arguing with myself, seeing which inner voice will win: confidence or doubt. Chanting gets me out of this thought pattern. It really is a magic portal into a kind of dreamland, where what Starhawk calls my "Talking Self" starts to quiet, and I actually feel like I'm connecting with my "Deep Self," the divine, wise, compassionate version of me that exists beyond time and matter. For a few minutes, I successfully feel light and woozy and one with all the atoms in my office. That is, until my throat starts to itch. I think the essential oil blend in the censer might be a little too strong.

Finally I pick up the citrine and quartz and shuffle them in my hands. I feel a warm sensation go through my body, a lightness, a relief—just like Liza told me she felt when she knew a crystal was working with her. I almost can't believe it. I try so hard not to question it. They feel like luck, like magnification.

I am not sure when to stop, so I keep cycling through the chanting, shuffling the crystals in my hand for a few minutes. Then I hear a voice in my head that comes through hard and clear, like a giant copper bell: *"If the rings are supposed to return to her, they will."*

I open my eyes. I am searching for that clicking feeling that means I was successful. I don't feel like I've clicked anything into place. But part of the spell I created involved burning the spell candle for a week.

There's still some time for the magic to build, to float into the world and do my bidding.

DAY 205

Connecting to your ancestors is the first step in your magical practice.
—LORRAINE MONTEAGUT

Today I am attending The Emerging Paths, a neopagan convention that effectively replaced Pantheacon—the largest neopagan convention in the country. Pantheacon shut down in 2020 after upheavals around transphobia, nepotism, poor treatment of presenters, and more. Sad to learn that this long-standing community gathering had self-destructed, I have been very excited to finally—finally!—attend a large gathering of neopagans and Witches with this new in-person con.

So today, when I am yet again staring at my computer screen, I'm trying very hard to remain excited and not bitter that the event organizers have done the responsible thing and moved the convention online due to Covid.

I have signed up for a few different panels. Today's is Starhawk's, titled "Wrestling with the Complexities of Heritage." The description reads: "What do we do when our feelings about our own ancestry are profoundly complicated? As a Jew, a Pagan, an advocate for justice for Palestine, and a woman, there are aspects of my heritage I [Starhawk] love and embrace with pride, and others that I find deeply oppressive. This workshop is an opportunity to honestly confront some of the complexities in our heritages through brave conversation, meditation, and ritual. Every heritage includes both those who fought for justice and those who perpetuated injustice. While this workshop is offered from a Jewitch perspective, it's open to anyone who wants to explore these issues."

After a talk about her personal thought journey around the Israeli-Palestinian conflict, and how we can go about embracing ancestors we also find problematic, Starhawk plays a gentle rhythm on a drum as our *Brady Bunch* face tiles crowd the screen. She leads us in a trace, inviting us to go deep into a cave, to meet our early ancestors, and hear what they have to say to us.

I want to go along with Starhawk, but there's a notable speed bump: I have absolutely no interest in talking to my ancestors. I mean of course I'm interested in knowing where I come from. But historically, whenever I have tried to find out more about my progenitors from those that are still living, I usually regret asking. Either nobody knows anything, or they start sharing anecdotes of abuse, neglect, and abandonment with the same ceremony afforded to a conversation about whether whole ear corn is on sale this week at Safeway. Thorn Mooney says ancestral connections are a critical part of the Craft. Lorraine Monteagut and Juliet Diaz have several methods for contacting your ancestors and cite them as the very source from whence a Witch (especially a Witch of color) can draw her power. But I am having trouble mustering the desire to want to talk to mine, because for the most part they seem like certified assholes.

That's one part of the problem. The second part is that I'm a white American. Which means I, like many children, spent a portion of my public education years sitting in a plastic school chair under fluorescent lights learning about things like the Trail of Tears, and the African slave trade, and the California governor's program whereby Europeans could exchange Native American scalps for money, while also being told to sit still, be quiet, and simply write this information down. In other words, I have been trained to recognize, but not engage with, my ancestors and their misdeeds. I remember feeling little internal moments of shock while sitting in class, and then the sensation of my mind backing off, preserving itself with distance. From there, the walls of logic are built over time, to keep the uncomfortable information at bay: "It was so long ago." "Things have changed." "It was a different world. It wasn't me, so it's not my mess to clean up." Thusly we give ourselves continued permission—I gave myself permission—to feel nothing about the very bad things my colonial ancestors very probably did. I pride myself on being a good student.

You could argue not *all* of my ancestors were complete assholes. That's just statistically improbable. One of them knit me a pretty incredible baby blanket. Maybe my long-ago ancestors faced harsh conditions and brutal migrations and had to overcome incredible odds to survive long enough to have the kids who would have the kids who would eventually have me. But that's me guessing again. And even if they did suffer, I'm not sure precisely what that excuses.

Which brings me to my final, and most fatal, point: I don't think my ancestors would like me. I'm not sure I can heal them, because I'm not sure if they want to be healed. The only thing I really know is that a vast number of them were Christians, and I cannot shake the certainty that they would not approve of what I'm doing, let alone let me borrow their power like some kind of metaphysical jet fuel. Maybe my female ancestors are cheering me on whenever I do things like drive a car or have consensual, premarital sex. Or maybe they think I'm a whore. Patriarchy is held up by women all over the world.

Of course, I would like to imagine there are some long-forgotten, ancient Witches in my bloodline. My great-grandmother had one green eye and one brown, and I inherited heterochromia from her in my own eyes. My sister sees ghosts. My mom brews herbal tonics. My name is Diana, for crying out loud. Surely this book should be about me uncovering my lost magical birthright. But I can't write that book. Probably because whatever shining conception of those ancestors I *want* to have seems too unbelievably flattering to be true. Of course, I want to feel like there is a hope that has been expressed in me, that generations of ancestors are counting on me, watching me, rooting for me to do better than they did before. But I can't. It feels too fantastically indulgent for me to believe there was some Stone Age matriarchal utopia from which I descended, and can find again, thousands of years later in my blood to help me navigate the future—no matter how bad I want it.

Because of all this, it's probably not surprising that when I make an earnest effort to fall under Starhawk's trance, go into my cave, and meet my ancestors, there is no one there.

I get tired of staring at the dark, so instead I open my eyes, and stare at my screen, watching her earnest, wizened face, eyes closed as she taps her drum, pretending I'm going along with it. Pretending I'm still not failing at this most basic connection to my ancestors; pretending I'm not failing at being a Witch.

I don't know why I was so worried about indulging in fantasy when I began the journey into Witchcraft, or why I was so concerned with the idea that I would be tempted into playing make-believe. The deeper I get, the more and more I find myself staring into the unwashed face of reality.

DAY 208

Diana went into the street; she took the bladder of an ox and a
piece of witch-money . . .
—CHARLES LELAND

I don't have a great desire to talk to my more recently dead ancestors. And I can't imagine the ancient ones. But I can't ignore this fundamental part of Witchcraft either. Maybe I can get something out of the land where my ancestors once walked.

On this justification, today I book a pair of plane tickets for Justin and me to visit the UK. This is the home, according to the people who analyzed my spit a few years ago, that some of my ancestors left behind when they came to America. England is also the home of Gerald Gardner, the father of modern Witchcraft, and sacred sites like Stonehenge. I can't think of a better ancestral pilgrimage.

I'm still waiting on the spell for the return of my mother's jewelry to finish percolating out in the world. It's been six days, and still nothing. A lot of things feel in process. So I spend an evening with friends at Eli's Mile High Club in Oakland to take my mind off things. This is the kind of place that offers Montucky Cold Snacks on tap and where you can barely find the toilet in the bathroom through all the graffiti. It's a mellow night—we sit outside with clusters of punks huddling under heat lamps. Eventually, the chill of the evening (low forties, somewhat radical for the Bay Area) gets the better of us and we call it a night.

I get into my car at 11:30 p.m., turn the key, and see my gas light illuminate. I sigh. It's been on since yesterday, but I keep dragging my feet on filling up. Inflation is reaching terrifying heights, and I've been holding out for a station that will still sell for less than five dollars a gallon. But now I don't have a choice. I decide to stop at the first one I see so I don't get stranded in the middle of the night by the side of the road, at the mercy of roadside assistance.

Driving down the vacant lanes of West MacArthur, I see a station. And the gas is $4.59. What luck.

Don't stop here, says a voice in my head.

I assume it's paranoia. It's late. This isn't a great neighborhood. But I need gas. *Don't be a baby. This isn't even the worst part of the city.*

I pull my car up to a pump. The station is desolate, fluorescent lighting glows like a barrier against the moonless night. I swipe my card in the machine and put in my zip code, imagining eyes on my back, trying to keep my spine straight.

As I turn around to put the nozzle in my car, I hear footsteps come up the sidewalk.

I tense. I pretend to look at the dim interior of the station's convenience store, catching the stranger out of the corner of my eye. "It's closed," he says, still walking toward me. He has his hands in his pockets and his hood is up.

"Yep, looks like it," I say, turning my head and looking him in the eye. My blood pressure rises, but I don't blink. This is what they tell women to do: "Look at the face, and they are less likely to attack you."

He breaks eye contact first and walks right past me, toward a trailer I suddenly notice is parked next to the gas station garage. I hear the trailer door open and then thwap shut. I realize he probably lives there.

I unclench a little, chastise myself for being so worried. My tank is half full, the pump is still going.

Then I hear a bike approaching. A man in a pink sweatshirt, on a small BMX, is pedaling toward me. *Is this the slowest gas pump on earth*, I think, watching the numbers on the dial crawl. I recall Thea Sabin and all her advice on shielding. I imagine beams of sparking energy radiating off of me, like a force field.

"You wanna buy a burger?" says the man on the bike. His speech is slurred. He holds out a milkshake and a greasy brown Burger King sack. His lips are lined in white.

"I'm good, thank you, though." I try to speak clearly and politely.

He scoots the bike closer to my body. He's three feet away from my face, and I feel myself lean back toward my car. He starts going off on a rant I can't entirely make out. He speaks too fast. I think he is asking me for help getting his backpack back.

"I can't help you with that, I'm sorry. I don't know where your backpack is," I say, shaking my head and trying to speak in a tone that evokes both kindness and "screw off." I look back to my gas pump, praying he will move on.

"You got a couple bucks you can help me out with?" he says, his voice suddenly crystal clear.

This is the part where later I will realize I fucked up.

"Yeah, you know what, I do," I say. Because I do. Because I feel bad for him.

I pull out my wallet. I grab two one-dollar bills and hand them over. He leans forward.

"What else you got in there . . ." he whispers softly, closing the distance between our bodies. He grabs my wrist.

"Hey," I say, and twist my wrist in his grasp.

He lurches forward toward the wallet, almost falling off the bike. His milkshake spills on my arm, sticky pink goo flying everywhere. He grabs my other wrist. I scream, "*Hey!*" ripping his hands off me. My legs scoot me back a few feet, away from my car, out of his grasp.

I look up. A beat of primal fear goes through me.

He is right next to my gas pump, the flow still open. My keys are still in the ignition.

He gives me one last hungry stare, glances behind me, then rides off.

I turn around and the man in the hoodie, the first man who walked up to me, is suddenly there. He's wearing a surgical mask and holding a thin broom upright in his hand, like a sword. He shakes his head toward the man riding away on the bike, then lowers the broom. He glances at me once, then turns around and starts walking back to his trailer.

I don't know what to say. I need to say something.

"Thank you," I finally call. "That was really nice of you, to come out,"

I nearly yell at his back. It feels pathetic. But I mean this more than I've meant anything I've ever said in my life. I think about offering him money, but two dollars feels more crass than kind.

He shrugs and doesn't turn around. I hear the door to his trailer thwap shut.

I'm alone again. The fluorescent gas station bulbs hum above my head.

I remove the gas nozzle and put it back in its holster. I duck inside my car and put my hands on the steering wheel, realize I'm tremoring. I wipe the milkshake off on my jeans. I want to burn my clothing.

Instead, I lock my doors and pull out onto the road.

I think about how much worse that could have been.

The man on the bike could have stolen my car. He could have doused me in gasoline.

I know better than everything that just happened. *Why didn't I listen to the little voice, why didn't I go somewhere else?*

I think about the man with the broom, and how I feel in his debt.

I think about all my anxiety, and try to turn it into a ball of glowing, happy light. I imagine it floating in front of me. Then, I send it to his trailer, like a streaming cloud.

It feels pretty feeble, in exchange for saving me. Especially considering I won't ever know if it worked.

DAY 209

The problem is . . . I'm a Witch, so by worrying about things, I
draw them to me, so then they actually happen.
—AUGUSTEN BURROUGHS

I wake up the next morning and text Lauren in bed, telling her I narrowly avoided a mugging on the way home from the bar. It seems too weird that my mother's house got burgled and I almost got mugged within the same couple of weeks. Old me would think it's a coincidence. New witchy me is convinced my family has been cursed.

That is a lot of crime in a short period of time, she texts back. *Could be Pluto return. Maybe we get you some new protection stuff.*

But I just bought a ton of protection stuff! I write back before realizing I've been using it all for the protection-and-property-return candle for my mom. I wonder if I accidentally gave her all my luck. This is the second time something bad has happened to me after I've tried a spell. And I'm not even trying to hex people. So maybe what's happening is what Blanca told me back in October: if you want to change the universe, you have to pay a price. So because I was trying to shield myself, protect myself, and get stolen property back to my mother . . . did I inadvertently bring about a stream of bad luck?

No, that makes no sense.

Maybe I manifested the mugging by my very trepidation about going to an empty gas station late at night in a bad neighborhood. If I hadn't worried about it, would that energy have been attracted to me in the first place? But by that token, wouldn't that mean everything bad that happens to anyone is their own fault, because their thoughts and fears brought it on themselves? No, that's not fair. That's the main critique against the law of attraction. But then . . .

"Oh fuck this," I yell, and shake the bed covers off me as if they were my own thoughts. It's too hard. There are too many options trying to trace why something could have happened. I feel paranoid. I'm getting exhausted with these circular ideas. How Witches don't feel dizzy every day with all this superstition, all these options about why something happened and what everything means, is beyond me.

It's coming to be an almost daily occurrence that if I think about something awful, I worry I am manifesting it, and so try to shut down the nasty thought as fast as possible. Instead of them getting better, I'm finding intrusive thoughts harder to control. The more I try to get away from one, the more it intrudes, and the more I become worried I am either manifesting it or sensing it happening in the future, and that I now must do something to prevent it. I then wonder if I am in fact on the path not to becoming a Witch, but to becoming a delusional megalomaniac. Since beginning Witchcraft, I am starting to fear being alone with my own mind.

According to psychologist Arlin Cuncic and psychiatrist Dr. Steven Gans, the belief in one's thoughts to manifest real-life outcomes is actually considered a part of generalized anxiety disorder. One type of magical thinking frequently seen in GAD is called "thought-action fusion," where the afflicted believes that "thoughts are the equivalent of actions and that thoughts can make actions come true."

But that's just Witchcraft, I think upon reading the second definition. The authors even acknowledge this, saying, "What one person calls magical thinking, another person calls a belief system. Sometimes, magical thinking helps us interpret the world around us in an adaptive way. If it causes significant distress or disruption in your life, however, it's advisable to reexamine your magical thinking."

In Witchcraft, I believe that the oft-repeated notion that thoughts are spells is intended to make us reconsider the negative things we think about ourselves and others. For example, if we continuously tell ourselves we are worthless, our reality will be that we believe we are, and thus our quality of life will plummet, and we will tolerate others treating us poorly. It goes hand in hand with modern Witchcraft's goals of self-empowerment. The direction in which I'm taking it—paranoia—is not the spirit behind the "thoughts are spells" message.

Still, I am now seeing the dark side of this philosophy. From day one, I have felt that in order to be successful at Witchcraft, I had to lasso my thoughts, cleanse my imagination, and have total control over my mind. This is how I would more precisely *see* my desires and manifest them into reality. Instead, I have become paranoid of everything I think. I don't feel empowered. I feel out of control.

What I probably need to learn, and what Witchcraft hasn't yet taught me (or I haven't been willing to learn), is how to embrace some stoicism, to accept the things I cannot change: to let the little things *go*.

Later that day, I unchain myself from my computer and go into the back garden for a splash of sunshine on my face. I'm leaning over a stump, picking clover tops to feed to the chickens, one of their favorite snacks. I do this almost every day. I find my mind circling the question of whether I am lucky or unlucky, if I am manifesting suffering or if everything lately has been a coincidence.

I grab a clover head and freeze. I stare at it, turn it around, blink a few times. I hold it up next to the other clover tops in my hand, just to be sure. I count the leaves one, two, three times.

It's a four-leaf clover. A one-in-ten-thousand occurrence.

I can't help it. I feel an immediate sense of relief, like something has been lifted off my chest. But whether I manifested it just by sitting here and thinking about luck, or it's a sign from the heavenly forces, I'm still not sure.

It means the bad luck is over, my subconscious says back. *Chill out.*

DAY 211

We should be at least a little suspicious of folktales about witches' hexes as purely malevolent for the sake of chaos and evil.
—CORY THOMAS HUTCHESON

I'm wondering if I made the right call by ~~being too chicken to~~ refusing to hex the people who burgled my mother's house. It's been over a week now, my spell candle has burned down into a Cronenberg mass of black wax and dried basil, but the missing rings have not yet appeared. So today I get Michael Hughes on the phone for a conversation. I do this because he has practically made a living out of hexing. He is the author of *Magic for the Resistance* and the organizer behind #bindTrump. Today I read in the news that Russia is still invading Ukraine, and his online groups are already planning a mass spell to hex Putin. On the phone, he listens patiently to my concerns about baneful magic, and seems to appreciate my skeptical approach to Witchcraft. I also am curious about why he prefers the term "Magician" over "Witch," and ask him about the distinction.

"I became disillusioned with Wicca when I found out it was a modern religion, invented by Gerald Gardner, cobbled together from Freemasonry and his own little kinks, based on faulty Margaret Murray history about this neolithic goddess cult and all that," he says. His voice is breezy, kind, casual. He talks to me as if we're coworkers having a beer after work. "I think Wicca kind of fell apart when people started having a better understanding of the history. Also, 'Witch' is such a profoundly laden term, there's just so much good and bad associated with it."

"I agree," I reply. "The more I get into Witchcraft, the more I find the principles behind Wicca, and Witchcraft in general, really beautiful. But Witchcraft is almost synonymous with rebellion. I'm starting to find this frustrating. Do you think Witchcraft can ever become truly mainstream?"

"Magic could become mainstream, because magic is just tools," he says. "I've always said that when my wife's Jewish grandmother lit a candle every time she knew my wife was getting on a plane, she was doing magic. We can come to grips with magic as a culture, but I think a 'Witch' will maybe always be seen as transgressive."

Then I get into the heart of my fears: "Have you ever felt any kind of blowback from your hex work that you feel like you can identify?"

"I've always been a proponent of nonviolence," he replies thoughtfully. "But at the same time, if Nazis are knocking down your door, then you get the baseball bat and you beat the Nazis in the head. I have a firm sense of ethics; I don't feel like I've ever done anything that would've generated blowback, because the things I do are generally protective of other people. I do feel like sometimes life is messy and there are unintended consequences. Self-defense can become a tricky thing—how far do you go? I've certainly done things in my life where I look back and wish I'd had a little more wisdom. But if you start from a place of protection and self-defense, no, I don't think you get blowback."

"Have you ever been threatened with a hexing or binding?" I ask.

"Holy shit, yeah," he says, and guffaws into the phone. "Every right-wing Witch, I'm sure, has tried to throw something at me. Someone made a Wanted poster of me for conducting 'black magic.' I've been told that there are some Russian occultists and Witches who have focused on me and our group and what we're doing. I've gotten hex threats and death threats."

"That must be stressful," I reply. Because what else do you say to someone who says they are getting death threats for psychic work?

"Well again, that's where my what could be described as illogical paradoxical thinking comes in," he says. "The thing I try to tell everybody who's getting into occultism, or Witchcraft, or magic: believe that your magic works, but don't believe that the people who are trying to harm you, that their magic works. I know that sounds like a contradiction, a paradox. But it's served me very well. My attitude is 'Fuck you. You can't touch me. I'm sorry. I'm invincible and nothing you're going to do is going to affect me.' Because when you start believing that people are after you or hexing you all the time, psychologically, you can become paranoid. Like every bad thing that happens is a curse. I think when you're doing good work, that has its own natural protective element. I believe there is a moral arc of the universe, and when we are doing righteous things, compassionate things for other people and for other beings, that is recognized."

The devil's advocate in me wants to point out that "good work" is frustratingly relative. What I think is a righteous act can be someone else's sin, even if it makes no sense to me. So how does the universe know which way to bend? We're just back at subjective square one: if I believe what I'm doing is good, it will protect me. And if I have a doubt (such as the baneful magic coming back to me threefold), I'll just end up paranoid.

I wonder how much of Witchcraft relies on hero-level self-confidence. I wonder if I'll ever get there.

I wonder if I want to.

MARCH

)) ● (((

DAY 215

Magic is something used by those who have no power.
—SUZANNAH LIPSCOMB

Today, my sister Nicole comes over to drop off some Girl Scout cookies. Nicole is seven years my senior, the leader of our family's sibling trio, a preppy, elegant brunette with a perfect smile who has been cooler than me for as long as I've been alive. I once hiked for twelve days in the Sierra Nevada. She hiked for a month in the Himalayas. She's been a nurse in Oakland for sixteen years (most of it in the ER) and is the mother of my niece and nephew. Although she's too classy to ever make fun of us, she at least seemed immune to the "woo-woo spiritual" bugs that bit Kim and me when we were teenagers. As far as I know.

I come downstairs to greet her and she's staring at her phone. Her face falls into a frown. She moans, "Oh *nooo*."

"What's up?" I ask.

"Someone at Miles's preschool has stomach flu."

She looks up at me. It's like I can already see the bags under her eyes. Miles, my nephew, is three. If he's up all night, she's up all night.

I want to say something that will help her. I feel impotent.

"I'll light a candle for you," I blurt.

"Oh my god please do." She says it quickly, like she means it. There's a beat of silence. This exchange seems to take both of us by surprise.

I don't think either one of us really knows what I mean.

But later that day, I go inside my office and pick up a white candle. I imagine the four corners, just a quick little summoning. I chant, "Miles will be healthy and happy, and he will sleep through the night." I don't know how many times, but at a certain point, I notice my mood shift, as if I have been briefly meditating. I have been told that this sensation—this certainty that settles over your brain and body—means your spell has worked, that you have successfully shifted the cosmos to your will. I light the candle and imagine my intention drifting away, toward the smiling face of my nephew.

If the Christian serenity prayer is "God grant me the serenity to accept the things I cannot change, courage to change the things I can, and the wisdom to know the difference," the Witch's serenity prayer is probably "Goddess grant me the serenity to accept the things I cannot change, courage to change the things I think I can't, and enough candles on hand to make a difference."

DAY 220

We used fetishes (objects fashioned of feathers, skins, and bones)
in ceremonies to honor our animal brothers and sisters, and in
an effort to communicate and bridge the gap between animal
and human, human and divine . . . it was believed that the fetish
put you in sympathy with the animal energy.
—SILVER RAVENWOLF

I go out into the yard just after dusk, to ensure all the chickens are safely inside their coop. It's a leftover habit from when they were younger and couldn't find it alone in the dark. At twilight, they would try to nuzzle behind their waterer, or jam their tiny heads between the fence and a rock. We would lift up their confused, peeping bodies and gently place them up in the safe dark of the coop, until they could figure it out on their own.

I walk up to the fence and immediately see something is amiss. The chickens are all inside, but they are not alone. There is a small gray pigeon walking around on the floor. He occasionally stops and bobs his head up at me, as if equally confused about how on earth he got there. I sigh and manually open the coop door, to begin the Benny Hill sketch of getting him out.

He darts and runs but does not fly. I watch his gait for a minute. His right wing is injured, mangled at the joint on his back.

A hawk has been in the neighborhood. Two days ago, it dove right into the chickens' run. From inside the house, I heard them squawking in a way I've never heard before. I quite literally ran outside, saw what was happening (or about to happen), and waved the hawk away. But I have seen it circling a few times overhead since. I have also seen it at Nicole's house a few miles away, trying to make a snack of the neighborhood mourning doves.

I have a feeling this pigeon in my yard was to be a tasty supper. But the hawk didn't complete the kill, and now it's my problem. Correction: I'm choosing to make it my problem. Call it an overzealous softness. I stare at the pigeon as it sits a few feet from me, cocking its head side to side. It should be in a nest, high in a tree, far away from me and fast asleep. I'm sure this is what we would both prefer. Instead, it is sitting in the dirt, defenseless, quietly waiting for something to come finish killing it.

After ten minutes of the two of us flapping and darting under bushes, I manage to catch it. I hold its wild body in my hands, feeling electric. I stride toward the house, its heartbeat fluttering against my palms faster than a kick drum. I'm afraid it will die from fear before I can get it into the towel-draped milk crate I've prepared on the deck. But eventually we both make it. I put in a small dish of water and a quarter handful of dried mealworms, cover the crate with a towel, and go inside and look up animal rescue centers.

Later that night on the couch, a thought occurs to me. I text Lauren.

ME: So here's a question, if you feel like weighing in. I attempted that spell to bring back my mom's stolen rings about ten days ago (they still aren't back). At the end of the ritual, I wrapped a black candle in red string, attached the hawk feather she gave me (to represent her), and lit the candle every day until it finished burning down, which was two days ago.

Since it burned down, a hawk has been visiting us. It tried to attack the chickens, and I just caught a pigeon with its wing half ripped off in the coop. I've also seen it at my sister's house.

LAUREN: Congrats, Diana. You found your animal spirit.

ME: The pigeon or the hawk?

LAUREN: Oh, the hawk. You are balancing your energies here. You summoned your rage, which is the hawk. A lot of you is respite and protection, which is the shelter of the coop.

ME: I was trying so genuinely hard not to be angry during the ring ritual, though. And I was very clear that the hawk represented my mother. Not an actual hawk. But now I'm wondering if I accidentally performed sympathetic magic.[*]

LAUREN: So, Diana. Here is what I've learned about you, in my limited expertise, so please correct me if I'm wrong. You project very accommodating and sweet (which is not wrong). But most of you is actually truly ferocious. Which is fascinating. So you being both shelter *and* hawk makes total sense to me.

ME: But it was supposed to be about my *mom*. Not me. Not animal spirits!

LAUREN: Some people fucked with your mom. You are going to put it somewhere.

ME: I didn't mean to take it out on a pigeon!

LAUREN: Your command of hawks will get stronger.

ME: Is magic just a potato cannon?

LAUREN: Sorta like buckshot, yeah. Is the hawk actually killing your chickens?

ME: It tried to.

LAUREN: But did it manage to?

---

* Sympathetic magic, according to Raymond Buckland, is the oldest form of magic, based on imitation and representation. For example, "If a life-size clay model of a bison was made, then attacked and 'killed' . . . then a hunt of the real bison should also end in a kill." In my case, I take it to mean: if you want something to return to your mother, use something from your mother. Not a hawk.

ME: No, the chickens are super protected. With fencing. The real kind, not psychic.

LAUREN: So the hawk is out for hurts but not kills. Which means you've jerked its chain. It isn't out of control, this rage of yours.

ME: So this whole scene with the hawk and the pigeon is just a reflection of my emotional state. Not really a "summoning"?

LAUREN: I mean define summoning.

ME: I don't really know. I didn't know "animal spirits" were a thing in Witchcraft. I think of that as a Native American thing.

LAUREN: They exist in all practices I know of. How they exist is variable. But a lot of us have . . . I don't want to say minions, but it's minions. Turns out you have a minion.

ME: Okay, how do I get my minion to stop hurting pigeons?

LAUREN: Eh, communication issue.

LAUREN: Also, hawks eat birds, so what you really want is to have it eat birds not in your yard.

ME: Is the takeaway here that I shouldn't try and do spells for other people even if they ask? Or that I should be way more careful what I use to summon things (i.e., not hawk feathers. I should have used my mom's hair or something.).

LAUREN: I think the lesson here is to build relationship. To me this is an on-ramp. It's you and this bird and your feelings. I recommend a candlelit meditation with the hawk.

LAUREN: Okay let's try this a different way. Why do you assume you did something wrong?

ME: I wanted stolen property returned to my mom. Instead a predator is in my backyard attacking my birds. This is not what I ordered.

LAUREN: One-third of my psychic events have not been useful at all. Like I see a fire and then it happens. But not in a way I could prevent. And that is most of power. It's slamming the damn thing on the counter and yelling, "goddamn it."

Later, I run all of this by Justin, who is slightly less convinced than Lauren that I am capable of summoning a hawk.

"Maybe," he offers, appearing to give his next words careful thought. "We live near woodlands that host raptors and happen to have their favorite snacks in our backyard."

"That's why we've lived here for two years and have never seen a hawk until last week?" I counter.

He shrugs. It's not enough for him.

I go to sleep, remembering that hawk feathers are also a symbol of Isis.

DAY 221

Crowley's book remains complex and perhaps a hazardous undertaking.
—GUY BERNARD AND ANTONY LAWRENCE

This morning Lauren follows up with me from our conversation last night, asking if my mother's rings have returned.

No, I reply, like I'm telling a teacher I didn't finish my homework. *It was too big of an ask.*

Do you want to try summoning a demon?

I pause.

Can a demon . . . help with this?

I'll bring over some materials, she texts.

Later that day, a Trader Joe's paper bag appears at my doorstep. I peer inside. There's a bottle of graveyard dirt, a vial of coffin nails, a mottled key-cross with a squirrel's spine tied up with ribbon, and two books: *Low Magick*, by Lon Milo DuQuette, and a copy of something called *The Goetia*.

Lauren has left me a Post-it note of instructions: "*Low Magick* pgs 19–31, 155–169 / apply to pg 42 of *Goetia*." I stare at the note. Then I stare at the books.

The Goetia—also known as *The Lesser Key of Solomon, Clavicula Salomonis Regis*, or *The First Book of the Lemegeton*—is hard to date officially. The version I have was translated from Latin, Greek, French, and Hebrew in Baroque England by the order of the Secret Chief of the Rosicrucian Order. Put simply, it is a manual for evoking the biblical King Solomon's seventy-two demons, which the medieval occult book the *Testament of Solomon* tells us he tamed to do his bidding.

This is it. That real Dan Brown shit. Just holding it in my hands feels like breaking into a museum with Nicolas Cage.

Opening *The Goetia*, however, is like running headfirst into a spiderweb of nineteenth-century pomp. The book tells me that the best time to summon a demon is on the eighth day of the month, a Tuesday, and during a waxing moon phase. By sheer luck, all three of those things are true today. But that's about where my luck runs out. For example, to create the Secret Seal of Solomon, an object I should have present for every ritual, I must begin that work on a Tuesday or Saturday at midnight while the moon is both waxing and in Virgo. The seal must be drawn upon virgin parchment paper using the blood of a black cock that has never ridden a hen, and then perfumed with "alum, raisin dried in the sun, dates, cedar and lignum aloes." The Seal of Solomon is but one object in a bank run of lion skins, silk cords, brass trinkets, and mathematical formulas I am told I need in order to summon any one of the seventy-two demons described in the ensuing pages. Before each summoning ritual, I must also ensure I have cleansed myself with fasting and prayer, and have not defiled myself "by any woman in the space of a month."*

In the introduction, Aleister Crowley admits freely that the demons described in the text are metaphors, "portions of the human brain." But that doesn't seem to stop him from insisting that you do, in fact, require all these instruments and astrological alignments in order to activate those parts of your brain.

Assuming you can build the recommended wizard's palace in your living room, then the actual conjuring of the demon begins. This consists chiefly of arguing with it. *The Goetia* lists eight different tirades (in order), with which the magician is instructed to lambast the demon about why he's not showing up yet. The seventh tirade actually has me threatening to bind him "into the Lake of Flame and Brimstone" unless he comes upstairs right now to do what I say (which begs the question about where he's coming from in the first place). This preplanned argument strikes me as presumptuous. In a word: rude.

I am not going to argue with a demon, I vow to myself. *I don't care what Aleister Crowley says.*

Lon Milo DuQuette's book *Low Magick* is a little more forgiving. He breaks down the bombastic tone of *The Goetia* into modern language and philosophies, explaining that Solomonic magic is, at its root, about humility. When Solomon sought to build the ultimate temple, he was able to harness scores of demons not because he asked God for power and strength, but because he asked for "an understanding heart."

This is the secret of Solomon, according to DuQuette: the realization that the demon and I are actually made from the same "capital-G Good stuff." Demons (as well as angels, and spirits of any kind) are colorful metaphors for the cascading hierarchy of all natural forces of the universe. Thus, "a true Solomon is a proactive citizen of both heaven and hell. A true Solomon is, in fact, encouraged by the Great G God Almighty to conjure the devils and put them to work doing good things!"

---

* I am a woman. I briefly wonder if masturbation counts. *The Goetia* does not specify.

So I have to summon a demon, believe there is good in him despite what everyone else says, and then, knowing I am pure of heart, send him out to run an errand for me.

I am suddenly reminded of several of my past relationships. *I have been training my entire life for this.*

I start prepping the circle.

First, I need a triangle with which to trap the demon. I go into the kitchen and grab an iron trivet, handmade and gifted by a blacksmith friend. I can't imagine anything better, whether or not it does occasionally balance pots of baked ziti. I find the symbol of my demon online and print out two copies—a florid ordeal with lots of curved edges and twisted lines—and smack one on my T-shirt with Scotch tape and place the other in the middle of the triangle.

My demon of choice, I should mention, is named Foras. Lauren picked him out for me. Among his many talents—like imparting knowledge of herbs, logic, and ethics—is helping you recover lost items. *The Goetia* provides an illustration of him: a short, stocky man with shoulder-length black hair and a Neanderthal brow. He seems deceptively, benignly human, with the notable exception of his erection, which is the width of his arm and stretches north from his pelvic bone to the top of his shoulder. He holds it up calmly with two hands.

I turn the lights off, cast my circle of protection, call the corners, acknowledge the land spirits, invoke the Goddess and the God, and then really because I feel like we've been talking lately, I call Isis out by name. The air is thick with the competing scents of juniper incense, sage, and frankincense.

I plop myself down into the circle, close my eyes, and start to think about my intention. I really, really think about it. I think about justice. I think about how I don't get any joy from malice. I think about King Solomon. I try to think about what it means to have "an understanding heart."

Then I open my eyes and try to summon a demon.

I start with argument number one. When I recite, "I am armed with the power of the *supreme majesty*," I mean it. When I command Foras to appear before me "without any deformity or tortuosity," I mean it.

When I say, "For thou art conjured by the name of the *living* and *true god, Helioren*, wherefore fulfil thou my commands," I stumble, because I am not sure I'm pronouncing "Helioren" correctly, but I do mean it. I'm at a point where I basically just assume everything and every god is a metaphor for Isis, and Isis is a metaphor for the interconnectedness of all life. The larger point I'm clinging to is that Foras and I are made of the same stuff, and that stuff is basically Isis, and Isis and I are cool, so Foras and I should be cool. The transitive property strikes again.

I stare at the paper circle with Foras's seal, sitting in the iron trivet. Nothing happens.

I start on speech number two, "The Second Conjuration."

I fumble on the pronunciation of "*Zabaoth*," which occurs in a paragraph where I am, for some reason, reminding the demon about the plagues of Egypt.

Be confident, I think, *be confident*.

But eventually I realize in order to stay confident, I have to put *The Goetia* down. The language of Aleister Crowley is exotic and wonderous, but his confidence does not make me feel confident. It makes me feel like Mickey Mouse screwing around in a tower with mops.

I also realize I'm going to have to start imagining Foras in the iron circle. He's not going to *actually* appear.* I'm not entirely sure I want a pint-sized Neanderthal with a thirty-five-inch erection to pop into my bedroom. So I make an effort to imagine a small version of his form there. He shows up blue for some reason. I don't question my mind anymore in ritual. Self-critique is for the daytime.

I say to the hologram, "Find the rings that were stolen from my mother and return them to her. Do not harm anyone in the process. You have one month."

I pick *The Goetia* back up and officially send him off with a grandiloquent speech, reminding him once again not to hurt anyone, and only to do the errand I specifically requested.

I uncast the circle and release the corners. I remove the tape from

---

* Right?

the Foras seal on my chest and the iron circle, then go outside to the firepit and burn them both. Just to be safe.

A few hours later, Justin comes home and sees me reading DuQuette in bed. I had mentioned I was going to attempt a demon summoning while he was gone.

"Is he still in the house?" Justin asks, peering down the night-dark hallway.

"No, I sent him off to do my bidding."

"How did you do it, anyway?"

I explain the process of summoning as instructed by *The Goetia*.

"Seems a bit rude to talk to a demon that way," he says.

"I agree" I say, happy that's he's taking my side instead of Aleister Crowley's. "So I didn't do it that way, not precisely. The whole point is I'm harnessing a demon for higher work, inspiring him to do better by performing a righteous task, not just yelling at him to do what I want."

"You sure he's not still here?" Justin asks, looking around the room.

"No, I told him to leave. Why? I thought you didn't believe in this stuff?"

"What you just did, *in our shared home*, is the beginning of every eighties horror movie ever," he says. "I'm an atheist, not an idiot."

DAY 226

Witches solve problems.
—CORY THOMAS HUTCHESON

I get a text from a friend asking if I can do a "repair" spell for her handyman. She writes it like I'm a deli, and she's ordering pastrami on rye.

This is what I do now. Take orders.

There are a lot of definitions of a Witch, but most involve the idea of a helper—especially one who steps in when all other help has failed.

I don't even know this handyman. Am I qualified to be helping other people at this point? By any "real" Witch's standard (and my own), the answer is a resounding no. I'm at roughly month seven in my year and a day. It's not imposter syndrome if you're actually an imposter. But I've made the mistake of telling too many people about this little Witchcraft project of mine. All of a sudden people are reaching out to me, asking for things that seem to surprise both of us. Melody, one of my oldest friends, came over last month, torn up over a potential career change. Of all the atheists I know (and I know a lot), Melody is probably the brassiest. Imagine Bill Maher trapped inside the body of a Torrid model. And she—she!—suggested we pull out the tarot cards. She meant it as a joke, I think. But she also didn't stop me when I got up to go get them. That's when I realized, when you're experiencing a big enough problem, the tiniest sliver of doubt about the realms of magic can suddenly look like a pair of open arms.

We sat on my couch, pulled the little tarot deck out of its black velvet bag, and did Skye Alexander's simple yes or no spread to help answer her question. When the cards created a no, I immediately turned and watched her face. Because the catch is: I have known Melody for fifteen years. I have seen her face express every gradient of emotion between sorrow, love, joy, worry, stress, curiosity, grief, and relief. Right then, she was cringing.

"Okay," I said. "So you need to do it. The answer is actually yes."

"But the cards said . . ." she began.

"Fuck the cards, look at your face," I said. "You are not going to be happy unless you say yes. The cards aren't revealing no, they are revealing that you don't want the answer to be no."

She seemed mollified. It was the first time I felt like I had actually helped someone. That's when I learned it's not really about my connection to the uncanny. More and more, I'm realizing, the most important Witchcraft skills are not mind reading and bird summoning. Those are parlor tricks. The line between "folk magic" and "folk therapy" is very, very blurry.

Occultist Lon Milo DuQuette has concluded, after a lifetime of magical undertakings, the only thing he can really ever affect with his magic is himself. So, at my most skeptical, I would say when someone asks me for help because they believe I am a Witch, they are engaging in an act of magic to help themselves. We both might be quietly believing that this is nothing but a LARP, an intentional placebo experiment wherein magic is the sugar pill, and I am its dispenser. But as my nurse sister Nicole is fond of saying, "The placebo effect is still an effect."

Also, it feels good to be able to help someone with nothing but a hunk of wax, a deck of cards, and a sympathetic shoulder. I can't help it. I like it.

"Okay," I reply to my friend on the phone, who is asking for help for her handyman and his sorrows. "Tell me what's going on."

DAY 230

The tools have no power save that which we lend to them.
—SCOTT CUNNINGHAM

Lauren and I are back at Eli's Mile High Club catching up. She asks me how things went with the demon summing earlier this month. I tell her Foras has yet to return with my mom's rings.

"I wonder if I should have used all the actual tools specified in *The Goetia*," I think aloud. "Do you use them?"

"Yes," she replies matter-of-factly.

"Well shit."

"Why didn't you?"

"Because I didn't have a virgin rooster? Or a lion pelt? Because how do you?"

"Eh. I've had some years to stock up."

"The other thing is," I venture, "I can't tell if using every specific item exactly as described really matters. All my Wiccan authors tell me that you can use whatever tools you want as long as your heart is in it. What do you think?"

"I don't know," she replies.

"What do you mean you don't know?" I say, annoyed.

"It's really up to you," she says calmly.

"I was hoping you would tell me it was okay that I used only, like, a quarter of everything *The Goetia* told me to use. Or, because I didn't do what it told me to do, that's why summoning Foras hasn't worked yet."

"Okay, so then go back and do the ritual properly."

"But I don't know where I would get the tools. Or when it will be both a Tuesday and the eighth and a waxing moon again."

"Okay, so then don't."

"Lauren."

"You just want someone to tell you what's correct, right?"

"Well, yes."

"But then when someone does, you get upset."

"When it's impossible, yes!" I say. "I'm torn between using the tools that actually mean something to me, or spending thousands of dollars on tools I'm not even sure are legal, let alone will work."

"Why don't you think they will work?" she asks.

A silence. I don't have the heart to look her in the eyes and tell her I'm still not convinced this isn't all total bullshit. Instead I say, after some sincere thought: "Because I think the tools that mean something to me will work better. Not the random tools some guy from three centuries ago told me to use, which were probably only called sacred because they were hard to come by. I can't explain why."

"Well, there you go."

"But using them didn't work!"

"Hm." She thinks for a moment. "Did you offer the demon anything?"

"An understanding heart?"

"What?" She makes a face at me.

"That's what Lon Milo DuQuette said to do. I was supposed to understand Foras's better nature. So I asked him nicely. I tried to inspire him with a task of justice. I didn't want to yell at him. Seemed rude."

"Oh my god. Diana, they are *demons*."

"I don't know what he's been through! Hell seems like a rough place!"

She shakes her head.

DAY 233

Take a moment to ask yourself: Whom does my Witchcraft
serve?
—THORN MOONEY

"I don't wanna go."

I murmur this into my pillow after slamming my alarm clock into silence. It's Sunday morning. I have signed up to attend an outdoor Ostara (vernal equinox) ritual, put on by a coven operating out of a metaphysical shop a few hours' drive away. I'm supposed to pick up Blanca along the way. If I want to get there on time, it is imperative that I get moving now.

I roll over in bed. Bird is curled softly between the pillows, glaring at me.

"Then don't go," Justin croaks. His back is to me. He is also upset that an alarm woke him up on Sunday morning.

I remember when I first started this year, the sabbats felt special, prized, like every moment of preparation was a sacred act. I was unsure of myself, but there was still a sort of bright anticipation.

How quickly my glittering spiritual journey has devolved into the trudge of obligation.

"I have to go." I say this as much to myself as to every other mammal sleeping on the bed. "Religion is important."

I throw the covers off, make a cup of tea, and get myself together. Twenty minutes later I'm in the car on my way out of town. I'm listening to NPR, a segment on how Ukraine is doing during the continued invasion. I think about Putin and wonder if Michael Hughes's group spell has had any effect.

Blanca hops in the car and we head to the metaphysical shop. The drive is breathtaking. At this time of year, the hills along the highways of California are not husk gold, but alive with leprechaun green, knee-high grass. Masses of it roll in waves, and starbursts of purple and white mustard flowers line the country highways like fur on the collar of a coat.

We get to the shop. It's easy to know we're at the right place, because the ritual is being set up at the far end of the parking lot. Folding banquet tables are covered in an array of sacred objects I'm coming to be familiar with—the chalice, the incense, the candle, the statue of the God and the Goddess. A plump woman in a fantastical tie-dyed dress and a golden crown greets us warmly. She has three helpers in jeans and T-shirts, busying themselves with bunches of flowers on the other table. One other attendee sits in a beach chair, reading a book. She doesn't look up when we approach.

Feeling a bit awkward, we pop some cash into the donation box and take our seats.

The priestess has us rise, form a circle, and call the corners. She invokes the God and the Goddess. She invites us to take a plant and infuse it with something we want to grow in our lives. Ostara is the season of growth, of life bursting forth (however, a deck of oracle cards can give us direction, if we find ourselves needing inspiration). This holiday is the twin of the autumn equinox. Light and dark are briefly balanced here, but instead of embracing darkness, it is time to shed our shadow skins, and embrace the coming life and rebirth.

We all approach the table of flowers. It becomes quickly obvious that the rest of the coven is best friends. They laugh and share inside jokes, but they also extend friendly words and help to Blanca and me. We toss shovels of dirt around and compare plants, jotting intentions on the sides of the compostable cups. I don't feel like I'm between the worlds. I feel like I'm at my first day of Girl Scouts. But it's pleasant, in an uncomplicated, summer camp way.

There are a million things I want to manifest. Money. Global peace. A less saggy jawline. In a struggle to pick one, I shuffle the oracle cards

and silently ask the Goddess to help guide me. I pull a card with a ser-
pent on it, which is to represent knowledge and healing. I pick up an
infant basil plant, and write the words "knowledge" and "healing" on the
side of the pot.

When we're done, the priestess passes around a tray of marshmallow Easter bunnies and Dixie cups of POG juice. I don't quite finish my
snack before we are closing the corners, and end up raising my arms
and intoning, "Hail to the guardians of the east, powers of change and
growth, we release you," with a half-eaten marshmallow in my left palm.

I watch Blanca take the last bite of her snacks by some oleanders lining the back of the parking lot. I remember I'm supposed to offer the last
bits of cakes and ale to the spirits and walk over to do the same.

Then we're done. Fifteen minutes, start to finish.

I did not feel the cone of power. I did not feel the sensation of being
between the worlds. The wind blew about a bit in the trees when the
priestess invoked the God, but, a truck was also driving by, so it's hard
to say what was what.

I feel grateful for the priestess's time and energy, for creating a welcoming space for covenless randos to simply walk in and join. I tell her
this, and she tells me she was glad I came. But on the drive home, I try to
think of anything profound about the experience, and find I'm coming
up bare.

Then I remember an anecdote from *The Year of Living Biblically*,
where A.J. Jacobs is quizzed by one of his spiritual advisers, a Lutheran-
leaning Orthodox rabbi named Yossi, on the best way to pray. Let's
say two men perform their prayers at work. One closes his office door,
silences his phone, and gives himself twenty minutes to have a deep,
therapeutic contemplation of God. He feels refreshed and blessed when
finished. The other man is so busy he only has five minutes, so he recites
his prayers superfast in a supply closet between phone calls and then
gets back to the grind. Yossi asks Jacobs who has performed the better
prayer.

Like most of us, Jacobs says the first man, who took the time to connect with the divine and feel its wonderful effects. But according to Yossi,

it's the man in the supply closet who is actually the winner—because he was doing it only for God, there was no benefit to himself. The lesson is that if you ask not what God can do for you, but what you can do for God, you'll start to discover the real meaning behind the concepts of selflessness and service, and thus divine connection. Jacobs reflects that ultimately, this probably would help him become a better person, but then worries he's back at the top of the circle, viewing his quest as nothing but self-help, despite the admonitions of Yossi.

I realize this is a deeply Judeo-Christian allegory, but at the end of the day, I think anyone who really tries to get into a particular spirituality, from Buddhism to Evangelicalism, is doing it for self-help.

But you can't do self-help every day. It's time consuming.

Maybe some days it's enough to just show up. To go through the motions without feeling them in your bones.

In a way, I realize while driving back home, this is the greatest test of all of my belief. Until now, the best part of spirituality has been these ecstatic states I find I'm able to enter in a closed office after twenty minutes of chanting and huffing toxic amounts of frankincense. At the peak of those meditation sessions, I can *feel* how I'm connected to everything, backed by a bit of scientific theory and a bit of imagination. The contemplation that we are all made of the same elements is an ecstatic one. And the idea that I, a conscious being made of those atoms, could willfully manipulate some of that flow, is suddenly not so far-fetched. The Gods and Goddesses are symbols, tools, metaphorical faces.

The idea that I can just show up to a parking lot, go through rote motions, eat a marshmallow and leave, and still please the spiritual energy of the universe—let alone manifest something—is a newly radical concept.

Maybe the magic isn't dependent on me *feeling* anything at all. Maybe all this isn't riding on the personal measurement of my inner faith or ecstasy.

Or perhaps that's not it. Perhaps it implies there is some sentient presence floating around in the clouds, just happy to have been remembered.

There is also a warmth to the idea of coming together with strangers to do something as personal as worshipping. I have spent so much of this year alone. I wonder if I will ever get to experience one of the most important parts of adopting any new religion: community. The one here today is nice, but it's hours away, and I don't think they have room for another regular.

When I get home, I once again start looking up public Witch communities.

I discover something called "Witch camps."

I send out some inquiries.

APRIL

〉 〉 〉 ● ⦗ ⦗ ⦗

DAY 250

Thou has distinguished between the Just and the Unjust.
—THE GOETIA

An old, old family friend texts me out of the blue, asking if I happen to have my father's wedding ring. I have never even *seen* my father's wedding ring. The suddenness, the randomness of this request strikes me like a bolt.

I have a thought. I check the calendar and confirm; today is the last day in Foras's one-month deadline to return my mother's rings. And today of all days I get a random request from a distant friend about another family ring I've never even seen before? No one knows I'm even trying to summon the rings except Lauren and Justin.

It's very clear what's going on. And it's that I am being fucked with by one of King Solomon's demons.

I go back into my office, grab the graveyard nails Lauren gave me, and say Foras's name out loud three times. I start shaking the tube of nails, stabbing the air with their pointy sides.

You. Little. Shit. Stop. Fucking. With. Me. And. Do. Your. Job.

I recall Crowley's lengthy, impassioned rants to intimidate the demon, the instructions on how to trap the demon in a box, and various other magical threats. I now understand why they exist.

My cause is just, I remind Foras (I remind myself). *I only ask for what is good.* I visualize the rings in my mind's eye. *Find what was unjustly stolen from my mother, and return it to her. Do not harm anyone in the process.*

The urge comes up for me to offer something. To make a deal. It's so funny that this urge rises in me. I remember DuQuette cautioning never to make a deal with a demon. I consider that perhaps I only want to offer Foras something because I'm not used to feeling like I deserve something inherently.

Perhaps this is a test of my resolve.

I ignore the urge to bargain, and hold fast to the divalike sensation of complete, unquestionable entitlement.

Now go, I say to the dead space on my wall that I've been staring at. *Get out of my house.* I huff, frustrated, and light a stick of incense to clear the air.

Assume with me, just for a moment, that I have made contact with Foras—that I'm not just playing make-believe. Why would he be messing with me like this? Maybe it's that I really did need a nine-foot circle and a seal perfumed with dates and lignum aloes to inspire him to do higher work. Maybe the rings themselves have a spiritually questionable history I don't know about; maybe the stones were mined unethically, or stolen from someone else first. Maybe it's because I am thumping my chest about how my family deserves some jewelry.

Is that the type of person who has an understanding heart?

I start to question my unquestionable entitlement.

Does my heart need to simply understand there are more important things in life than heirlooms? Is that the lesson here?

I turn this over in my head.

No. It feels too much like an after-school special. I don't want the answer here to be something intangible. I want results. The physical kind.

DAY 264

*Contemporary witchcraft has long had a love affair with the
very concept of "The Celts."*
—KATHRYN GOTTLIEB

I'm packing for my trip to the UK, land of my ancestors, and birthplace of Wicca. To prepare for this sacred pilgrimage, I have been listening to the Riverdance twenty-fifth-anniversary album for approximately seventy-two hours straight.

I'm not going to Ireland on this trip, only Scotland and England. So it might not immediately make sense why I'm listening to Riverdance, but hear me out.

As a child, I was enamored with my family's VHS tape of the original 1995 Riverdance show. It was recorded live off a PBS special broadcast and worn thin from me and my sister Kim watching it 1.7 million times between 1996 and 2002. We did this because Riverdance is a picture book of white people magic. I will never forget Jean Butler gliding onto the stage in cream-colored lace, a princess from another realm, her face aloof against the bombastic applause that accompanies each weightless step. In the penultimate act, the stage goes black, and the music goes silent. Michael Flatley struts to the top of the stage, raises his arms before a curtain, and reveals an army of backlit step dancers clad in black velvet. On his command, they stride forward out of the darkness and into the light, stomping the ground in perfect time, like spirits rising from the grave, like an army that knows they are igniting a ten-year (minimum commitment) obsession with Celtic culture for an entire generation of American girls. "There's no going back from here, lassies,"

Michael's pendulous silk sleeves seem to babble to the screen. "It's clad-dagh rings and Loreena McKennitt from now until you're twenty-five. Oh, PS—you're a fucking Witch."

The disappointment I felt when I discovered later in life that I didn't have a single drop of Irish blood in me cannot be overstated. Irish myth and lore is all over European-American Witchcraft, probably because it's one of the few white ancestries that is not associated with pure evil. Ireland's history isn't complicated by colonial war crimes and genocides—in fact the Irish spend most of their history surviving English tyranny by the skin of their teeth, keeping the hearth flames of pre-Christian Celtic lore alive as it's stomped out across the rest of the main continent. According to historian Kathryn Gottlieb, the Celts did in fact live throughout most of Europe but their traditions slowly died out as different tribes dominated and intermingled with them. Ultimately, the Celts were pushed farther and farther west, right to the edge of Europe itself. Which is why today they are associated almost exclusively with Ireland, the unbowed, unbent, unbroken land of the Tuatha Dé Danann, floating just off the coast of the world's largest imperial power, perpetually flipping it the bird.

Maybe I should be going to Madeira to connect with my Portuguese ancestors, since it's my only ancestral location I'm actually 100 percent confident in (my great-grandmother had "native of Madeira" written in boldface print on her tombstone). But there's just one problem: Madeira doesn't have much of a Witchcraft scene, at least not that I can find.

But the Celts?

The Celts are waiting, like an army of practiced step dancers, stomping a capella in black velvet, to enfold me back into the mystic past.

))) ● (((

DAY 266

Going back to the roots of our culture, even if we were not raised
with those roots, we can help create a spiritual depth and bond
between our spirit and our flesh.
—TEMPERANCE ALDEN

I land at London Heathrow and take my first sip from the spring of my
ancestors.*

After spending ten minutes figuring out the difference between the
train and the Tube, I get on the right form of public transit and step
outside of Farringdon station. It's bright, partly cloudy, the sidewalk still
puddled from an earlier rain. The cars are smaller than I'm used to, the
street signs unfamiliar despite being in English. I hear three different
languages spoken at once. Everyone is from somewhere else. It's wonderful. London is the new Rome.

In preparation for my time in Wicca's homeland, I asked around for
the "witchiest" sites in this vast, eternal city.

"Go to St. Bride's Church," was Meg's response. And a little research
makes it easy to see why.

St. Bride's is a modest (by European standards) sized church on London's Fleet Street. The current, wedding-cake-spired building dates from
the seventeenth century, but this is at least the seventh house of worship
to have been on the site since its original founding by Saint Bride herself.
This woman wears so many hats and name tags I can barely keep them
straight. Bride, I learned, is pronounced like "breed," and is another
name for Brigid, the Celtic goddess of spring, fire, healing, domesticated
animals, and fertility who is celebrated at Imbolc (aka, St. Brigid's Day).
Brigid is also the name of one of the Tuatha Dé Danann, the original

---

* The water fountain next to the bathrooms in Terminal 2.

mystical people who conquered Ireland, and then were driven underground themselves, to become, depending on whom you ask, the fairies.
The foundation of the St. Bride's Church I'm walking toward today rests
on an unknowably ancient spring, which archaeologists agree was a site
of worship from prehistoric England through Roman occupation. Many
neopagans believe it was for Brigid—before she became St. Bride.

The church closes at 5 p.m., and it's already 4:10. I am speed walking through London, marveling at the city as it whizzes by: glossy, sleek
office buildings rub shoulders with studded medieval spires. Minimalist
gray boutiques share walls with cozy wood-paneled pubs. I walk past
something I am convinced is actually Camelot, before discovering it's
the Hall of Justice. Finally, with twenty minutes left before the church
closes, I scramble through a courtyard and arrive at the front door of St.
Bride's Church. A sign tells me it is the church's silent hour, when anyone
is welcome to come in for prayer, or just to enjoy a moment of peace. I
take a deep breath to quiet my hammering heart, stamp my puddle-wet
boots on the welcome mat, and open the wooden door.

The church is completely empty. A whitewashed vestibule radiates silence above the altar to my left, and the lightly checkered waxed
floor gleams so bright I can see my reflection in it. I take a few ginger
steps toward the wooden pews and scan the back wall. Not even a timid
docent appears. There is no one here but me.

There's a sign pointing toward a downward staircase: "Roman
museum and medieval chapel open, free for all." Excited, I make my
way down the stairs, into the foundations of the church, and hurry past
the Roman coffins and brickwork. I don't want to diminish their significance, but I'm in a hurry to find the well.

After weaving around the cramped hallways downstairs, I find a
sign that tells me the St. Bride's well dried up centuries ago. I come to a
screeching halt. I am crushed.

I slowly retrace my steps around the basement and find myself entering the area that served as the chapel during medieval times. Today it is
a low-ceilinged, alabaster cellar, with a few backlit images and a simple
wooden cross in the center of the far wall. There's a bench placed across

from it. I imagine this is as good as it's going to get, in terms of ancient connections today, so I plop onto the bench and try to get in my witchy zone. I take a few breaths. But, it doesn't come. I stare at the cross.

I realize I feel angry at it.

The full impact of what this symbol stands for hits me. Maybe it's just that I've spent the last week researching pagan gods turned into Catholic saints, but the truth is so much history has been destroyed in the name of Christ, in the name of "saving" others from pagan ways. Christ taught compassion and brotherly love. But an appalling number of his follow- ers have spent their lives running around raping and killing people, and destroying their culture in his name. I have to content myself with the burned scraps they left behind. His house is everywhere, in every city. He has all the hegemony, all the tidy history, all the normalcy. To many people, neopaganism is a laughingstock because it's new. Because the followers of this symbol made it be something that had to be new.

I stare at the altar and wonder what the world would have been like if Constantine never painted a red cross on his shield.

I don't know why I have this feeling now. It takes me by surprise. But eventually I realize getting mad in a church is a bad idea, period. I get up and leave the chapel.

Then, across the far wall of the main exterior chamber, I see it.

I can't remember what it is at first, but it looks familiar. I walk closer. It's a four-pointed St. Brigid's cross, a real one—the one I tried to make on Imbolc with Liza in her living room, and failed, but still hangs over my desk at home anyway. This one is hay colored, modest, sitting behind an altar table with two unlit candles on it. I approach the area slowly, and see that behind the little table is a stone outcropping. Within the cavity of stones there is a hollow, an obvious path where a thick stream of water used to flow up from the depths of the earth. It now contains a small white candle, burning steadily.

This is it. This is St. Brigid's well. And the church workers are keep- ing the flame lit.

I sit down in the one of the plastic chairs in front of the altar, feeling electric. This is not make-believe. This is the actual well of an ancient goddess, preserved over centuries. For the first time since I began this journey, I am looking at a verifiable pre-Christian worship site.

I close my eyes, and imagine my taproot coming out of my tailbone with each exhale, and a white cone of light opening above my head. I am anxious about the time, but resist the urge to check my phone. I should have at least ten minutes before the church closes. If anyone comes down here, I tell myself it will just look like I'm praying to Jesus.

I think about Brigid, sheer white skin, lamb in her arms, smile on her face, surrounded by billows of red hair.

I remember you. I remember you. I remember you.

Eventually I open my eyes, and am given an image of the rocky outcrops surrounding the well pulsing red, the color of fresh blood—the color of life. I think about the energy of Brigid. I ask her to help fuel my creativity, my next steps going forward.

I recall reading somewhere that ancient women would pray to Brigid for fertility. This persisted through centuries—the Catholics believed this very well was a holy site that could bless a supplicant with pregnancy.

I should mention I don't want to get pregnant, I think to Brigid with a touch of alarm. At that precise moment, I get a very small uterus cramp. My period is at least a week away.

Okay, and we're done. I open my eyes and stand. I am not going to sit here and get myself knocked up because I accidentally prayed to a fertility goddess with a bit too much enthusiasm.

Just then, a young blond woman comes downstairs and pauses, surprised to see me. She says she's locking up, but offers me more time, since she can infer I just arrived. Christians are so nice.

"That is kind of you," I say, and I mean it. "But I should be going anyway."

I walk back upstairs, open the church door, and exit onto Fleet Street. While I was inside it rained again. Everything is freshly washed, the trees of the courtyard sparkling with refracted light. I once again step into the bustling scene of London during rush hour. Next I'm headed to Covent Garden, to visit the occult bookshop The Atlantis. This is where Gardner himself used to hold coven meetings in the 1940s, when Witchcraft was still technically illegal.

I feel a little dehydrated from the flight, but once again, I only have an hour before my destination closes, so I put my feet to the pavement. Traffic is clogged, tiny cars blaring their horns in front of rusty medieval doorways, Victorian brick buildings, and a series of modern Pret a Mangers; I'm convinced London has every kind of building that's ever been built, crammed in together like Tetris pieces. For such a massive city, I expected to see more trash piled up around the gutters, but the streets are so clean I feel embarrassed for America.

After dashing through the obscenely charming, ivy-lined cobblestone alleys of the theater district, I approach The Atlantis bookshop. Once again, it's twenty minutes before closing. I all but run to the door and step inside. The store is a modest little thing, the front room not much bigger than a bedroom, colorful bookshelves snuggled together like best friends at a sleepover. The woman up front is busy chatting with another customer. It's pin-drop quiet otherwise. I try to slow my postrun panting in the crushed space and feel my cheeks burn red. On the back wall, there's a spiral staircase with the word Exhibition painted above it. I teeter down the narrow iron steps, step into the empty basement, and let out a huge breath.

I am alone in Gerald Gardner's old meeting space. It's a simple, small room with cheap pine flooring and lightly warped white walls. It reads less "grand wizard's palace" and more "accounting office at a failing law firm." On the walls is an exhibition of paintings of Beowulf, done by local artists Joe Machine and John Matthews. They're quite good. I sit down in one of the two chairs and take them in.

Then, in the far corner, I see a tall glass cabinet of objects. I get up and approach, curious. In the top chamber is a picture of Gerald Gardner, with that same mad expression on his face, like he just looked up from a batch of bubbling experiments, unsure if you can handle the answer to the cosmic question for which you dared to query him. Next to him is a portrait of Doreen Valiente, Gardner's right-hand woman. She seems the opposite of Gardner: soft-cheeked, happy, round glasses framing crinkling eyes, looking at the camera as if she's just about to let you in on an inside joke.

On the other shelves are reverently laid relics from Wiccan founding family members like Morgan McFarland and Alex Saunders. The chalice they passed mouth to mouth, the wand they used to cast circles between the worlds. The portrait under Gardner states that his coven used to hold ritual in the very space I'm standing in.

I turn back around and face the humble room with new eyes. I try to imagine Gardner and his coven, swathed in black robes, illuminated by candlelight, walking widdershins around a candlelit altar, holding their arms to the sky as the sounds of chanting and the smoke of incense swirl in the air.

This is where it all started.

I blink. I try to hold Gardner's coven in my imagination, but I can't help but notice the crummy white-walled room itself.

I don't write this to offend the proprietors. The room is clean and tidy. They clearly have been taking care of it. It's just not the kind of place you'd associate with the revival of arcane European myth and magic. But I suppose all those places belong to the Catholics now.

I feel a sense of camaraderie with Gardner for the very first time since I began this journey. It is validating to know that even the fearless founders of this neopagan Witchcraft revolution were practicing their Craft in a crammed office. After all, I practice in a crammed office. On a cardboard box.

Even before this, I have only ever practiced Witchcraft in borrowed living rooms, shared bedrooms, Ikea coffee tables transformed into altars with tapestries and candles. In fact, I know very few Witches who actually practice skyclad, outdoors, or who have permanent ritual altars set up anywhere. Even Gardner and Valiente came into this little basement, to do what they could, where they could. Where they were allowed. Where they wouldn't be misunderstood.

I murmur my respects to Gardner's coven, then head back upstairs and peruse the books. I feel the urge to buy something, to pay a tribute. The necklaces are the same pendants you see at every Renaissance fair or New Age shop in the US. I observe a statue of Brigid that looks like a Victoria's Secret model striding the runway while breastfeeding.

Eventually I grab two books that look interesting and head to check out. The woman up front is named Geraldine. I tell her I'm working on a book about Witchcraft, and thank her for preserving the room and the relics in the basement. She tells me about the time when she, as a little girl, met Gardner, coming up the stairs after ritual, and how full of life he seemed. I insist on shaking her hand, then, feeling the person in line behind me huff at being made to wait, head back outside into the light of present day.

DAY 271

I think the use of the witches' circle, in magic, may have come
from the Druid, or rather the pre-Druid people who built
Stonehenge and Avebury and who made use of it to concentrate
the powers generated.
—GERALD GARDNER

"A nd *don't* take your clothes off."

A ripple of laughter goes through the passengers on the bus. Our guide, a thickly accented, red-haired British archaeologist, is explaining the rules.

"This is Stonehenge," he says in acknowledgement of our collective middle-school giggle, "Listen, people do a lot of things here."

He is explaining a bit about the history, what is and isn't known about this Neolithic monument we are speeding toward through the English countryside. Stonehenge was built about five thousand years ago, two thousand years before the Roman Empire touched British soil. But it is still active in terms of current worshippers. Neopagans, especially Druids, consider it a present-tense sacred site, and the English Heritage nonprofit that manages its preservation seems to understand this fact.

"Stonehenge is sacred to a lot of people," says our guide. "Please behave as you would if you were in a church. You can't get naked, but you can take your shoes off, absorb the energy and what have you."

Justin—who flew in last night to join for this part of my journey—whips his head to look at me.

"What?" I whisper. "Are you gonna take your shoes off?"

"You should," he whispers back.

"I'm wearing tights," I say, gesturing to my skirt and boots.

"How often are you at Stonehenge?" he says.

How are you the atheist in this relationship?

I bite my tongue and murmur, "We'll see."

The bus parks, and we shuffle off like a herd of excited puppies. A wall of cold wind hits us, and I huddle into my jacket. Justin is the one who convinced me to spend the extra cash and book a private tour. Most tourists who visit Stonehenge today see it only from a guarded perimeter (unless you can manage to get here on a solstice, when the Druids apparently take it over). It didn't used to be this way, but in 2014, the managing nonprofit deemed there to be too much damage to the stones for the public to continue to have direct access. People were scraping them, hugging them, carving graffiti on them—basically everything people do to ruin natural, ancient things for other people. But with a private tour (or some preplanned taxi services), you can step behind the ropes, after the main gates have closed.

We walk across the undulating green carpet of Salisbury Plain in spring. Something you never hear about Stonehenge is that it's surrounded by livestock pastures. Next to us, on the left, are about a hundred white, fluffy lambs, oblivious to the fact that they are pooping right next to one of the wonders of the ancient world. At one point a runner bounds past us on the path we're walking up. I try to imagine what my life would be like if my daily exercise involved a little jog past Stonehenge.

Then it appears on the horizon, growing in size as we get closer. I feel adrenaline build inside of me, my pace quickening. Eventually we get to the ropes. The stones loom above us like mute giants, serene, spectacular in size, covered in mint-green splotches of lichen. I open my mouth, and to my sincere surprise, a sob escapes. I was not expecting to be this emotional.

When we step over the rope and walk toward the henges, I am positively vibrating. The thing about the stones in Stonehenge is that you wouldn't have to know anything about them to know they are important. The place has an unquestionable vibe of "sacred." When we step inside the actual stone circle, the wind hushes a bit, despite the doorways of airflow between the stones. I check in with my body, as if perhaps this is the moment when I'll suddenly gain fantastical X-Men powers. I do, in fact, feel an electric buzz all over. But it's impossible to separate this from my dorkish excitement at being at an archaeological mystery site.

I turn to the guide and ask him, "What do you think they did here? Not the historians, but you, personally, the person who comes here almost every day."

He rubs his chin. Then says, "I think it was used for ancestor worship, and revering the spirits of the dead. The way the sun rises on the winter solstice is more impressive. It hits this stone, at the front." He points to the tallest obelisk, the one that looks like it's wearing a little pointed hat. It was the first stone I noticed when we entered the ring, and it struck me as different than the others—almost sci-fi in its shape. "There was an altar here, in front of this stone. We don't know if it was used for sacrifices of course, but I think knowing what we know about the winter solstice, this was more death than sex or whatnot. Then on the summer solstice"—he turns 180 degrees to point to the smaller stone at the opposite edge of the henge—"I think it's about the return of life."

I walk around for a bit, thinking about my pre-Roman ancestors, the people who probably walked this land who would eventually give rise to me. I think this is how I wanted to feel in Salem but failed. Here, it's happening. I sense the miracle of my existence. That I am one in an unbroken line of survivors of nightmarish winters, famines, abuse, conquests, and erasure. They survived so I could thrive. That the neolithic magic that was here could still be in my blood, too, if I want to believe.

I lift up my leg, grab the top of my boot, and pull the zipper down.

I feel for the underside of my foot, collect a handful of nylon in my fist, and tear.

The soles of my bare feet meet the cold, green grass. It feels rubbery. I wiggle some of the blades between my toes. I don't really feel different than I did with my shoes on, *energetically*, but I do feel like a more proper pilgrim.

The stones at Stonehenge feel like hugs. I don't know how else to describe it. You step inside, and you feel like you are being watched.

No.

Protected.

DAY 274

It was also well known that at times six thousand people were
present at one sabbat.
—GERALD GARDNER

Justin and I have made our way from London to Edinburgh. After spending a few days poking around the Royal Mile—including visiting the Witch's Well—we are now on our way to Calton Hill.*

It takes us twenty minutes just to get to the end of the line. City officials in orange blazers herd us as we walk up the cobblestone streets away from the city below. Official barricades organize the leagues of human bodies into a queue, preventing us from spilling out into the road. I feel like I'm at an arena concert.

When I bought my tickets for the Beltane Fire Festival, I thought I was going to be sitting on a hill in the rain with three hundred stoned

---

* The Witch's Well is a minuscule cast iron plaque that serves as Scotland's official apology for murdering thousands of women for Witchcraft. It's hidden behind an ice cream shop at the top of the Royal Mile, and reads something to the effect of "Our bad. Some of you meant well."

hippies, shivering and counting the minutes until I could retire to a pub and a bowl of warm fries.

I couldn't have been more wrong. There's at least a thousand people just in line with me, chittering, buzzing, oblivious to the rain. Teens with glitter-painted cheeks and running eyeliner walk alongside retirees in sensible gray rain jackets. Neon-coated frat boys sip cheap cans of beer and rub shoulders with quiet Chinese tourists tucked under umbrellas. Scots, Brits, Germans, Spaniards, Japanese, Mexicans, Americans—the entire world is here. By the time we get our tickets scanned, my hair is dripping with rainwater, as if I've just stepped out of a shower. We walk under bowers of sweet-smelling green leaves inside the park and continue spiraling upward toward the darkening sky at the top of Calton Hill. Eventually we round the corner and the flat peak comes into view. My breath catches.

This is impossible.

There must be ten thousand people up here in the rain. They are all here to see the May Queen.

The Beltane Fire Society has been putting on their eponymous festival since 1988, a restoration of the ancient Celtic holiday that marked the start of summer. Beltane's connotations of luck, beauty, and lust are all over Western history. It's a common weekend for bachelorette parties to roam the streets in Europe, and many American schools still crown a "May Queen" at a spring semester dance. In old times, people would jump over the great flames of the Beltane fire for luck and protection, and couples would hop together to strengthen their bond. My Welsh grandfather's own favorite saying (as quoted at his eulogy) was "First of May, first of May, outdoor fucking starts today."

Once upon a time, fires used to light up the sky in nearly every town in Scotland on the night of April 30. Farmers would drive their cattle between the flames, as a form of ceremonial (and arguably technical) purification. It was a bit of country fun at once openly Celtic in origin, but not explicitly at odds with Christian faith. However, in the nineteenth century, the fires stopped being lit. It is not immediately clear why. Maybe farmers discovered alternative pest treatments for their livestock that didn't involve the drama of driving them through (from the cow's perspective) the flaming gates of hell. Maybe there was a sudden Puritan influence. Maybe they ran out of trees.

At any rate, in 1988, the Beltane Fire Society decided that was enough time off and made a plan to bring the bonfires back.

According to their literature, the modern festival began as the dream child of industrial musician Angus Farquhar, with support from Professor Margaret Bennett and the School of Scottish Studies at the University of Edinburgh. The fledgling group used to hold the event at Arthur's Seat in Holyrood Park, the topmost point of Edinburgh's much larger, older green space. But Edinburgh's appetite for the festival outgrew the infrastructure of Holyrood, so the rite is now celebrated here, on the wide, flat top of Calton Hill.

The fact that the city got involved is the most fascinating part to me. There is no pagan ritual that takes place in the United States so massive that the local government has to be notified lest there be chaos. Their involvement implies a certain amount of buy-in; a critical mass of public eagerness; the government giving the people what they want.

This is precisely what is making me feel so overwhelmed. For the past few weeks, I have been standing on my toes to peer at off-limits archaeological sites, trying to worship at dried-up wells paved over for church foundations, sitting alone in windowless office basements, and communing with crumbling stone circles that I'm not allowed to touch—all against the backdrop of Christianity's cathedrals and statues and living grandeur. I have been doing what most neopagans do: working with whatever I can find, whatever wasn't burned or destroyed or forgotten—whatever someone will let me have. I have been trying to sate myself with table scraps.

But now I am here. One of ten thousand people crammed onto a hill in the damp twilight, waiting for a pagan queen to rise out of the night sky and usher in the summer. This is not a table scrap. This is a *feast*.

I try and explain this to Justin, the emotional magnitude of a pagan festival with this kind of production value and public appeal.

"Yeah but, how many people are here for the spectacle, and how many people are here because they're actually religious?" he says.

"I think it's more significant that it's on a stage, getting respect, getting screen time. I don't care about measuring the belief in everyone's heart," I reply. "I've just never seen this many neopagans who didn't feel like they had to hide. They don't have to hide here." *I don't have to hide here.*

The daylight grows dimmer and dimmer. Justin and I are sipping wine from a plastic bottle and chatting with our neighbors, two retirees from Oregon who are traveling the world. The crowd of heads and umbrellas is laid out in front of the Scottish National Monument like a multicolored carpet. The building itself is a quarter-finished replica of the Greek Parthenon that was abandoned when the builders ran out of funds in 1829. The fact that it's unfinished only makes it look more antiquated. The crowd's eyes are fixed on it now, bored, waiting, eager.

Finally, from between the columns, tiny humans dressed in black make their way forward and down the steps, lining up in rows, drums facing out against their chests. The crowd shifts in response, and some people begin to whoop. After what feels like ten minutes of us watching stagehands shuffle around, a massive trellis is raised between the two-hundred-foot-high columns of the fake Parthenon. A moment later, it explodes into live flame. The crowd gives one more eager whoop. My Californian sensibilities shudder with forbidden pleasure at the sight of so much fire on public property.

From under the flaming megastructure, I suddenly realize there is a woman in a white dress kneeling with her back to us, almost blending in with the beige stone. A massive crescent moon is rising from the bottom of her skull into a thick halo, the tips kissing twelve inches above her head.

She rotates her bent body slowly toward the audience and then stands, and I can see her more clearly. She looks like the Borg Queen had a baby with the moon. Her hair is bound flat against her skull, and she appears to have been dipped head to toe in white paint, except for the brown tufts of hair under her armpits, the red-fruit slash of her mouth, and the pink stain spilling from her pelvis to her toes.

The May Queen raises her thin arms into the air in a high V. Twenty drummers slam into their instruments. The crowd screams. And I burst into tears.

I'm overwhelmed. I'm embarrassed. I'm in the moment. I don't care.

I do not know if I will achieve a level of belief needed to be a real Witch, an effective Witch. I can't turn off the part of my mind that doubts, that searches constantly to prove. But here, in Scotland's rain, in front of a mortal woman dressed up as a pagan goddess, standing in an ocean of voyeurs and believers, the crux between religion and spirituality, and neopaganism and Witchcraft, is finally clear to me: *I want this*. The value of neopaganism, the value of religion, of community, of feeling like you are a small part of a greater thing, and that greater thing wants to reclaim lost power, have a harmonious relationship with the earth, foster peace over domination, repair past wrongs both familial and global—those values don't have to be hidden in a basement any longer. They are on a stage. They are here for anyone who wants to reach out and be a part of them. You don't have to be a perfect believer. I cannot pinpoint precisely why, but I feel like I have been waiting for this moment my entire life. I do, finally, feel like a version of Indiana Jones: the one in the temple, water running down his chest as he clutches a tarnished cup, and the old knight tells him, "You have chosen wisely."

Over the course of the next three hours, Justin and I do our best to follow the May Queen as she makes her slow, slow (slow) procession around the night-dark hilltop with her entourage of moon-colored attendants and drummers. She really is committed to the "move like you're carved out of marble" act. I should be bored. I'm exhilarated for every second.

Along her route, the May Queen encounters the four elements, which are pods of actors, dancers, and acrobats dressed as elemental spirits. The fire group is more or less in their underwear, juggling flaming batons and hopping about and sticking their tongues out at us. It's probably not much above forty-five degrees out here and still raining. I am impressed at their commitment.

"I think she has to kind of battle the elements, or borrow their power, to bring the Green Man to life. That symbolizes the start of summer," I say to Justin when he asks if I know what's going on. In Wiccan lore,

Beltane is the day the God and Goddess make love, and she becomes pregnant with the God. This story is pulled from ancient rock carvings that were found in Scandinavia, depicting a sacred marriage between the human representatives of the God and Goddess in the spring to fertilize the land. What precise version of the myth the Beltane Fire Festival is going to play out, I couldn't say. I am aware that what I'm watching isn't a perfect historical re-creation of a three-thousand-year-old ritual. That's okay. I don't want it to be. I want it to be relevant to the people today.

However, the one thing about the Beltane myth is that it always ends in a union. Whether the Green Man and the May Queen are going to literally or metaphorically consummate that union on the very large stage I see at the far end of the hill remains to be seen. At first, I think of course they wouldn't, but then I remember I'm in Europe, where toplessness is basically the equivalent of wearing flip-flops, and I wonder where the night is headed.

Justin and I skip through the dark, from one "scene" of elementals to another, bobbing our heads above the people in front of us, and trying to get up close to see the action. It's a lot of hurry up and wait, stamping in the wet grass hoping for a glimpse of the queen as she approaches. When she does, she nods to the elements. And then moves on. It's not exactly cinematic. Nevertheless, I am thrilled.

Justin turns to me and says, "You know what I love about this? I don't have to be worried about loving it."

"What do you mean?" I ask him.

"Usually when you see white people doing stuff like this you have to wonder who they stole it from. But this is, like . . . actual indigenous white people stuff. I have never seen that before. I like that I can just enjoy it."

After three hours, near midnight, the May Queen approaches the wooden stage, swirls in a circle to pounding drums, and plays out a scene of reviving the fallen Green Man. He lies play-dead on the stage floor, a slender, athletic body covered head to toe in swamp-green paint. She raises her arms to each corner and throws invisible force down toward him. The actors all breathe as one as the Green Man raises his ribs to the sky and she metaphorically fills him with breath. Eventually, he rises from the ground. He dances. He kneels before the May Queen, then stands to meet her eyes. A moment of silence. They kiss, and the crowd breaks into applause. For the first time, I see the May Queen's red mouth break its statuesque stasis and turn upward in a smile. Then the two characters jump off the stage and dash up to a swimming-pool-sized pile of kindling. Despite the rain, it lights rapidly, ten-foot flames surging into the sky, and once again I have to remind myself I'm in Scotland on a hill of wet mud, not in dry California where this would be illegal to even think about.

We walk down the hill at 1 a.m., my feet tired, but my spirit giddy.

MAY

DAY 277

*Dreams used as visions and prophecy were common in the
ancient world.*
—SILVER RAVENWOLF

We return home from Europe.

Justin and I make the decision to fly to Seattle in July, to look at rentals. Just to look. I'm not yet making any promises about moving. But I owe him a glance.

That night, I have a dream all my chickens die.

DAY 289

When you perform a magical act in accordance with your true
will, you are in harmony with deity.
—THEA SABIN

I'm standing in front of my altar in my bedroom. It's dusk. In my right hand, I'm holding an abundance manifestation candle given to me by a friend last Christmas.

In about an hour, something called a "super flower blood moon" will peek over the horizon. Literally, that's what it's called, according to the astronomers. But unlike the scientists, I don't just want to admire it, I want use it. Because I might have failed to summon a demon to help with stolen property, but maybe I can manifest a dream rental in Seattle.

Lunar eclipses aren't always positive in Witchcraft. Some people say they aren't a good time to perform magic, bringing too much chaotic energy into your crafting, and Witches would do better to focus on reflections and shadow work. Others say eclipses are ideal times to work magic, as they can give your spell some extra oomph. Once again, it's up to me to decide whose magical theory I'd like to believe in. (I'm deciding to believe in oomph.)

Timing is key here. I said I'd watch the eclipse with Joanna tonight, and the last thing I want to do is bail on one of my closest friends in order to cast a spell about, well, leaving her. I have to figure out how to be good friend and good Witch with only so many full moon hours to spare. Also, anything I want to rent in three weeks is probably being prepped by its landlord now. I need time for paint to finish drying, carpets to finish steaming. You can't cast a house spell and expect the house to be ready for you in less than twenty-four hours. I mean, that's just wishful thinking.

Eventually I decide to put the candle down and go outside to sit with Joanna and use our phones to confirm with each passing minute, yes, the moon is still hiding behind that gigantic tree in our neighbor's yard and we can't see anything at all. Regardless, it's nice, and I try not to think about how much I'm going to miss her and everyone else down here. I don't regret delaying the spell.

We get into the car and try to chase the moon until about 11:30 p.m., eventually giving up that we won't see it behind the clouds on the horizon. I get home, and I'm wiped, but I'm committed. I want to manifest my dream house. Augusten Burroughs did it in *Toil and Trouble*. I have failed at so many other spells. But this one feels possible. It's realistic. I just want some luck in my corner. I want to manifest a house so good it will distract me from leaving the world I know behind.

Once again, I approach my altar and grab the abundance candle. It's warm, dark yellow, and smells like fresh beeswax. I also decide to use the hawk feather in my spell, to represent air. I don't always know what it's going to do, but it's clearly powerful. And we've installed a mesh ceiling on the chicken run after what happened last time.

Tonight I'm using Juliet Diaz's Candle Spell for Manifestation, the one listed in *Witchery*. Well, mostly. I don't have the dried cornflower, High John the Conqueror root powder, dried goldenseal, or dried yellow-dock that she specifies. I also don't have two of the essential oils. If you cut half the ingredients out of a cake recipe, you'd probably end up with something like oversweetened scrambled eggs. But this isn't a cake recipe. This is Witchcraft. For something to work, I have to believe it, I have to know it works for me. So, since I've come to accept that plant energies don't talk to me, despite my efforts, rather than ruin my good full moon timing in order to obtain all the herbs tomorrow, I'm just going to go ahead tonight with what I have on hand. I like to think Juliet (and the Goddess) would understand.

I pick up *Witchery* and follow Diaz's instructions, putting pen to paper and writing down what I want to manifest—something realistic, but at the upper end of what's possible. I write down words like "backyard," and "gas range," and "skylights," and "in-unit washer-dryer." I write "in Seattle." And just to be safe, I finish with: "A place where Justin, the animals, and I are safe and happy."*

I fold the paper toward me as Diaz instructs, and then breathe onto the candle to infuse it with my intention. As I breathe, I really try and imagine everything I want flowing out of my breath into this honey-sweet candle. I try and hold the image of my dream house in my mind. But it's actually very hard to try and imagine something you've never seen before, at least in great detail. I'm trying to be realistic, avoiding fantasies of houses surrounded by orchards and full of spa tubs. But everything I end up imagining is either something I've seen on a Pinterest board or a part of some Airbnb my friends and I pooled our money together to rent in the past. Instead, I decide to focus on the feeling. When Justin and I were first moving in together, we toured a house that was so idyllic I thought I was in a fairy tale. The owners loved us. Everything was perfect. Two weeks later, we got an email that a pipe had burst, and we wouldn't be able to move in for many months. And we ended up moving where we are now instead. But tonight I focus on that feeling I felt touring that picture-perfect home in the Oakland Hills. *I am bringing that feeling to me now.*

After a few minutes meditating, something happens. Something inside of my body breaks open, and a wonderful sensation pours out. I have the feeling that my request has been received and has been granted. I simply now need to be patient. I can't explain it. Just suddenly I'm sure this is going to happen, the same way I'm sure the sky is blue and that fire is hot. Certainty is not a feeling I am accustomed to, especially in Witchcraft, and it's wonderful, like a kiss from a new lover. When is the last time you felt *certain* of something? It makes me smile, even though I'm completely alone. A Witch once told me, "You can feel it, when a spell is going to work. It's like something clicks into place in your mind and you just *know.*" I nodded, even though I wasn't totally sure what she meant.

Now I know.

Finally, I wriggle a single hair strand free from the hair tie on my

---

* The last thing I want is a dream house with an exploding oven because I specifically forgot to write, "No exploding ovens."

wrist, and begin to try to tie it around the candle, as Diaz instructs. I don't know if you've ever tried to tie a single hair around a candle in the dark, but in fact it is no easy feat. I spend about five minutes struggling under the light of the Guardians of the Watchtower of the South candle before I finally get a knot. Diaz also suggests I drop a few bits of my menstrual blood onto the hair, but unfortunately, I'm midcycle, so the hair alone will have to be good enough.

I uncast the circle, release the directions, and go into the kitchen to drink a glass of water and eat a leftover slice of taco pie. I light the candle in the corner of the bedroom window, and watch the little flame talk to the moon.

Now all I have to do is wait.

JUNE

$$\text{)}\ \text{)}\ \text{)}\ \bullet\ \text{(}\ \text{(}\ \text{(}$$

DAY 324

Magick should just flow, it should just be there inside you . . .
It's certainly not something that should one day suddenly go
missing. On the day you happen to need it the most.
—AUGUSTEN BURROUGHS

I'll replay the events of this day over and over in my head for the rest of the year. Because I'm sure it was my fault somehow.

There is an odd linkup in the timing. It's one year to the day since we adopted them. On the way home, a mourning dove will fly in front of my car, and "Amazing Grace" will start to play on the random radio channel I put on Spotify. Maybe it's because my phone is listening to me, hearing me cry. Sometimes it's impossible to tell the difference between acts of witchy serendipity or digital marketers serving you curated content.

Aaron Turner is in the trunk of my car, dead. To clarify, Aaron Turner is one of my chickens. I am driving her home from the vet.

In American society, chickens are fungible. We eat them. I eat them. But this is my first flock, and she was one of my first girls, and so I loved her. I made the mistake of loving something as futile as a chicken. I don't think you can clean up something's poop every day for a year and not love it.

She didn't run up for treats in the morning, like her sisters. I couldn't even see her in the coop at first. For a moment I thought she had escaped. Then I found her in the back, hiding behind a bush, face pale, breathing like an invisible weight was on her downy gray back, eyes half closed. I took one look at her, and I knew something was very wrong.

As I drove to the vet, I told myself she's fine; she just needs antibiotics. Or maybe it's sour crop, which is a common ailment, but I don't have a seasoned farmer to walk me through the home cures. It seems wise to not start pumping vinegar down something's throat unless you're 100 percent sure that's what you're supposed to be doing. I sped down the freeway, glancing at her in her crate, her bleary eyes blinking at me. As I drove, I tried to manifest some kind of healing for her. This is the moment that counts, I thought. I have read story after story about preindustrial folk-healers casting spells to protect livestock; it was practically their primary job. *Am I a fucking Witch or not?* I tried to breathe and focus my mind while also focusing on the road, to reach out for that feeling of "click-ing" into success that I experienced with the house manifestation spell a month ago. I reached and reached, and eventually convinced myself I felt the click, that everything was fine, that I had manifested her healing. I just had to get through the vet visit. Everything was going to be okay.

In the vet's office, we waited in a sterile room for thirty minutes, me getting more and more agitated, watching her labored breathing against the slits in the plastic animal crate.

Suddenly she started thrashing like she was having a seizure. I lost all propriety and ran into the hallway of the vet's office, locked eyes with the first human I saw, and cried, "Can someone help me in here please?"

Two women in scrubs dropped their watercooler chat and rushed toward the door. Aaron flailed in the vet's arms. They asked me her symptoms and I tried to explain. The room was a sound bath of flapping wings and screeching and my blubbering speech. Then silence. Aaron went limp.

"I don't hear a heartbeat," said the tech, looking at me with raised eyebrows and a stethoscope to Aaron's body. The tech ran to the other side of the room and slammed the door closed so the rest of the patients couldn't hear me sob.

We played a game of back and forth, where I tried to figure out what just happened. Yesterday she was fine, eating, drinking, running around, beating up her sisters. How could she be dead today? The doctor said it's too hard to say what happened. She kept telling me it's not my fault, but since we don't actually know what went wrong, it's hard to trust the kindness of that message. I asked if the rest of my flock was going to be okay. I got a referral for an autopsy and was told not to eat any of their eggs for a while. The vet and the tech left the room, giving me a few minutes to collect myself.

I stared at a handful of grey and brown feathers, peeking out of the yellow towel they wrapped her in, willing them to move.

The drive home was a watery blur.

I got home, told Justin. We contacted the autopsy office. We cleaned the coop and sterilized the food and water dishes, because we didn't know what else to do and felt like we had to do something. I went back inside, and Basil came up to me and meowed, nuzzled my leg. I picked up his teddy bear body and whispered in his ear, "You're never allowed to die on me, okay?"

I've known Witches who have lost pets right before or after a move. Sometimes they bolt through an open door, sometimes it's a freak accident, as if the animals are symbols—victims—of the lives they are leaving behind. I had a dream about all my chickens dying just a month ago.

I think again about Witchcraft's idea that your thoughts and emotions can affect what's around you. I know that this can get dangerous, the reverse implication being that bad things happen to people simply because they aren't being positive enough. But it's hard not to be tempted by this thought right now. I have been so stressed about moving, so sad at the idea I might not be able to take the chickens with me. I was thinking about it nonstop.

Did I manifest her death?

This is the part where I'd love to give over to a higher power and say this is all happening for a reason, and I had nothing to do with it at all.

I remember the brief feeling of certainty that overcame me in the car on the way to the vet. I made myself *know* that she would be fine; I was simply a new chicken mom overreacting to a minor illness. I tried so hard not to have one doubt. I bullied my emotions into a corner until they yielded.

I was wrong. My hurried spell didn't work. I just used the pretext of Witchcraft to con myself into denying the harder truth I felt in my gut: she was doomed.

Either way, as I near the end of this Witchcraft experiment, I'm starting to think I'm not manifesting much at all. If anything, the world simply reflects what's going on inside me. I feel less like a divine creator and more like a broken mirror.

I sit on the floor of my bedroom, exhausted from worry. My Witchcraft altar sits against the back wall. The lights are off, the sun is low. I stare at it, the candles, the wand, the athame, the iron nails and graveyard dirt, the crystals, the bells, everything, everything all awash in dim blue twilight.

"You are completely fucking useless," I whisper.

DAY 326

It was sunny, but in a bad way.
—LORRAINE MONTEAGUT

Because we are still waiting on the autopsy results for Aaron Turner, I am watching the remaining chickens like, well, a hen. Josie is now laying shell-less eggs. I'm told this can happen in small flocks. If one dies, the rest of the hens may begin to exhibit unusual behavior in response. In other words, Josie may be grieving. But she's also impossible to comfort. Because she's a chicken.

The alternative, of course, is that she's sick with the same ailment that killed Aaron Turner. My mind is dizzy with options of what could be wrong, and I am itching to do something helpful. But I've only been at this chicken mom game for a year, and I have all the avian medical knowledge of a lampshade. I have of course interrogated Dr. Google, and I have called a few more experienced friends who have had chickens in the past. But, like Witchcraft, chicken raising is a hobby with a frustrating number of options. Based on her symptoms, Aaron Turner could have died from seven different unique illnesses, half of which are contagious, half of which aren't. I'm also reminded by Blanca that "chickens just die sometimes." Seriously. Sudden chicken death syndrome is a real disease. It is accepted that chickens, with no preamble and little fanfare, will sometimes simply stop being alive.

Today is also Litha, the summer solstice, the longest day of the year. According to the neopagans, Litha is the last holiday before harvest begins. Elves and fairies are said to roam in great numbers, and I am to set about celebrating life, fertility, growth, and new beginnings. I can't help but feel like that's exactly what Beltane and Imbolc were supposed to be about, almost word for word. I'm having some trouble really feeling the differences in all of these Wheel of the Year holidays. Witches seem to be in a bimonthly cycle of catharsis. According to Krystle Jordan, author of *The Wholesome Witch* blog, Litha is an auspicious, easy, and momentous time to start something new. Justin and I are circling the drain on moving; our rental hunt begins next month. But new beginnings aren't always fun. So much has to die for something to be born.

I'm tired of searing epiphanies and bright beginnings. Just for a moment, I'd like everything to stop changing.

I stare at the football-feather bodies of the hens through the lattice of their run as they peck around in the dirt, oblivious to my worry. The sun is absurdly hot today. It feels like Apollo is drunk and blasting a ray gun onto my scalp.

I am still feeling jaded about Witchcraft. I absolutely convinced myself I had protected Aaron Turner in the car on the way to the vet. An hour later I was putting her dead body in the trunk of my car.

But also, because I feel powerless, I want to reach for Witchcraft. Because spellwork is something I can do that probably won't hurt the chickens, the way an incorrectly administered cure that I read about online might. The worst thing that will happen is nothing.

So, later this evening, I pull out *American Brujeria* by J. Allen Cross. I am hesitant to do this, because I'm not Latin American. But in the front matter of the book, Cross makes it very clear you don't need to be Latin American to practice the contents of his book, on the conditions that you don't use it to make money, you don't start blending it willy-nilly with Wicca, and above all you approach all the work with sincerity. He also has an elegant spell for reversal water, which is ideally used for trapping and banishing evil, negativity, and *mal de ojo* (the evil eye).

In my mind, there is a legitimacy to Brujeria that Wicca lacks. I am tired of shaking the skirt hems of dead Celtic gods, asking to be let in on the lost secrets of my European ancestors. Brujeria is not a reclaimed tradition. Its followers rarely bicker over scraps of historical accuracy, or spend hours debating if it's pronounced ATH-a-may versus ath-OU-may. Mexican folk magic is a blend of indigenous and imported colonial customs, sure, but as Valeria Ruelas told me, "Our traditions are unbroken." Neil Gaiman once wrote in *American Gods* that the deities we believe in grow strong from our faith, and the ones we ignore grow weak. The book is fiction, but the metaphor is real. And so, I believe the gods of the Brujas are wide awake, thumping their chests on almost every street corner of California, fueled by the prayers and candles and traditions of the millions of abuelas who attend mass thrice weekly.

After Justin is asleep, I get up from bed and go into the kitchen with Cross's book, carefully reading the instructions over and over.

I grab an empty mason jar from the cupboard and fill it with water, then wash the toast crumbs off my favorite flowered dessert plate from Goodwill. I also need a small white candle. I understand now why so many Witches have overstuffed cabinets of spell materials on hand at all times. You never know when you're gonna need a white taper candle at 10:30 p.m. on a Tuesday.

I dart around my kitchen before remembering there's a Renaissance fair lantern outside with a white votive candle in it—the exact kind you see at a Catholic church shrine. Perfect. I snatch it out of the lantern.

For the first time since this year began, I don't put on my pentacle necklace, or start listening to my witchy Spotify playlist. I don't take my hair down, or take a spiritual-themed shower. I'm just standing in my still-eighty-degrees kitchen with my hair in a messy bun, wearing an oversized pajama shirt emblazoned with the pinup-girl logo of the spaceship *Rocinante* from *The Expanse*. As Cross requested, I'm not blending his spells with Wicca. I'm trying more than ever to do precisely what he describes.

The book won't stay open on its own on the kitchen counter, so I prop it up with the butt of a hand mixer. According to Cross, I have to bless all the items first and cleanse them of negative energy, and this is where things get tricky. In the beginning of the book, he suggests smoke cleansing with herbs of my choosing. But in this particular spell, he also instructs readers to recite the Padre Nostro or Dios te Salve over the items. I am not Catholic; I don't know these prayers by heart. He reminds me I don't have to be Catholic to recite them. But I do have to be sincere. La Virgen and los santos will know if I'm lying.

I decide to start with the smoke, since I'm more used to it. I light a bundle of dried cedar and rosemary, and wave it over all my items, imagining I'm pulling out muck-colored energy, and throwing it into the air to be recycled. I pick up the bottle of salt next to the stove and pause. I don't really want to bless the kitchen salt; that feels kind of profane. Instead, I grab a dingy bottle of lavender salt I made one night after reading something on Pinterest about oven-roasted lavender sweet potatoes. I spend extra time smoke-cleansing it, pulling out all the bickering it has seen, all the curse words, all the drama that happens in a home kitchen. (And also rubbing off the grease it has absorbed, living right above the stove.)

Then I bend over each item and say, "I bless you in the name of the father, and the son, and the holy spirit."*

---

* I do this because I think this is the Dios te Salve.

The weirdest part about this is that I don't feel like an imposter. This takes me by surprise. I was expecting to feel the same bits of silliness I felt when I called the corners for the first time back in August. But that's not what's happening here.

The only thing I can think of that explains this is that even though I'm not Catholic, my entire mother's side of the family is, going back for generations and generations. Granted they were French-Canadian (I think). But they were still Catholic, and maybe some part of me feels like I'm invoking the power of my ancestors by invoking the divine Catholic power they used to connect with. (Or maybe it's because I've seen Catholic prayer on TV a lot of times, and I remember it's supposed to be very serious and lead to a positive plot turn for the main character.) For whatever reason, it feels *right*.

I add three pinches of lavender salt to the water, then hold the jar in my hands. I murmur, "Trap all bad magic, all bad spirits, all bad energy, and send it back to where it came from." I repeat these instructions over and over, like a chant. It's not hard to mean what I'm saying.

Next is a bit of a circus act. I am supposed to set the plate on top of the water, then flip them both upside down. I take my mason jar of water and Goodwill cake plate over to the sink, just to be safe. I hold my breath and flip them over. Barely any water comes out. I feel victorious.

Next, I place the candle on top of the upside-down mason jar of water and prepare to say a prayer.

I flip to the front of the book. There's a section called "Prayers."[*]

I move past the Dios te Salve, and head straight for the Oracion a San Miguel Arcángel. According to Cross, San Miguel (also known as Saint Michael) is "a powerful angel of protection who is called on to fend off evil spirits, protect from bodily harm, and cast out demons." Cross also tells me he is "friendly, humorous, and boundlessly energetic." Just the sort of angel I need right now. I flip back to the spell page to make

---

[*] This is where I realize the Dios te Salve is, in fact, a Hail Mary, and not whatever I just did.

sure I'm doing this right, then carefully light the votive candle while trying to read:

"St. Michael the Archangel, defend us in battle. Be our defense
against the wickedness and snares of the devil. May God rebuke him, we
humbly pray, and do thou, O prince of the heavenly hosts, buy the power
of God, cast into hell Satan, and all the evil spirits who prowl the world,
seeking the ruin of souls. Amen."

The words feel foreign, but the truth is I do want to cast out evil, so
the hyperbole is comforting.

I pause. I remember Cross encouraging me to be sincere.

"I'm sorry, Michael," I add quietly. "I know I never speak to you. But
my grandmothers did, and their grandmothers did. I really, really need
help right now. Please protect the animals, protect this house, protect all
who dwell in it. I don't know what evil is here, but please send it back to
wherever it came from."

I pause again. This doesn't feel right. I feel like a beggar, a mooch,
asking for something without giving anything. Why should Miguel listen
to this white girl in her kitchen in her pajama shirt?

I shake my hands out and take a big breath. I try to stop thinking and
dig deep into my soul. I interlace my hands over my heart and put my
chin down. I close my eyes, wait a few moments.

"Michael, I know that prayer isn't everything. I know I don't have
a pure heart, but I hope you can see I'm trying. I'm asking you for help
because I don't know how to help the creatures that are relying on me
to protect them right now. If you cannot save them with just a prayer,
please grant me the knowledge I need to save them. Please help me protect the innocent things that are relying on me to keep them safe."

I open my eyes and watch the candle burn, feeling peaceful for the
first time today, the first time since Aaron Turner died.

I unlatch the kitchen screen door and walk into the dark of the backyard, sharply reminded that I'm still not wearing any pants. It's still so
hot out here. My hands clamp down against the jar and the plate to keep
the water from spilling as I teeter down the creaky wooden stairs into

the backyard. I set my reversal water on a planter box near the gate of the chicken run, where it will stay level.

I feel tingly. Every little crack of twig, falling leaf, and rustle of a tarp sends my spine shivering.

I look at the water jar one last time, then speed walk back into the house, away from the sizzling air.

DAY 327

Abuela spent her life among creatures that most of the world would dismiss as legend, fairy tale, or myth.
—J. ALLEN CROSS

Justin is outside doing some yardwork. By that I mean he's doing something with his tarps. He always seems to have six on hand and is shuffling them about for reasons I can no longer keep track of. I've come to learn that Washingtonians just really love tarps.

He shouts up to me on the deck, "You know, there are better ways to trap flies than that."

"What?" I say, squinting up from my book.

He gestures to my overturned spell jar, sitting on the corner of a faded blue planter box by the door of the chicken run.

"Oh. That's um . . . that's some spellwork. To protect the chickens. Please don't touch it."

Justin, who was partially raised by his abuela, stares at me for a moment, then says, "It also scares flies. It's a thing in Mexican culture." Then he goes back to shuffling his tarps.

"Did your grandma ever use it for . . . anything else?" I prod.

He shakes his head. "Not that I know of."

"Huh," I say, turning back to my book. "What a coincidence."

>))) ● (((

DAY 328

The tools are unimportant; we have all we need to make magic:
our bodies, our breath, our voices, each other.
—STARHAWK

I step off the roasting asphalt of the summer highway and into the AC paradise of my car. My hatchback is crammed with sleeping bags, tents, bags of crystals, backpacks full of costumes, and two nonbinary teenagers named Hawthorne and Marigold. I've offered to carpool with them because it's a long drive, and sharing the journey seemed like a nice way to make friends.

I'm about to spend seven uninterrupted days with them and eighty or so other complete strangers at an event called a "Witch camp." This will be my first multiday gathering of Witches. I've been waiting all year for this kind of secret coven gathering in the forest. I am excited.

Witch camps take place across the world, put on by the Reclaiming branch of Witchcraft. Reclaiming was founded in 1979 by Witches Diane Baker and Starhawk, and her pioneering guide *The Spiral Dance* is based on its philosophies. I wonder, with a spark of excitement, if I will get to meet Starhawk. However, I'm quickly told by Hawthorne not to make the mistake of fangirling around any community elders at Witch camp. The Reclaiming movement is a nonhierarchical, politically intensive, consensus-based, antiracist, queer-centered, nonviolent, earth-first form of neopagan Witchcraft. Hero worship is discouraged.

After a few more hours we peel off the freeway and roll down a pebbled road, tree branches growing thicker and thicker around my car until the boiling sun of the freeway has been diluted into innocent rays of forest light. We park in front of a wooden cabin, and I am checked into camp by a series of kind elder hippies. My shoes give a satisfying crunch of dirt with every step, and the scent of summer-warm tree bark radiates in the air.

At the newcomers meeting, I hold my hand out to several smiling people, mostly white, mostly female, mostly queer, but of various ages, standing around in alternating pairs of German hiking sandals and off-brand combat boots. They introduce themselves with the names of birds, plants, stones, and Greco-Roman figures. I am in Birkenstocks and use my real name. I fit right in.

Most of the two-hour newcomer meeting is a review of rules, specifically concerning fire safety, hydration, and when it's okay to touch other people ("never, unless they say so"). This last point is reiterated a disconcerting number of times. I am also told that something called "the Bower" and an activity known as "the chocolate ceremony" are not happening this year out of an abundance of caution around Covid. Drugs and alcohol are forbidden. Nudity, however, is fine. More than fine, actually. I am told it is our gods-given right, and, if I am new to nudity, a great way to get started is to ask someone if they'd like to take a shower with me. As we are a community, we must sign up for at least three volunteer shifts, as shared work ensures not only rich people get to have leisure while poor people work hard. It is then mentioned that for an extra $170 we don't have to do any chores. There are no clocks, but we must be on time for everything. There is a pay phone. It is broken. There is no cell service.

After I set up my tent, I head to the main ritual circle at dusk. I have brought my drum from home, a Gawharet El Fan doumbek with a PowerBeat skin, coated in mother of pearl and blue ceramic tiles. I bought it in Egypt when I lived there ten years ago—not at the tourist souk, but a real music shop in downtown Cairo. It cost a painful amount of money on my college budget, and I told myself I would grow into it. I have played it all of thirty hours in the ten years since. However, "portable instruments" were on the suggested packing list for camp, so I popped it into the car.

Tonight two drummers at the head of the wide circle start playing, and it's one of the beats I actually know. And I only really know three.

This one is Masmoudi Sogheir, also known as Baladi. The head drummer, a trim woman in her sixties with a flame of pink hair, sees me and my drum, and gestures for me to join in. My hands hit the drumhead, joining their beat. For the first time since arriving, I feel like I might belong.

Then, sixty minutes of invocations begin.

Different people enter the center of the circle, pacing around a carefully tended bonfire, and lead us in various exercises. A dreadlocked yoga instructor conducts us through a taproot dropping routine, the same one I learned in a book from Thea Sabin way back in August last year. This is the first time I've ever done this outside of my own home, with other people near me. They make noises. They sigh, they yelp, they exhale performatively as they send roots of dark energy into the earth and cones of light into the sky. Another person steps forward and invokes our collective ancestors, and to my surprise, Isis, who just so happens to be on the list of ever-rotating deities that the camp focuses on each year. We chant, "In a crumbling empire, let us remind ourselves, we are initiates into the mysteries of love." A spindly man in a midnight-blue cape runs around the circle and shouts, "We are not alone. We are not victims. Let us remember: *We. Are. Witches*," and everyone whoops and cheers.

I have a strange sensation running up and down my body, and it takes me a moment to pinpoint what it is: for the first time in a year, I feel unalone. I feel outside validation for the things I have previously only felt in my own home, worried if the neighbors can see me dressing up a cardboard box and rocking back and forth in front of it like a possession victim. It's like I've been doing independent study my whole life, and someone just dropped me off at a university on rush week. I feel collective effervescence, the glow of shared purpose with strangers.

We grab each other's hands and walk around the circle in my first Spiral Dance. We sing. We chant. We call the connection in our blood that goes back, back, to the doorway of the beginning of the universe. I still don't feel anything when I reach out for my ancestors, but it's difficult to get upset when there's this many sincere people dancing around me in the here and now.

After three hours of circling with other Witches, I go back to my tent and have a surprisingly good night's sleep.

DAY 329

Working alone is not ideal . . . Those who travel the uncharted
pathways of the mind alone run more risk of being caught in
subjectivity. Also, working with other people is much more fun.
—STARHAWK

I awake with the light of dawn to the sound of birdsong, and my camping neighbors having sex. I fart half a gallon of last night's vegan risotto into my sleeping bag and roll over.

My hip hurts. It still hurts. Less than it did in November, but it's still there. I really would love for it to stop. I wonder if it ever will.

After breakfast, we break out into groups, and I sit in a quiet grove of trees with about twenty other Witches to be introduced to the core concepts of Reclaiming. The pink-haired drumming woman from last night is leading the talk. She explains, "We are the hunter-gatherers of spiritual practices. We pull a lot from different places, and we are eclectic by necessity. You can blend traditions, respectfully. Sometimes you have to. But also it is really important for white people to connect with their indigenous roots. This is how we don't steal." She tells us that humans are hardwired for ritual, and also reminds us again that before we do anything to each other, we must have consent. The repetition of this point has officially crossed from comforting to alarming. She finishes with, "If you accidentally cross a boundary and hurt someone, it's very important that you don't focus on repair." I bristle at this. *Hippies never want solutions to anything,* I say to my own head, stabbing a patch of dirt with a stick. *Everyone just wants to spoon-hug their trauma and call it self-discovery.* Then a British man in short shorts sitting across from me chimes, "I like the idea of having a safe space, but also a fear space. No real work gets done in if you're in a safe space all the time. But also, you can become traumatized if you're forced into a fear space for too long. I'd love it if we could find a consent-based balance between these two spaces. Like a yin-yang." I stop poking the dirt. I stare at him. He has casually vocalized something I have felt for years, but have never been able to articulate. I decide he is my camp crush, despite the fact that he is both twenty years my senior and exuberantly gay.

At lunch, I load my plate with perky mint-and-cardamom-scented salad greens and a bowl of butternut curry soup that would cost thirty dollars in downtown San Francisco. I approach a table of strangers, ask if I can sit, and am heartily waved in. I'm discovering the nice thing about going to a place where you don't know anyone is that you are free to make friends with anyone, you aren't tempted to only stick to the people you know. The conversation steers around doubt and skepticism, and how these are very natural feelings in Witchcraft—really, any spiritual undertaking. I open up about my struggles between the desire to surrender to a higher power and the desire to create, to be in charge of everything, and how paranoid that has made me. My neighbor, a stooped woman in her sixties with mermaid-like silver hair, simply says, "Why are you setting it up as an either/or, as if this is a polarity? We are cocreators with the universe." The word "cocreate" rings in my head like a bell.

I've been at Witch camp for less than twenty-four hours and am already having conversations that solve problems I spent months trying to untangle alone, in my office, with my books. I have always been shy of covens, the terrifying intimacy that can unfurl there, more deep than a love affair, more vulnerable than a friendship. But now I understand there are more benefits to working with a group than just intimacy exposure therapy. A coven can get you out of the worst fights with your own head.

During my free time that afternoon I run into Yin-Yang at the arts and crafts table. He tells me he came to the US from England ten years ago because he felt called to the land, and because there was a stronger

Witchcraft community here. My eyebrows shoot up to the sky. I try to express to him the irony; that some English Witches look down on American Witches, they see our practices as inauthentic because we are removed from our "homeland." This makes his eyebrows shoot up to the sky. He tells me about all the work he has done with the indigenous communities that used to steward the very forest we are sitting in. He knows four different medicinal uses for banana slugs. The only thing I know about banana slugs is how to test if someone is a sociopath by asking if they want to put salt on one. I feel embarrassed at my comparatively paltry connection to the land I grew up on. I try to imagine what it would feel like to be so certain you're not supposed to be where you are, to be called to a new land.

DAY 330

Interconnection demands from us compassion,
the ability to feel with others so strongly that our passion for
justice is itself aroused.
—STARHAWK

Today we are studying fire in my group at Witch camp, which means we sing one three-minute song about how "everything in the universe is fucking" and then spend two hours on the importance of consent and other people's boundaries. Literally. I am teamed up with a seventy-year-old elf-sized woman in top-to-bottom denim for an exercise in projecting and feeling out each other's personal boundaries. I do not like the idea of standing in front of a perfectly nice senior citizen in a forest with no cell service, testing the limits of her personal space. But, to my surprise, I mostly correctly guess what her projected shield looks like (a thick, cold graveyard stone), and she mostly correctly guesses mine (a clear white bubble with spikes).

Later that night there is a dance party. It's just past sunset, and only a small gaggle of people are surrounding the bonfire, awkwardly shuffling. This is the law of dance parties: they are lame in the beginning, until at least thirty people show up or it's after 10:45. Then there is collective permission to actually get down. Turns out this is true even for Witches.

The music, however, is too good, and I am breaking the rules and actually dancing. This is because I love to dance. I love to dance carefully, focusing on my feet and arm placements, and I love to dance badly, getting completely lost in sound. Usually I do this alone at home, when I'm sure Justin is in the other room locked into a video game, or at a club with friends, after at least two rounds of drinks. But this is Witch camp. I'm supposed to be free to do whatever I want, as long as I don't touch anybody without their consent. So I'm dancing. I'm the only one dancing, and I feel like the One Who Is Different. But with this feeling also comes the realization that no one is looking at me. No one cares. I'm just another Witch being herself.

To feel different, and to have no one notice, no one care, is inexpressibly liberating.

After ten minutes or so, I turn around and see one other person dancing, a six-foot-three topless trans woman bobbing back and forth with her hands in the air like she's on a surfboard. Like me, she feels the rhythm. I sidle up to her, give her a high-five, and scream, "Why is nobody fucking dancing but us?"

And instantly feel like I just stepped in dog shit.

I slow my dancing. I look around. No one is looking back at me. Maybe nobody heard me. But I have this plummeting feeling like I have crossed a line. This is it, this is when everyone realizes I'm a fraud, a grinch, and I don't belong. The one rule at Witch camp is to let people be and do whatever they want without shame; harm none and do what ye will. And here I just shamed a whole bunch of people for not dancing? I meant it as a joke, of course, but no one is sarcastic in utopia. Even joking about shame makes me feel like I might as well have just screamed, "I love fracking!"

I feel bad, because I realize I feel oddly protective of this place. Eighty percent of everyone here is queer; I've been in spaces where being nonwhite was the majority, but I have never been in a space where being queer was the majority. The people here are seeking to better know themselves, understand their power, and discover their true will, so they can better create magic—which is to say, create a world where they won't feel like they have to hide who they are. Because that's what Witches do: they don't beg for help, they manifest it. I heard someone shout a curse to Mitch McConnell in the fire last night and rolled my eyes. I don't like him, either, I thought, but can't we just have a good time out here instead of reminding ourselves about the unsympathetic politics of the mundane world?

Tonight I realize it doesn't work that way. You can't be a Witch without being political. There is no such thing as an apathetic Witch. It's the same reason this place feels less like spellwork camp and more like group therapy camp—it explains why so much of Witchcraft feels like therapy, which has driven me crazy from day one. Witches seek to create what they want, but in order to do that, you have to know what you want. What you *really* want. This means knowing your boundaries, your will, your desires, your uncomfortable truths—it means knowing deeply who you are. At least who you are right now.

In a world simultaneously full of options and oppression, that is much harder than it seems. How can you know what you want when you are changing all the time? No wonder we are told to treat each other like we are already bruised. No wonder we are told part of our job is to keep each other safe.

DAY 331

To communicate with the Deep Self, the Goddess/God Within,
we resort to symbols, to art, poetry, music, myth, and the actions
of ritual that translate abstract concepts into the language of
the unconscious.
—STARHAWK

At my breakout group in the forest today, the element we are studying is water. This will involve going into a deep trance. Our teacher
explains that for some people, falling into trance is easy, for others, it is
extremely difficult. There is usually not a lot of middle ground. Another
person raises their hand and asks if we must sit still, and the teacher says,
"No, although most people find this easier."

I pipe up and add, "I thought trance wasn't for me, because I have
trouble sitting still. Then I found I could do it if I allowed myself to move,
either standing or sitting. Actually, that was the only way I could get it to
work." I feel a little presumptuous saying this, because I think I've only
ever had one successful trance in my entire life, and I'm talking over a
guy who looks like he's been organizing ecstatic orgies in yurts since
1989. But the teacher nods at me, and thanks me for sharing. If I can
give someone else permission not to feel like they have to be still to be
spiritual, it's worth speaking up.

There's a swift rush of fabric moving and chairs creaking as everyone
sits down. I stand, along with one other person.

I close my eyes and a drumbeat starts. I sway back and forth, letting the teacher's voice and the sound of the beats become my entire
world. We are instructed to go on a path inside ourselves, where we
come across a tree, one that has existed inside us forever. We walk up
to it slowly, taking in its grandeur. We are told we notice a door at the
base of this great tree, and to open the door and go inside. We walk

down past the "earth people and the crystal people," down, down, following a river that grows wider and stronger as we descend, down, down, down, to a dark, hidden place. Then I am told I see a door blocking my path. "What is this door, what is it made of?" the teacher's voice floats into my ears. "What is this door made of?" The drumbeat is steady, like a heartbeat.

I imagine that the door blocking my path is a thicket of sticky, gooey cobwebs. It's disgusting and putrid. "What is this door? What is the door that keeps you from following the water?" the teacher asks again.

The fear that I'm an inherently bad person, bubbles up an answer from the back of my mind. *I can't ever just be myself, because I will hurt other people.*

I feel some tears well up in my eyes. This is a bit of a relief. I am worried my teachers think I'm phoning it in because I'm just swaying back and forth like a drunk teenager. I let the tears fall, as a show of effort.

"How does the water get through this door?" the teacher asks again, more urgently.

In my mind's eye, I see the door. It's not totally solid.

"How does the water get through this door?" the teacher repeats, over and over.

It flows. This word echoes through mind like it's on a pair of golden wings. I know this doesn't seem a like a big deal. But it feels like I'm summiting Everest.

Water flows around things. That is the secret of water. It seeps through the spaces you can't see, weaves through obstacles like silk. It moves unpreventably toward the place where it will be easiest for it to rest. It does this without effort, as a natural act. So I watch the water simply flow through the repulsive door, and I flow through with it.

"You follow the water to another door," my teacher continues, the drumbeat still going. "This door is thicker. The water can't get around it. What is this door?"

My mind offers me an image of a cement door now, in the underground tree cave of my mind. It's watertight, the river rising around the base, the inside of a sinking ship.

"How is the water going to get around this door?"

The water can't flow. This door is solid, there's not one crack.

"What is this door?" he repeats. "How is the water going to get around this door?"

"How are you going to get around this door?" he says again. I'm starting to worry we're not actually supposed to figure it out.

"What is this door?" He is almost yelling. I'm starting to panic.

If I was who I really want to be, no one would love me, says a little voice inside my head.

I'd be more embarrassed about crying at this point except that someone two paces to my left sounds like they're having a DEFCON 1 breakdown. We're all basically a heap of weeping toadstools on the forest floor at this point. I keep my eyes glued shut.

But the cement door opens, as if the password was just a matter of me recognizing some of my more embarrassing personal fears.

"You are now on the other side of the door, at the shore of a great ocean," the teacher says. "The place where the river has been, and always will be flowing toward."

In my mind, I walk toward the ocean—clear and lukewarm, the sandy beach golden and clean. The sky is frozen in a peach cream sunset. There is a twinkling, fairylike garden surrounding the beach, like the backdrop of a Keebler elf commercial. I walk into the water, and something reaches up and holds me, tight and warm as my mother when I was a baby.

"I will always be here, and I will always love you," says a voice in the water, the water that has been flowing inside me the entire time I've been alive. I understand, without being told, that I can come back to this water anytime I want. There is no scarcity of this resource. I think about the water that exploded in my house around my dad's birthday. I think about the water that always seems to explode around me when I'm happy or relaxed. I think about how water has always scared me.

After some time in the healing love ocean, we are instructed to journey back up the path we came, past the now-open doors, past "the crystal people and earth people," back up to the tree roots, back up to the sky, and back to reality. "Open your eyes," the teacher says.

I open my eyes, and see a circle of tarot cards has been laid out around the cold bonfire circle at our campsite. People pat their jeans, wipe their faces, avoid each other's gazes as they adjust back to reality.

"Water is the element most associated with divination," my teacher continues. "As well as the powers of the subconscious mind. Pull a card and see what your subconscious wants to tell you now."

I wipe my eyes quickly and walk up to the circle of stones, bending down to grab a card. I have a feeling it will be a sword. I turn it over and am greeted by the six of swords: two women in a boat, rowing over a lake of dark water. One is sitting at the far edge, her back to the viewer, shoulders hunched in pain and exhaustion. The other woman stands above her, oar in hand, a protectress. She stares up at me measuredly from the card with large, dark eyes. She knows how to get them both across the water.

I don't have to look up what it means.

DAY 333

The secret itself may be meaningless when out of context.
—STARHAWK

Tonight, at the end of our regular nightly ritual, the whole camp is led through another deep trance. At the end, the Witch leading the ritual tells us the veils have become thin between the worlds, and asks us to look for omens. A few minutes go by, with nothing but the sound of crackling logs and rustling leaves, as we all wait in the dark forest for a sign of something. We are instructed to shout any vision into the fire.

A mosquito lands near my mouth. I try to flick it off and end up splatting it on my cheek. It feels like a raindrop. I cringe with disgust.

I wonder if this is my sign.

"Rain," I speak into the darkness, toward the fire, feeling foolish.

DAY 334

Wiccans therefore first come to accept that words are only valuable as signposts and guides that point toward mystic experience.
—TIMOTHY RODERICK

It's the last day of Witch camp. Marigold and Hawthorne pile back into my car, a tired bundle of sweat and sunshine and feet. I come home, walk into my front door, and Justin greets me with a "hello, Witch." I cover him in kisses. I am unashamed to tell him how much I missed him. I notice an absence of my normal urge to feel self-conscious about sharing how much I care about another person; if I'm revealing too much, if I'm coming off as clingy. Who cares?

He asks how camp was and I try to tell him things like how important it is that there's a cis man named Daffodil who wears sundresses and conducts healing rituals and cries openly in front of bonfires. How important it is to live in a world where you can leave your backpack on the ground outside overnight and know it will still be there the next morning. How I understand the water inside of me.

None of it sounds right. Every time I tell a story he nods politely and says, "That sounds cool," which is how I can tell I'm not explaining it correctly. If I was, he'd be asking me how we can make the world like this all the time. Which is all I want to figure out.

DAY 335

There are still some states that have laws against practicing divination.
—MAJA D'AOUST AS QUOTED BY FRANCES F. DENNY

I wake up to puddles. It has rained. It has rained in Oakland, California, in the middle of summer. This does not happen.

To be clear: I don't mean it's foggy. I don't mean it has drizzled. I mean it has *rained*. Rain like what happens sometimes in winter. Rain like I said into the fire at Witch camp.

I go outside and stare at the puddles and smell the petrichor coming off the asphalt.

Maybe it really is just a freak coincidence.

Regardless, I can't help feeling like a real Witch.

JULY

))) ● (((

DAY 340

I have noticed one key factor in my students' struggle to manifest
their spells and intentions, and that is that they all have
expectations.
—JULIET DIAZ

When I was doing a dating tour on OKCupid back in 2018, I was methodical. I had criteria. I was no longer interested in men who had zero career motivations, no hobbies besides video games, and had not yet realized that hating everything isn't, in fact, the same thing as being intelligent. I wanted someone who had found the optimistic side of nihilism, someone who loved his family, had a job (literally any job, just a job), a creative hobby or two, and no addictions except perhaps coffee.

I was cursed with success.

"Wow . . ." Justin gasps in the foyer of the house we're currently touring in Washington, his gaze fixed on an Art Deco sconce on the far wall. It's a former bed-and-breakfast, built in the late 1920s, meticulously

preserved and recently upgraded into a few apartments. We are looking at the "manor" unit. It has three hotel-sized bedrooms, an industrial
kitchen, a private sauna, a bathtub the size of a paddleboat, and (I have
to look up the definition of the word just to be sure I'm using it right) a
solarium. The floors are painted with sunlight, thanks to a ceiling that
seems to be more skylight than actual roof. There's a pair of French doors
that open onto a fifty-foot wraparound deck. This allows the house's residents to gaze out over the canopy of evergreen trees surrounding the
manor, which appears to be the Pacific Northwest's response to *Fern-
Gully*. There is a private orchard.

The trouble with dating someone who actually loves his family, and
has a job and creative hobbies, is that he will want to be near that family, need a place to do that job, and have room for those hobbies. Justin
and I have spent the last weekend on our rental hunt in Seattle, and it
is abundantly clear we have missed the boat on affordable housing. This
was not supposed to happen. We are supposed to be dreaded Califor-
nians, fangs dripping with kale juice, terrorizing the rental market with
tech-inflated bank accounts and immunity to five-dollars-per-gallon
gas. However, the houses we have toured in Seattle at our price range
are a joke. One had a bedroom Justin couldn't stand up in. In another,
none of the windows opened. We aren't rich. But we aren't in our twenties anymore, either. We have standards. They include opening windows
and standing up.

So now we're in Bremerton, Washington, ninety minutes away by
car from Seattle ("one hour if you take the ferry!"), looking at a house so
comically majestic and so painfully in our price range I feel myself on the
verge of a panic attack.

He is going to make me live here.

Half his friends and most of his family live in Kitsap County—this
county—not in Seattle, so living here would actually make him closer to
his loved ones. He's an aficionado for anything Art Deco and Art Nou-
veau, and this place comes with original 1920s light fixtures, Escher-
style woodcut carvings, and hundred-year-old oak bureaus framed with
swirling stained glass. There's room here for all his hobbies. I think I'm

going to have to invent new hobbies just to justify my presence. You could park a fully armed artillery tank in the kitchen. I don't even know what to do with that much space.

The property manager walks us into the solarium. A pair of butter-yellow and sea-green cranes shimmer in the floor-to-ceiling windows on the farthest wall, framed by the forest outside. Justin puts a hand over his heart.

Fuck.

This isn't what was supposed to happen. I was meticulously clear in my spellwork. I wanted a house that had a bedroom, a home office for both our jobs, decent light, maybe a couple of trees nearby, and access to a washer-dryer that didn't require coins. This is all of those things, and a bag of cedar chips. But I *very specifically* wrote "in *Seattle.*" I don't know anything about Bremerton other than it's a naval shipyard town where one in five people are living below the poverty line. There's a military base twenty minutes north. Both the upstairs and downstairs tenants of this place are in the armed forces. Meanwhile, I think war is stupid. And I like talking about how I think war is stupid. It literally might be danger-ous for me to live here.

But all of Justin's community would be nearby; the closest thing I have to a community outside of California. And this house is practically spun from the raw fibers of his dreams.

I manifested Justin's dream house, I realize, staring into the ivory pit of the Jacuzzi tub off of the master bedroom. I recall what Lauren said about magic being a potato cannon.

Augusten Burroughs spends part of *Toil and Trouble* talking about how he used his magic to coax his unwitting husband to leave Man-hattan and move into a spectacular vintage mansion in the middle of nowhere. They tour a series of dilapidated estates with waning enthu-siasm before finding the house that is the manifestation of Burroughs's spell: regal, ancient, hand-crafted, sturdy, with original leaded glass win-dows, cauldron-sized fireplaces, sunrooms, hardwood floors, antique cabinets, a pharmacy-sized kitchen, and fairy-tale green landscaping. In other words: a Witch house.

Maybe Witches are only capable of manifesting one kind of house, I think as I consider that the downstairs shower has the same floor dimensions as my first bedroom after college. *Or maybe Justin is secretly a better Witch than me.*

Or maybe it's all for a reason. Pam Grossman, host of *The Witch Wave* podcast, once said that in your spellwork you should "leave some room for spirit to have a better idea than you do."

But that's bullshit, Pam, I think. *Witches don't ask for things; they create them.* I learned that months ago from Thea Sabin. She describes it as the key difference between prayer and spellwork, which are often conflated. When you pray you are asking God to make something happen. When you perform a spell, you are *telling* (not asking) the universe to make something happen. You can ask a god or goddess for a boost, but it's you, the Witch, who is in charge. Assuming this house is a product of divine intervention assumes that the divine knows what's better for me than I do. Which, I would immediately agree it does. But that's the former Sunday schooler in me talking. Assuming the universe knows what's better for me than I do feels so very . . . Un-witchly.

It's not that I don't like the house. Of course I like the house. Living here would be like living in an Airbnb. And not a normal Airbnb—one of those houses you put on a Pinterest board titled "dream wedding" that rents at eighteen hundred dollars a night and the landlords force you to sign a triplicate waiver before they send over the lockbox code. The issue is the location. I was already compromising by moving to Seattle, away from my closest friends and family, but at least Seattle is a big city where I could distract myself and make new friends. I was already going to be a stranger in a strange land. I don't want to be a stranger in a strange forest an hour outside of a strange land.

But I have not seen Justin this happy in literal years. All the Covid changes hit him harder than me: his band, his friend group, his in-person job all basically dissolved. I don't have it in me to tell him he can't have this, that he has to get rid of half his stuff and move into a glorified shack with windows that don't open and a bedroom he can't fully stand up in—all so I can feel like I'm a big girl in a big city doing . . . nebulous big-girl city things.

I know if I insisted that we live in Seattle, in a shack, he would do it. He would do it for me, because I'm moving up here for him. We're not supposed to say that out loud, of course. It puts too much pressure on the relationship. I'm supposed to be moving up here entirely for myself, as if he is in a space vacuum and I am living out some girl boss fantasy that requires displacing myself eight hundred miles from my immediate family and job network. Of course, I'm moving here for him. I wouldn't even be here, staring wistfully out at the Puget Sound from a private wraparound deck on the side of a mansion, if I didn't know him. But I do know him. So, I am.

I wanted a man who loved his family, had real hobbies, and real dreams.

And unfortunately, that is exactly the kind of shit men like that will make you do.

Well, and the ace of wands.

I think about how it's not too late for me to bail, to say no, for us to have a tear-filled breakup and go our separate ways, me in California, him in Washington, wishing each other the best. I have been in a few serious relationships in my life. All of them had a glass ceiling: he was an addict; he was anti-choice; there was nowhere for us to live. Now I'm with someone who is telling me he wants to build a real life with me in a palace. I don't have it in me to refuse this.

I remember the warm, golden feeling that flooded over my skin during the house manifestation spell, when I really let go, felt my doubt evaporate, and I believed completely that it had worked. I had done it; I had truly manifested something. I thought it was the sensation of success.

It wasn't success. I realize, watching him float down the stairs toward the property manager to ask, to beg, to know what we have to do to lock this place in.

It was love.

DAYS 350–361

You bond with the land you live on.
—THORN MOONEY

The rest of the month is a blur. Justin and I rope two friends into helping us move everything into a pod. The Oakland apartment seems to keep vomiting up more things: forgotten collections of books, missing sets of tools, CD cases I kept from high school but don't even have a drive to play on anymore. I sell things, I drop off things to donation stations and am greeted by hipsters in Doc Martens and oversized dad jeans, frowning at me for bringing them yet another trunk of trinkets I can't bear to send to a landfill. I have a squeeze of sorrow when I send off the cardboard box that served as my altar for a year. There are people in this world who own nothing but a pot, a bed, a power strip, and a Mickey Mouse wall clock. I start to envy them. I feel like I am being punished for my Western decadence.

Joanna spends two days with me on the I-5 locked in my hatchback while Bird and Basil tremble in their crates, listening to me worry that my deathly bald tires might pop in the 110-degree heat around Redding because I didn't have time to get them changed before we left.

We cross the Columbia River bridge and I drive under a sign that says Entering Washington. The reality of what I'm doing hits me, no longer able to hide behind the logistics and deadlines of moving a household across state lines. I start to cry behind my sunglasses. I really, truly don't want Joanna to see. We are alone in a sardine can. She sees.

"Okay. It's okay," she says, like she's coaching an eight-year-old through a skinned knee. "We have two hours to get all of this out, until you get to the new house. You can get all of it out here."

"What the fuck am I doing?" I squeak.

"You had to do this. If you didn't do it, you'd be in California asking yourself 'what if' for the next five years, and with love, I do not want to listen to that."

I've been repressing my emotions around this move. I refused a goodbye party when Eleanor offered to throw one. I told people to think of it as a year abroad. When Melody came over for a final dinner, we hugged for a few moments too long before she said into my shoulder, "Nothing special about this, I'll see you soon, and I'm saying I love you for no reason at all. Nothing is about to happen!" I think if I had to face what I'm doing head-on, I wouldn't do it. Most skydivers close their eyes right before they jump out of the plane. You have to trick yourself into big things sometimes.

But now we are here. I walk into my new home, and it smells like warm cedar and clean carpet, the windows opening out to the forest. We walk down to the beach at the end of the property, the calm, inky silk of the Puget Sound caressing the stones along the shore. The water is so clear I can see tiny fish swim, and clams snoozing in beds of sand at the bottom. A seal peaks its head above the water and stares at me.

That night, Justin and I curl up in bed in our new bedroom. *You're here, you lucky duck. You're here. The hard part is over.* I drift off to sleep.

We are awakened at 2:00 a.m. by a rocket-launch-volume hiss from the far wall. It sounds like someone just stabbed the Night King. We get up to investigate. We can't figure out what made the noise, but nothing seems to be on fire. We get back in bed. The air mattress starts leaking. At 3:00 a.m., Basil decides to sing us his new song titled "I Hate This Place, and I Hate You." At 4:00 a.m., the sun rises, blasting nonconsensual angelic light into the curtainless bedroom. I don't fall asleep again until 6:30 a.m. At first I think all of these problems are my fault; it's my anxiety being reflected back at me. The law of attraction strikes again. Then I remember my friend at Witch camp saying I'm a cocreator, not a perfect mirror. I let go of blaming myself.

The next morning, we see a river otter scooting through the backyard. All seems well until water starts leaking out of the kitchen ceiling, a steady stream pouring out of one of the light fixtures, below a shower upstairs. I panic. *Not again.* I thought water and I were on good terms. I thought I understood the secret of flow, or whatever.

We text the landlord and a plumber appears within an hour. He cannot re-create the leak. He removes the light and everything is dry. He gets on a chair and pats his hand around to confirm. "If you hadn't shown me a video, I'd say you were hallucinating," he tells me. "There is no leak here."

We find out that the moving company won't have our things delivered for three weeks past when we were promised. I have one pair of pants and two pairs of underwear to last me that time. I recall telling the universe that I wanted to live simply and in nature. The universe seems to have replied: "Cool! All your shit is gone. Here's an otter."

Later that day, I realize I still haven't cleansed and greeted the house. Spiritually, I mean. I was waiting until I was in a better mental state, but I'm starting to think I have the cart-and-horse configuration backward, and I should do it now in order to improve our relationship.

Despite the terrifying hissing sound that came from the bedroom our first night *and* the brand-new air leak in our mattress (which was fine in Oakland) *and* the mysterious water from the ceiling *and* Joanna's proclamation that "this place is definitely haunted"—I think this place has good vibes. Houses with this many skylights can't be haunted. At worst, it witnessed some Bing Crosby–era domestic abuse. But all the paint has been changed since then, so really what's holding on?

I dissolve some peppermint essential oil in propylene glycol and mix it with water and salt in a spray bottle. I packed these things in my car expressly for this purpose. When Liza moved into a new house in the Bay Area several years ago, our tiny coven walked sunwise inside and around the house, one person spraying peppermint oil, the other sprinkling saltwater, another following with a smoking bundle of herbs. It was to cleanse the space of any bad energy or spirits, and to greet the structure itself. As we walked, I saw a few spiders escape the corners and run for the door. Years later, I read that peppermint oil is a highly effective spider deterrent.

I go around the house and start spraying, imagining shadows

being chased away. I say, "Hello. I am here. I would like to be friends. I intend to take care of you. Thank you for welcoming me." I am feeling pretty good, until the sprayer breaks in the middle of bedroom number two.

I don't quit that easily, I think. I open up the bottle and pour the liquid into my palm, flicking drops over the floorboards and into the ceiling corners.

My palm burns with peppermint oil for the rest of the day, no matter how many times I wash it.

If I was one for reading into signs, I'd say this place, despite a lovely welcome from the landlords and a tarot reading that basically told me to move up here, was not particularly thrilled to see me.

But the primary force behind Witchcraft isn't intuition. It's will.

And according to my astrological chart, I am very, very charming.

DAY 366

This magic did not involve the supernatural. It involved an understanding of psychological and environmental processes.
—MARGOT ADLER

This is it. The final twenty-four hours in my year and a day trying to become a Witch.

All I can think about is how much more there's left to read, how many people I didn't talk to, how many traditions I didn't explore, how many stories are still out there. And above all, how many questions I still have unanswered.

At the end of this year, I was hoping to finally be able to erase the doubt in my mind that magic was real and accessible to me. I am not sure I accomplished this. But today I have a phone call with Raven Hinojosa, a woman I met at Witch camp, author and creator of *The Re-Enchantment* art vlog series on YouTube. I want to follow up with something she said one day when our teachers were explaining the importance of feeling certain about an outcome to ensure success in spellwork. Raven poked her head up from her journal and said: "You don't have to believe in magic for it to work. Your spell will still work, even if you have doubt." I just stared at her.

Back in December, I discovered that "honest placebos" can still be effective; theoretically I could not believe in magic, but my spell could still very well have the desired effect. But this is hardly a common idea in modern Witchcraft—most people still agree magical success hinges on belief. Intrigued by Raven's position, I asked if I could call her after camp.

Today, we get on the phone, and in her soft soprano voice she tells me, "When I began, I started with that idea that I really had to believe. A lot of people start there. But you don't. You literally don't have to do that at all. My introduction to spellcraft came through chaos magic, the postesoteric way of doing things. People in the early twentieth century were kind of rebelling against the Hermetic system, saying that, 'We don't have to be so particular about this specific demon and that specific planet.' They were coming to see that all of these things were just energies. People were starting to understand the power of thought meeting the interconnected web of circumstance that we're all in.

"So the logic thread here is that if in my consciousness I'm creating a version of reality, then there is something that happens simultaneously on a larger and larger scale. My little thought bubble that's infused with whatever this material is that touches everything at once—it scales out and out and out and reverberates, like rings in the surface of water, throughout the universe. That's how I interpret 'as above so below.' And I don't think that requires my faith to work. I think that's a bit grandiose, actually. Like I might be an agent of change, but I'm throwing pebbles in a pond. How I feel about throwing pebbles in the pond is not significant."

"So then, how does it work?" I ask her.

"How does magic work? Is that what you're asking?" She chuckles.

I pause.

"I guess it is."

"Witchcraft is a mystical tradition," she says thoughtfully. "And by that I mean, experiential. I don't believe in any single thing that I haven't experienced. It's not because I'm a skeptic and I think everything needs to be proved to me. I've just experienced a lot of weird shit, so I believe in a lot of weird shit. And I'm naturally inclined to it, sure, but you know, that's what makes Witchcraft a tool of personal transformation and personal power: it's about your own immediate experience.

"I'm not surprised that at one point in your journey, you started to feel this pressure to be in charge of everything, and then got anxious and paranoid. There's an overwhelming sense of being in control of everything in modern Witchcraft; I see it pressed on new Witches. I think one thing that the Christians do have, that I wish we had more of, is the idea of service and surrender. That's a really powerful and central part of being a spiritual person, to have a sense of dedicating your life to something bigger, centering your life in service of the larger life force experiment, to help create harmony and evolution. I think that's actually what makes Witches healers. In fact I think eventually, it's almost inevitable. I don't know if it's possible to be a Witch and not be a healer."

We get off the phone, and I think more about how internal my year has been. Aside from a handful of volunteer work sessions, and a couple of fulfilled requests to light candles, I haven't done much for the outside world.

I wanted community. I never asked myself what I had to offer a community.

I know I want to live in a world where the values of Witchcraft aren't considered rebellious.

I start to wonder what it would take to create that world.

EPILOGUE

For me, reviewing old magical diaries is never a pleasant experience . . . I am paralyzed by a combination of nauseating embarrassment and amazement.
—LON MILO DuQUETTE

It's a clear, warm day in mid-August. Justin gifted me a kayak for my birthday, and I'm not totally sure how to use it, but I put my butt in the seat and flap the oars about and seem to get somewhere.

Today, I finish work at six and the sun is still hours from setting. I walk down the grassy hill to the water's edge, untie the massive plastic toy of a boat, and slide it into the water, where it floats expectantly. I straddle the kayak, it wobbles, and I hear the bottom crunch into rocks and seashells. Then I haul my legs in, and eventually push off into the dark water of the channel. I'm afloat on my PVC magic carpet, peering at the world a few feet above the surface. I don't have a waterproof cover for my cellphone, so when I'm on the kayak I'm truly alone. There are no distractions beyond what's in front of me (or anyone to call if I capsize). It's just the lapping water, the seagulls, the salt-and-kelp-scented air, my arms, and my thoughts.

I think about how a year ago, I would describe myself as someone who is afraid of water. Now, in Washington, I'm virtually surrounded by it. It's at the end of most roads, like a protective moat. It falls every other day from the sky and makes the world refract with celestial light. The Puget Sound is dark, and hundreds of feet deeper than the San Francisco Bay, but it doesn't scare me the way dark water used to.

The nature in Kitsap County is so green, so lush, so splendid and dense that it's causing me some anxiety. Every day I don't go outside I feel bad, as if all this beauty is going to get snatched away any moment, and I'm sinning by not enjoying it to its fullest while I can.

I think about this as I paddle, keeping my eyes on the horizon, trying to train my arms to work evenly so my kayak goes straight. I don't think I realized what an inherently guilty person I was until I started this Witchcraft journey. Witchcraft is not a guilt-stricken religion. It's the designated opposite. A Witch is supposed to be unapologetic, self-actualized, and confident; strength of belief is what powers magic, and what is belief if not spiritually flavored confidence? I think a lot of people expected that I would "Eat, Spell, Love" my way into my most authentic, unapologetic self during this year. But if anything, the opposite is true. I overcame the guilt I felt toward not living up to my father's perceived legacy, and there was healing in that. But that's about it. My guilt around my role in climate change—however insignificant it is as a single human—at some point exploded into eco-anxiety. Maybe it was the day I spent volunteering to pick up trash at a marsh, or maybe there was an underlying eco-guilt in my personality that drew me to tree-hugging Witchcraft in the first place. Whatever the reason, during the year I found myself hardly able to throw anything into a trash can without a whirlpool of guilt running through me. I had a lot of trouble shopping for everything my spellbooks required of me without feeling like I was just generating more trash in the name of a religion that's supposed to prioritize environmentalism.

And this wasn't the only area where my guilt actually increased. The more I tried to explore ancestry, the more I felt blocked by my guilt because of the actions of my colonial forebears. Through the year, I kept trying to write specific sections about "shadow work"—that sticky part of our souls, our past, our heritage that we'd rather not deal with, and that modern Witchcraft urges us to contend with. But no passage was ever quite right. It took me even longer than my 366 days to I realize that this entire book is shadow work. I don't think shadow work is ever truly finished.

What I also realized, somewhere along the way, is that guilt is like fuel. Sitting by itself, it is useless and dangerous. Put it to action, and it is power.

I find I am thinking more about politics. I consider more deeply the lifecycles of my food. I read up on the initiatives of the Suquamish, the local indigenous tribe on whose land I'm now living, to see what I can help with. I am signing more petitions and donating more money than ever before, especially to individuals in countries that my ancestors colonized. It doesn't feel like work. It feels good.

I've been paddling for about fifteen minutes, but my arms are already getting sore. I'm probably not using my core enough, relying too much on my arms to paddle. I take a break and watch some seagulls in the distance, floating on the wind.

When Justin and I finally got our pod back from the moving company, one of the first things I unpacked, without much thought, was my Witchcraft altar, and the bookshelf it lives on. I know I don't need to have this up anymore; my experiment is done. But I'm not ready to stop seeing it every day at the edge of my bedroom. To the unsuspecting eye, it probably just looks like a shelf of knickknacks and beach trash anyway.

As I unpacked the actual books that live inside the bookshelf—wiping the covers of old high school journals, my father's Bible, my childhood CD of Shel Silverstein's *Where the Sidewalk Ends*, letters from past beloveds, cards from my mother, photo albums from friends, pictures of old father figures—I realized that by instinct, I first built my altar on top of all of this. Which means all my ritual items have been getting charged by the love sitting beneath them, all year. I cherish these objects; I treat them with care. They have been nourishing my mental health for a long, long time, before I even began this spiritual experiment. Whenever I tried to reach out for my blood ancestors during my year and a day, I never felt anything I trusted.

It occurs to me that perhaps my ancestors—my chosen ancestors—

have been here the whole time on this bookshelf, simply waiting for me to notice they've already been in every part of my magic since before I officially tried to start using it.

I start paddling again and see that another boat is heading toward me across the channel, a large white yacht. They slow, I assume they see me. I've learned that a few minutes after a larger boat passes me on the water, waves of wakes rock my little kayak, bouncing me up and down like a plastic rubber ducky in a bathtub. I haven't been pitched overboard yet, but I'm too new to know what my little boat can actually take, what *I* can actually take. I appreciate the larger, nicer, automatic aquatic vehicle for slowing down so the wakes won't be large. People around here are generally nice like that.

I've had a few weeks now to discover my new home on its own terms. When I tell people outside of Bremerton that I moved to Bremerton, I am usually met with two reactions: "Where?" or "Why?!" People from Seattle talk about it like it's a barren strip of big-box stores, a meth hub devoid of meaningful culture. So allow me to share some things I like about the place: The Seattle Freeze does not apply. People say hello to you, and actually expect you to respond. I can park my car downtown and don't have to worry about the window getting smashed for no reason. I don't need to find a Whole Foods because I can get cheaper and fresher produce directly from farmers; I have two neighbors who sell succulent houseplants and eggs out of their garages, respectively. I feared I would be spit on in public if anyone found out I was from California. Instead, half of everyone I meet is from California, or at least somewhere else but here. I assume the military base plays a large part in the culture of welcoming strangers; everyone is coming and going.

There are other adjustments. Bremerton is more politically purple than I'm used to. I know conservatives exist in Oakland; I think they are just smart enough to keep their mouths shut. I'm no longer going to be able to laze in the knowledge that most people around share my politics, which means I'm going to have to actually listen to others' differing opinions and vocalize my beliefs.

At Kitsap county's only grocery co-op, I saw a flyer wall of advertisements for house cleaners, lawyers, tutors, and something called a "tan-tric earth magick" workshop. Later that night I went home and fell down an internet wormhole into Kitsap's tiny occult community. I remember Blanca telling me that the thing she missed most about being a Jehovah's Witness was the ironclad sense of community. She could go anywhere in the country, in the world, and be greeted like family by a group of people who all shared the same spirituality. If you told me a year ago that I would be seeking out the Witchcraft community to ground me while I adjust to life in Bremerton, I would have stared at you as though you had said, "Next year, you will become a tiny elephant."

On the kayak, I stare at an uninterrupted length of evergreen forest to my left, watching a pair of seagulls take turns fighting over who gets to peck at the carcass of a crab. I think about a conversation I have seen budding on social media over the past year, where Witches accuse other Witches of focusing too much on casting spells, rather than leaving their homes to create change out in the world. This is a false, and infuriating, dichotomy. You can do both—in fact, I'd wager you need both. You need spiritual work to calm you, to inspire you, to remind you we are all made of the same capital-G Good stuff. This is how you can keep rolling up your sleeves and doing work in the real world, without it feeling like work.

Experiencing the sensation (while sober!) that all objects are inter-connected, is perhaps the greatest way that this year changed me. I can-not unsee it, I cannot unfeel it. Alone in nature, it's easy to gaze out at the trees and get lost in the sound of the sea lapping against my boat and feel at one with everything, but that's not what I'm talking about. I'm talking about feeling connected to the plastic threads of the kitchen broom I purchased at the hardware store, the feathers left outside my front door by the local owl, the people who processed the salmon I unpack from a Styrofoam container, and the Styrofoam container itself, and the landfill it will end up in, and the seagulls that may peck at it, and on and on. I think about the lifecycles of everything. I can't turn it off. I don't know yet if this is good or bad for me.

The yacht has passed, and I can see the wakes rushing toward me. I turn the bow into them, which I've learned through experience makes my boat wobble less. The long, snake-like waves hit the bottom of my boat, and the horizon bounces up and down a few times. Then they pass. That wasn't so bad. I turn the bow back north and start paddling again. I have been trying for a few weeks to make it to the head of this channel. The water is rougher up there, but I'm getting stronger, and I want to see what's around the bend.

People have started asking me if I believe in magic, and if I will be continuing spellcraft, now that I'm not writing about it anymore. The answer is that I'm not entirely sure, because there's really two questions there: the first is whether magic is real, and the second is whether it's actually fun. I'm still a little nervous around my tarot cards. I may still have qualms about crystals and astrology, but my tarot readings, more often than not, were uncanny. It's not always nice to know what the future holds, nor is it always enjoyable to place your subconscious in front of a mirror. As for Crafting: I tried to manifest four major things over the course of my year. Only two materialized. That's a 50 percent success rate—technically a failing grade. Any person I lit a protection candle for remained healthy and happy, but I don't think that means I get to pin a ribbon on myself. It's very hard to prove magic is the reason something bad didn't happen.

What this year has taught me is how to truly meditate. It's not always easy, but I am no longer afraid of silence. I think spellwork was demonstrably helpful in getting me through the worst of my back injury. And I am certain that there is value in adoration of the divine. Every time I sat down and reached out to Isis, or the God or Goddess, whether or not I even performed magic, for the next few days, I would feel peaceful, happy, calm, and a thousand small coincidences and pleasantries would greet me. There's no other way to say it: I felt plugged into the flow of the world. I still don't know if those coincidences were objectively happening or I was seeing patterns that weren't there. But I know I'm going to keep adoring the divine either way. There are so few things in life that bring us uncomplicated pleasure. We should savor the ones that do.

I spent part of last week calling all the Christians I know and apologizing to them for ever implying it was dorky that they prayed. They didn't exactly tell me they related to my experiences chanting the name of a pre-Babylonian goddess for two hours, but they seemed to accept my new perspective with a kind of cautious grace.

Another common question I get is: Will I be calling myself a Witch, now that everything is done? Have I successfully converted? The answer, which I know sucks but is unfortunately true, is that I'm still not sure. The word "Witch" can mean almost anything depending on whose mouth it's in. I know some people will look at my Witchcraft journey and only see everything I did wrong, everything I missed. Others will be confused why I'm running from the label.

But if forced to choose: No. I don't think I am comfortable calling myself a Witch. This is because we still define a Witch as a rebel: a woman living alone in a cabin in the woods; a woman who has self-agency despite the norm of patriarchy; a woman who peddles power the good girls are told not to partake in; a woman who represents opposition to the mainstream. If this is the case, I don't want to be a Witch. It's not because I fear being an outsider. It's because I want Witchcraft's values to be mainstream as fuck. I'm talking outright *blasé*. I want to live in a world where nonviolence is normal, everyone is making an effort to right the path of our ancestors, and we see the earth as a something that would behoove us to protect and live with harmoniously. I want everyone to be talking to the fucking trees. In other words, I want Witchcraft to be the dominant culture, in principles if not in name. To quote Starhawk, "At twenty-eight, I didn't mind being a rebel. The secrecy around witchcraft just added to its charm. But at forty-eight, I find the necessity for fear and secrecy around our tradition intolerable." I also think it's critical we don't characterize Witchcraft as solely about female empowerment. There is so much here for men, so many incredible lessons and examples. While it has helped women considerably, it's a disservice to pretend this whole spirituality is only for one gender.

My kayak approaches the top of the channel, and the current changes, gets stronger. My heart starts beating faster, every muscle in my upper body brightens into life. Little waves start to jostle my boat around, and I have to work hard to paddle straight. I am momentarily nervous. Then I remember I have a life jacket on. I'm not too far from shore. Who cares if I get a little wet, or I flip a moon jelly onto my face.

After about ten minutes, I reach a calm section and rest my paddle on my thighs, staring at the spectacle around me. I'm completely alone. The sun is framed by the edge of the treetops to my left, casting wide, golden god rays on the surface of the sound. Everything is blue and green and glittering white. I feel ridiculous, like I'm in an Eddie Bauer commercial. I do not know what is coming next. I do not know how long I'll be able to stay here in this paradise. But I am certain it was the right choice to come.

Maybe, I think, I'd ultimately be more comfortable calling myself a simple neopagan, a subscriber to "green religion." I would like to see green religion grow over the world. I know a lot of us are hungry for it. I think it's possible to do this without wanting to run backward into the past or into fantasies of Luddism.

Maybe this is what I'll pray for.

A seal pops her head up out of the water, about twenty feet from my boat. I hold my breath. Her wet black eyes stare at me, curious. She swims parallel with me for a few moments, then dives back into the cold dark.

ACKNOWLEDGMENTS

There's a weird moment in writing where the thing you've been working on, alone for months, wondering if it's any good at all, suddenly becomes this huge group project. At first it's disorienting, but these are the people who actually get the book past the finish line out into the world. I'd especially like to thank Danielle Svetcov, without whom I'd be nowhere. Ronnie Alvarado, and the whole team at Simon Element, for taking a chance on me and letting me convince them this was a good idea. My mentors who let me pester them with Witchcraft questions at all hours of the night: Meg Elison, Lauren Parker, Liza Ryus, "Theodora," "Madeleine," and "Emma." Huge thanks to Eric Scott, Sylvie Althoff, Marie Vibbert, and Louis Evans for beta reading—the book would be nothing without you. I am especially grateful to Valeria Ruelas, Raven Hinojosa, Michael Hughes, and Oberon Zell-Ravenheart for sharing their thoughts with me. I encountered so many radically generous Witches this year: the woman who gave me crystals on Lakeshore Ave.; the women who welcomed me to their Samhain ritual; Mark, Ella, Electra, Helen, and so many others from Witch camp. If I don't mention your name here, it's not because I forgot you, but more an abundance of caution for your privacy: Know that I see you. Thank you to all the girls in high school who gathered to play at magic in our parents' living rooms (you know who you are)—including, of course, the parents who let us turn their living rooms into makeshift occult shops. I'd also especially like to thank Joanna Robinson, for listening to me vent about this process for eighteen months. And, of course, Justin Castilla, for always cheering me on.

BIBLIOGRAPHY

Adler, Margot. *Drawing Down the Moon: Witches, Druids, Goddess-Worshippers, and Other Pagans in America*. New York: Plume, 2001.

Alden, Temperance. *Year of the Witch: Connecting with Nature's Seasons through Intuitive Magick*. Newburyport, MA: Red Wheel/Weiser, 2020.

Alexander, Skye. *The Modern Guide to Witchcraft: Your Complete Guide to Witches, Covens, and Spells*. Holbrook, MA: Adams Media Corporation, 2014.

———. *The Modern Witchcraft Book of Tarot: Your Complete Guide to Understanding the Tarot*. Holbrook, MA: Adams Media Corporation, 2017.

Allen, Charlotte. "The Scholars and the Goddess." *Atlantic Monthly*. January 1, 2001. https://www.theatlantic.com/magazine/archive/2001/01/the-scholars-and-the-goddess/305910.

Allen, Lasara Firefox. *Jailbreaking the Goddess: A Radical Revisioning of Feminist Spirituality*. Woodbury, MN: Llewellyn Publications, 2016.

"ARCHIVES Blacklist." n.d. Google Docs. Accessed September 8, 2021. https://docs.google.com/document/d/1UbUyQPdKnZWwQo0rk7IjfOMevSE4Fuhmb2jQYnHUuX4/edit.

Asprem, Egil. "The Magical Theory of Politics Memes, Magic, and the Enchantment of Social Forces in the American Magic War." *Nova Religio: The Journal of Alternative and Emergent Religions* 23, no. 4 (2020): 15–42.

Auryn, Mat. *Psychic Witch: A Metaphysical Guide to Meditation, Magick & Manifestation*. Woodbury, MN: Llewellyn Publications, 2020.

Basile, Lisa Marie. "Astrological Shadow Work: Healing Writing Prompts." *Luna Luna*, September 9, 2019. http://www.lunaluna magazine.com/dark/tag/grimoire.

Bernard, Guy, and Antony Lawrence. *The Goetia Ritual: The Power of Magic Revealed*. Self-published, Magi Majesti, 2017.

Beyer, Rebecca. *Wild Witchcraft: Folk Herbalism, Garden Magic, and Foraging for Spells, Rituals, and Remedies*. New York: Simon Element, 2022.

Buckland, Raymond. *Buckland's Complete Book of Witchcraft*. Woodbury, MN: Llewellyn Publications, 1986.

Burroughs, Augusten. *Toil & Trouble: A Memoir*. New York: St Martin's Press, 2019.

"Casting Spells for and against Trump Divides Neopagan Community." n.d. Religionwatch.com. Accessed December 1, 2021. https://www .religionwatch.com/casting-spells-for-and-against-trump-divides -neopagan-community.

Centennial Magazine. *Witches: The Truth Behind the Legends & Lore*. New York: Centennial Media, 2021.

Chamberlain, Lisa. *Wicca Spellbook Starter Kit: A Book of Candle, Crystal, and Herbal Spells*. Self-published, Chamberlain Publications (Wicca Shorts), 2018.

Conway, D. J. *Wicca: The Complete Craft*. Freedom, CA: Crossing Press, 2001.

Cross, J. Allen. *American Brujeria: Modern Mexican American Folk Magic*. Newburyport, MA: Red Wheel/Weiser, 2021.

Crowley, Aleister, Hymenaeus Beta, MacGregor Mathers, and Samuel Liddell. *The Goetia, the Lesser Key of Solomon the King: Lemegeton, Book 1 Clavicula Salomonis Regis*. Boston: Red Wheel/Weiser, 1995.

Cunningham, Scott. *Living Wicca*. Woodbury, MN: Llewellyn Publications, 1993.

———. *Magical Aromatherapy: The Power of Scent*. Woodbury, MN: Llewellyn Publications, 1989.

———. *Wicca: A Guide for the Solitary Practitioner*. Woodbury, MN: Llewellyn Publications, 1988.

Denny, Frances F. *Major Arcana: Portraits of Witches in America*. Kansas City, MO: Andrews McMeel Publishing, 2020.

Diaz, Juliet. *Witchery: Embrace the Witch Within*. London: Hay House UK, 2019.

Divinebyjo. "Recover Your Stolen Money Spell." HubPages. March 21, 2012. https://discover.hubpages.com/religion-philosophy/Recover -Your-Stolen-Money-Spell.

Draco, Mélusine. *Pagan Portals: The Inner-City Path: A Simple Pagan Guide to Well-Being and Awareness*. New Alresford, England: John Hunt Publishing, 2020.

Dugan, Ellen. "Spell: Spell to Find a Lost Item." Llewellyn Worldwide. September 19, 2016. https://www.llewellyn.com/spell.php?spell_id =6461.

DuQuette, Lon Milo. *Low Magick: It's All in Your Head . . . You Just Have No Idea How Big Your Head Is*. Woodbury, MN: Llewellyn Publications, 2010.

Eason, Cassandra. *A Little Bit of Wicca: An Introduction to Witchcraft*. New York: Sterling, 2017.

Farnell, Kim. *Simply Runes*. New York: Sterling, 2006.

Gardner, Gerald. *Witchcraft Today*. New York: Citadel Press, 2004.

Gottlieb, Kathryn. "Cultural Appropriation in Contemporary Neopaganism and Witchcraft." Honors thesis, Honors College at the University of Maine, 2017. https://digitalcommons.library.umaine.edu /honors/304.

Hearn, Spencer. "45 Different Types of Witches." *Letters to Lilith*. July 1, 2020. https://www.letterstolilith.com/blog/the-different-types-of -witches.

Hood, Abby Lee. "Buying Ethical Crystals Shouldn't Be This Hard." *Cosmopolitan*. November 16, 2020. https://www.cosmopolitan.com /lifestyle/a34441511/ethical-crystals.

Hughes, Michael M. *Magic for the Resistance: Rituals and Spells for Change*. Woodbury, MN: Llewellyn Publications, 2018.

Hutcheson, Cory Thomas. *New World Witchery: A Trove of North American Folk Magic.* Woodbury, MN: Llewellyn Publications, 2021.

Hutton, Ronald. *The Triumph of the Moon: A History of Modern Pagan Witchcraft.* London: Oxford University Press, 2001.

IrieDiva. "Manifestation and Law of Attraction: What's the Difference?" *IrieDiva* (blog). October 1, 2020. https://www.iriediva.com/manifestation-and-law-of-attraction/.

Jacobs, A.J. *The Year of Living Biblically: One Man's Humble Quest to Follow the Bible as Literally as Possible.* New York: Simon & Schuster, 2008.

Joho, Jess, and Morgan Sung. "How to Be a Witch without Stealing Other People's Cultures." Mashable. October 31, 2020. https://www.mashable.com/article/witchtok-problematic-witch-cultural-appropriation.

Kelden. *The Witches' Sabbath: An Exploration of History, Folklore & Modern Practice.* Woodbury, MN: Llewellyn Publications, 2022.

Kelly, Aidan. "About Naming Ostara, Litha, and Mabon." *Including Paganism with Aidan Kelly.* May 2, 2017. https://www.patheos.com/blogs/aidankelly/2017/05/naming-ostara-litha-mabon.

Koronka, Poppy. "Paganism's Culture War: The White Supremacists Versus the Liberal Left." n.d. Shorthandstories.com. Accessed December 1, 2021. https://swlondoner.shorthandstories.com/paganism-s-culture-war--the-white-supremacists-versus-the-liberal-left-/index.html.

Leland, Charles G. *Aradia, or the Gospel of the Witches.* Newport, RI: Witches Almanac, 2010.

Lipscomb, Suzannah. "Why Are Women Becoming Witches?" *UnHerd.* December 24, 2021. https://unherd.com/2021/12/why-are-women-becoming-witches-2.

Lyte, Fire. *The Dabbler's Guide to Witchcraft: Seeking an Intentional Magical Path.* New York: Simon Element, 2021.

Mankey, Jason. *Transformative Witchcraft: The Greater Mysteries.* Woodbury, MN: Llewellyn Publications, 2019.

McLoughlin, Lisa A. 2019. "US Pagans and Indigenous Americans: Land and Identity." *Religions* 10, no. 3: 152. https://www.doi.org/10.3390/rel10030152.

Mercury, Kelden. "Rethinking the Sabbats." *By Athame and Stang*. April 24, 2018. https://www.patheos.com/blogs/byathameandstang /2018/04/rethinking-the-sabbats.

Monteagut, Lorraine. *Brujas: The Magic and Power of Witches of Color*. Chicago: Chicago Review Press, 2021.

Moon, Hibiscus. "Is Crystal Collecting Ethical?" Hibiscus Moon Crystal Academy. July 2, 2012. https://www.hibiscusmooncrystalacademy .com/ethically-mined-crystals.

Mooney, Thorn. *The Witch's Path: Advancing Your Craft at Every Level*. Woodbury, MN: Llewellyn Publications, 2021.

Mulvey, Alora Paulsen, and Jessalynn Keller. "This Halloween, Witches Are Casting Spells to Defeat Trump and #WitchTheVote in the U.S. Election." *The Conversation*, October 29, 2020. http://www.the conversation.com/this-halloween-witches-are-casting-spells-to -defeat-trump-and-witchthevote-in-the-u-s-election-148213.

Murphy-Hiscock, Arin. *The Way of the Hedge Witch: Rituals and Spells for Hearth and Home*. Holbrook, MA: Adams Media Corporation, 2009.

———. *The Green Witch: Your Complete Guide to the Natural Magic of Herbs, Flowers, Essential Oils, and More*. Holbrook, MA: Adams Media Corporation, 2017.

———. *The House Witch: Your Complete Guide to Creating a Magical Space with Rituals and Spells for Hearth and Home*. Holbrook, MA: Adams Media Corporation, 2018.

Myers, Brendan. *The Earth, the Gods and the Soul: A History of Pagan Philosophy: From the Iron Age to the 21st Century*. Alresford, England: Moon Books, 2013.

Orapello, Christopher, and Tara-Love Maguire. *Besom, Stang & Sword: A Guide to Traditional Witchcraft, the Sixfold Path, and the Hidden Landscape*. Newburyport, MA: Red Wheel/Weiser, 2019.

Pike, Signe. *Faery Tale: One Woman's Search for Enchantment in a Modern World*. New York: TarcherPerigee, 2011.

RavenWolf, Silver. *Solitary Witch: The Ultimate Book of Shadows for the New Generation*. Woodbury, MN: Llewellyn Publications, 2003.

Ricketts, Rachel. *Do Better: Spiritual Activism for Fighting and Healing from White Supremacy*. New York: Atria Books, 2021.

Roach, Mary. *Spooked*. Read by Bernadette Quigley. Newark, NJ: Audible, 2005.

Roderick, Timothy. *Wicca: A Year and a Day: 366 Days of Spiritual Practice in the Craft of the Wise*. Woodbury, MN: Llewellyn Publications, 2005.

Ruelas, Valeria. *The Mexican Witch Lifestyle: Brujeria Spells, Tarot, and Crystal Magic*. New York: Simon Element, 2022.

Sabin, Thea. *Wicca for Beginners: Fundamentals of Philosophy and Practice*. Woodbury, MN: Llewellyn Publications, 2006.

Schiff, Stacy. *The Witches: Suspicion, Betrayal, and Hysteria in 1692 Salem*. New York: Back Bay Books, 2016.

Shaw, Christopher. "A Theft of Spirit?" *The Tracking Project*. November 5, 2012. https://www.thetrackingproject.org/a-theft-of-spirit.

Sheppard, Kathleen. "Forced into the Fringe: Margaret Murray's Witch-Cult Hypothesis." *The New Inquiry*. April 21, 2017. https://www.thenewinquiry.com/blog/forced-into-the-fringe-margaret-murrays-witch-cult-hypothesis.

Starhawk. *The Spiral Dance 20th Anniversary Edition*. San Francisco: Harper, 1999.

Steiner, Andy. "The Wicca That Never Was." *Utne*. October 23, 2007. https://www.utne.com/community/the-wicca-that-never-was.

Stonestreet, John. "The Weight of Too Much 'Choice.'" *Breakpoint*. August 24, 2022. https://www.breakpoint.org/the-weight-of-too-much-choice.

The Norwegian American. "Yule Ale: A Tradition Older than Christmas." *The Norwegian American*. December 12, 2017. https://www.norwegianamerican.com/yule-ale-a-tradition-older-than-christmas.

Urquhart, Alaina, and Ashleigh Kelley. "The Salem Witch Trials." *Morbid*. October 16, 2018. https://podcasts.apple.com/ca/podcast/the-salem-witch-trials/id1379959217?i=1000421987015.

Walker, J. D. *A Witch's Guide to Wildcraft: Using Common Plants to Cre-*

ate Uncommon Magick. Woodbury, MN: Llewellyn Publications, 2021.

Whitmore, Ben. *Trials of the Moon: Reopening the Case for Historical Witchcraft. A Critique of Ronald Hutton's* The Triumph of the Moon: *A History of Modern Pagan Witchcraft.* Auckland, New Zealand: Briar Books, 2010.

Wigginton, Eliot. *Foxfire 1.* New York: Alfred A. Knopf, 1972.

Zapata, Kimberly. "How to Manifest Anything You Desire." *Oprah Daily.* December 17, 2019. https://www.oprahdaily.com/life/a30244004 /how-to-manifest-anything.

INDEX

ABOUT *the* AUTHOR

Diana Helmuth is a nonfiction author. Before delving into writing, she studied anthropology and Arabic at UC Berkeley and worked in Silicon Valley's startup land for several seed-stage companies. Her first book, *How to Suffer Outside*, won a National Outdoor Book Award, and her freelance writing on travel, nature, and millennial cultural trends can be found in various anthologies and online magazines. When she's not writing, she helps produce the occasional podcast. Helmuth was born and raised in Northern California.